Domestic strategies offers a new reading of the historical sources in order to understand the social relations and strategies of labouring families towards the organization of productive processes and institutional arrangements in early modern Europe. In contrast to many other works, the essays in *Domestic strategies* place labouring families as the actors on the historical scene, utilizing existing opportunities, rather than as passive recipients of historical changes. Conceptual insights derived from both anthropology (e.g. from Sahlins and Geertz) and sociology (e.g. from Bourdieu, Elias and Mary Douglas) are applied to individual case-studies of social groups from north-central Italy and the French Alps, and the whole offers an important new perspective on the working lives of European families during the early modern period and beyond.

Studies in modern capitalism

Domestic strategies: work and family in France and Italy 1600–1800

Studies in modern capitalism. Etudes sur le capitalisme moderne

This series is devoted to an attempt to comprehend capitalism as a world-system. It will include monographs, collections of essays and colloquia around specific themes, written by historians and social scientists united by a common concern for the study of large-scale, long-term social structure and social change.

The series is a joint enterprise of the Maison des Sciences de l'Homme in Paris and the Fernand Braudel Center for the Study of Economies, Historical Systems, and Civilizations at the State University of New York at Binghamton.

This book is published as part of the joint publishing agreement established in 1977 between the Fondation de la Maison des Sciences de l'Homme and the Press Syndicate of the University of Cambridge. Titles published under this arrangement may appear in any European language or, in the case of volumes of collected essays, in several languages.

New books will appear either as individual titles or in one of the series which the Maison des Sciences de l'Homme and the Cambridge University Press have jointly agreed to publish. All books published jointly by the Maison des Sciences de l'Homme and the Cambridge University Press will be distributed by the Press throughout the world.

For other titles in the series please see end of book

Domestic strategies: work and family in France and Italy 1600–1800

EDITED BY STUART WOOLF

Professor of History, European University Institute and University of Essex

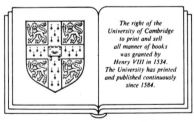

The right of the
University of Cambridge
to print and sell
all manner of books
was granted by
Henry VIII in 1534.
The University has printed
and published continuously
since 1584.

CAMBRIDGE UNIVERSITY PRESS
Cambridge
New York   Port Chester   Melbourne   Sydney

EDITIONS DE
LA MAISON DES SCIENCES DE L'HOMME
Paris

Published by the Press Syndicate of the University of Cambridge
The Pitt Building, Trumpington Street, Cambridge CB2 1RP
40 West 20th Street, New York, NY 10011, USA
10 Stamford Road, Oakleigh, Melbourne 3166, Australia
and Editions de la Maison des Sciences de l'Homme
54 Boulevard Raspail, 75270 Paris Cedex 06

© Maison des Sciences de l'Homme and Cambridge University Press 1991

First published 1991

Printed in Great Britain at the University Press, Cambridge

Typeset by Servis Filmsetting Ltd

British Library cataloguing in publication data
Domestic strategies: work and family in France and Italy,
1600–1800. – (Studies in modern capitalism. (Etudes sur le
capitalisme moderne)
1. Western Europe. Capitalism, history. Sociological
perspectives
I. Woolf, S. J. (Stuart Joseph), *1936–* II. Series
306.342094

Library of Congress cataloguing in publication data
Domestic strategies : work and family in France and Italy, 1600–1800/
    edited by Stuart Woolf.
        p.   cm. – (Studies in modern capitalism = Etudes sur le
    capitalisme moderne)
        ISBN 0 521-39164 4
        1. Work and family – France – History.   2. Work and family – Italy –
    History.   3. Guilds – Italy – History.   I. Woolf, S. J. (Stuart
    Joseph)   II. Series: Studies in modern capitalism.
    HD4904.25.D66   1990
    306.3'6–dc20   89-13997   CIP

ISBN 0 521 39164 4 hardback

ISBN 2 7351 hardback (France only)

Contents

Contributors

Sandra Cavallo is a Fellow of the Wellcome Institute for the History of Medicine in London

Simona Cerutti is Jean Monnet Fellow at the European University Institute in Florence

Laurence Fontaine is at the Centre National de la Recherche Scientifique in Paris

Carlo Poni is Professor of Economic History at the University of Bologna

Osvaldo Raggio is at the European University Institute in Florence

Stuart Woolf is Professor of History at the European University Institute and the University of Essex

Acknowledgements

The essays in this volume come out of a research project on 'Work and Family in Pre-Industrial Europe' funded by the European University Institute between 1984 and 1987. The project was deliberately exploratory and open-ended, dependent on regular meetings of a small group and conferences on specific themes involving broader participation. The directors, Stuart Woolf and Carlo Poni, are extremely grateful to the EUI for its generous support. They hope that, besides the present volume, the project has justified itself for the successive cohorts of research students in the Department of History and Civilization who followed and participated in the conferences and discussions.

Their thanks also go to Maurice Aymard and Jacques Revel, whose interest in the project led them to accept this volume for publication in the series Studies in Modern Capitalism.

1 ❧ Introduction

Stuart Woolf

It is a truism that historical (like all social science) research is influenced by the preoccupations and moods of the society in which the historian works. (In this sense, as Croce put it, all history is contemporary history.)[1] The direction of research is oriented by concepts whose pervasive influence is based on affirmations of widespread, if not universal validity. Inevitably the assumptions underlying such affirmations subsequently emerge as at best limited in space and time, at worst doubtful or unverifiable, while the nature and type of explanation appears as conditioned more or less heavily by contemporary concerns. To identify such phases of research and place them in their precise historical context can be of practical use (beyond its intrinsic historiographical interest) as the very underscoring of the limits of previous work facilitates the identification of new objects, concepts or methods of research.

As the pace of change has accelerated in all domains so dramatically in our lifetime, so arguably the aims, methods and strategies of historical research have shifted at a faster pace than in the past. Most striking has been the move away from the optimistic assumptions of the 1950s and 1960s, codified in the dominant academic modes of historical research, to the more sceptical, self-enquiring and necessarily pluralistic approaches of the past decade. This is not the place to engage in a discussion of the theoretical, epistemological and philosophical bases on which historians base their research. Few reflective practising historians

I wish to thank Maurice Aymard, Sandra Cavallo, Simona Cerutti, Laurence Fontaine, Carlo Poni, Osvaldo Raggio and Jacques Revel for their comments on earlier versions of this Introduction. The comments about the European University Institute research project on work and family expressed here are shared by all the authors, although responsibility for the views expressed in the Introduction as a whole remains entirely mine.

[1] B. Croce, 'Storia e Cronaca', *Teoria e storia della storiografia* (1st edn 1917), Bari 1973, pp. 3–17.

today would deny the cumulative effect on their establishment of the sapping operations of neighbouring disciplines, from linguistic analysis to economics, from sociology and anthropology to political philosophy and scientific logic. At the same time, the reluctance of historians – quintessentially 'national', for the most part, in their reading and teaching – to interest themselves in developments in their discipline beyond their frontiers has become at least slightly less impermeable as a result of the increase in the availability of published work in translation throughout the western world. Paradoxically, the very crisis of universities (especially in Britain) may have accelerated the receptivity of the younger generation of historians towards the implications for their discipline of the contributions of one or another of outsiders, such as Karl Polanyi, Norbert Elias, Michel Foucault, Marshall Sahlins, Clifford Geertz, Pierre Bourdieu or Mary Douglas, to mention only the most obvious names.[2] Interest in the analyses and interpretative models developed by such authors, or more generally by social scientists, does not of course imply passive receptivity. When tested against the empirical evidence of historical sources, the models have often proved insufficient, even misleading. But they have acted as a powerful stimulus by offering new or alternative possibilities in interpreting the documentation utilized by historians.

Perhaps such remarks are unduly optimistic. Maybe they underestimate the resistance to change of academics in their struggle for predominance within their disciplines, which Bourdieu has dissected so pitilessly.[3] But at least they should serve the purpose of situating the change in approaches towards economic and social history in the broader context of an undeniable evolution, marked by horizons of the intellectual and academic debate. For it is in economic and social history, alongside cultural history, that the changes have been most marked.

Economic historians have never denied the close relationships of their discipline with economic theory. The two derived from the common

[2] K. Polanyi, *The Great Transformation*, New York 1944; N. Elias, *The Court Society*, Oxford 1983; M. Foucault, *Disciplinary Power and Subjection*, Oxford 1986; M. Sahlins, *Stone Age Economics*, London 1974; C. Geertz, *The Interpretations of Cultures*, New York 1973; P. Bourdieu, *Outline of a Theory of Practice*, Cambridge 1977; M. Douglas, *The World of Goods*, New York 1978.

[3] P. Bourdieu, L. Boltanski and P. Maldidier, 'La Défense du corps', *Social Science Information*, 10:4, 1971, pp. 45–86; P. Bourdieu, *Homo Academicus*, Cambridge 1988. Without excessive polemical intent, it is relevant to quote the common reaction of a political and an economic historian, both very distinguished, to the contributions of exponents of other disciplines (in particular philosophers) to historical methodology: 'The problems and meaning of endeavors to rediscover the past have for some time formed a favorite theme for certain philosophers whose profound and original analyses do not always seem relevant to the working historian', R.W. Fogel and G.R. Elton, *Which Road to the Past? Two Views of History*, New Haven, CT 1983, p. 1.

matrix of eighteenth-century political economy; economic history, in its evolution, has consistently incorporated advances in theory. Indeed, the increasing insistence on econometrics and mathematical modelling in the one field has led to parallel developments in the so-called 'new economic history'. If, in recent years, a small but growing number of historians has moved away from the dominant modes of analysis in economic history, it is not because of the lack of conceptual or methodological tools. The reasons are to be found elsewhere, in dissatisfaction on the one hand with the assumption of a linear evolution towards an 'Atlantic' model of mechanized industrialization, and, on the other, with the inadequacy of explanations of rational behaviour that find their origins in the classical economists.

Nobody would deny the major advances in our understanding of the formation of the contemporary western world that have resulted from the historiography of economic growth of the 1950s and 1960s.[4] Our knowledge of English and American economic history has increased enormously, the range of sources has widened and their utilization to answer questions of theory has become incomparably more sophisticated. The reservations, that have been formulated with increasing clarity, relate to three assumptions implicit in the analytical framework of the economic-growth school. The first questions the applicability of the model itself to the economic history of all states, and in particular of the extra-European countries of the Third World. Within Europe, as Milward and Saul have shown,[5] the assumption of a single model (with or without the variants of 'first-' and 'second-comers') forces a range of very differing experiences into a constrictive mould. Even more, viewed through the lens of 'successful' industrialization and 'take-off' into self-sustained growth, the extra-European world is reduced to an undifferentiated and passive object of European penetration: all cats are black in the night of economic backwardness.[6]

The second reservation relates to the interpretation of economic

[4] A. Gerschenkron, *Economic Backwardness in Historical Perspective*, New York 1965; W.W. Rostow, *How It All Began. Origins of the Modern Economy*, London 1975; H.J. Habakkuk, *American and British Technology in the 19th Century*, Cambridge 1962; D.S. Landes, *The Unbound Prometheus*, Cambridge 1969.

[5] A.S. Milward and S.B. Saul, *The Economic Development of Continental Europe 1780–1870*, London 1973.

[6] D. Seers, 'The Limitations of the Special Case', *Bulletin of the Oxford University Institute of Economics and Statistics*, 25:2, 1963, pp. 77–98, and 'The Congruence of Marxism and Other Neo-Classical Doctrines', Discussion Paper, Institute of Development Studies, University of Sussex, 1978; J. Knapp (ed.), *The Teaching of Development Economics*, Cass 1967 (including P. Streeton, 'The Use and Abuse of Models in Development Economics'); Milward and Saul, *The Economic Development of Continental Europe*.

growth in terms of industrialization, and in particular mechanization and the factory mode of production. Criticism has focussed increasingly on the teleological implications of a history of industry that regards the mechanized factory as a necessary point of arrival. The 'proto-indus-trial' exponents and many others, like Maxine Berg, point to the long history of manufacturing before the factory; Samuel to the continued importance of manual and dispersed production, Sabel and Zeitlin to the success of alternative technologies in the factory age.[7]

Finally, reservations are increasingly expressed about the adequacy of purely 'economic' explanations of processes of economic change. The 'residual', that category which economists fill with what they cannot classify otherwise, has tended to assume ever larger proportions in historical explanations of economic processes. It is not without signifi-cance that those economists and economic historians – such as Hicks, Jones, North and Thomas, even Rostow – who have had the courage to risk a world's eye view of the history of economic development have been forced back on institutional and social explanations, which usually lack the quantifiable characteristics of more purely 'economic' factors.[8] The issue of quantification is an important one, as it is accepted as the necessary basis for verification of hypotheses.[9] It relates essentially to the macro level of the economy. But analyses of economic growth remain rooted in explanations of individual rational behaviour whose origins are to be found in the classical political economists and Walrasian equilibrium theory. They assume, on the one hand, a coherence and systematicity of the market system and, on the other, a form of behaviour of individuals that corresponds to the tenets of economic rationality. Failure to meet such expectations of rationality are accounted for in terms of other elements, such as 'custom'. The implicit opposition of custom (or other unexplained behaviour) to economic rationality casts it into the category of the anomalous 'residual'.

Quantification has not been, of course, the prerogative of English and

[7] M. Berg, 'Political Economy and the Principles of Manufacture 1700–1800', in M. Berg, P. Hudson and M. Sonenscher (eds.), *Manufacture in Town and Country before the Factory*, Cambridge 1983; R. Samuel, 'The Workshop of the World: Steam Power and Hand Technology in Mid-Victorian Britain', *History Workshop*, 3, 1977, pp. 6–72; C. Sabel and J. Zeitlin, 'Historical Alternatives to Mass Production', *Past and Present*, 108, 1985, pp. 133–76.

[8] J. Hicks, *A Theory of Economic History*, Oxford 1969; E.L. Jones, *The European Miracle*, Cambridge 1981; D.C. North and R.P. Thomas, *The Rise of the Western World*, Cambridge 1973; Rostow, *How It All Began*.

[9] R.W. Fogel, '"Scientific" History and Traditional History', in Fogel and Elton, *Which Road to the Past?*

American economic historians of growth. Nor indeed has it been the reserve of economic historians. The deployment of time-series analyses of massive data sources is equally the characteristic of the Braudelian *longue durée* approach, practised by the *Annales* historians of society and culture, as much as of the economy.[10] Evidence based on statistical series, however crude and imprecise, is of the essence of the structural approach as the series provide indicators of dimensions and trends. Few would deny the necessity of statistical series for certain types of research and its utility for many others. Even in so treacherous a field as the history of criminality – where the data are more closely the product of those who formulate the object than an accurate indicator of what is counted – their careful use to provide a preliminary framework of long-term trends can be defended.[11]

Nevertheless, outside the field of economic history, the adequacy of the statistical approach raises doubts. Social and cultural phenomena cannot be understood in serial form like population and prices, essentially for two reasons. First, because by definition the scale is large, which has the effect of flattening out and losing the specificity of the historical situation. Second, because their very expression in statistical form creates stable and unchanging categories, as if historical reality could be defined and divided up once and for all. The models of causality, for which historians have constructed their statistical series, are usually constructed around too-simplistic correlations. The time-series are both too rigid and too macroscopic, as they assume that what is most repetitive and least individualized (the statistical mean or mode) is representative. As historians of society and culture, like Ginzburg and Grendi, point out, to understand and analyze in their specificity how social realities were constructed requires a reduction of scale and a search for alternative approaches.[12]

This is the historiographical context within which two historians

---

[10] P. Chaunu, 'L'Histoire sérielle. Bilan et perspectives', *Revue Roumaine d'Histoire*, 9, 1970, pp. 459–84; P. Chaunu, 'Un Nouveau Champ pour l'histoire sérielle: le quantitatif au troisième niveau', *Mélanges en l'honneur de Fernand Braudel*, Toulouse 1973, vol. II, pp. 105–25; F. Furet, 'Le Quantitatif en histoire', in J. Le Goff and P. Nora (eds.), *Faire de l'histoire*, Paris 1974, vol. I, pp. 42–61.

[11] L. Stone, 'The History of Violence in England: a Rejoinder', *Past and Present*, 108, 1985, pp. 216–24.

[12] C. Ginzburg and C. Poni, 'Il Nome e il Come: Scambio Ineguale e Mercato Storiografico', *Quaderni Storici*, 40, 1979, pp. 181–90; E. Grendi, 'Micro-analisi e Storia Sociale', *Quaderni Storici*, 35, 1977, pp. 506–20. Although his concerns are different, Roger Chartier's critique of the approach to cultural history of the 1960s to 1970s seems to me to point in the same direction: R. Chartier, *Cultural History between Practices and Representations*, Cambridge 1989, pp. 1–16.

brought up in the earlier tradition of economic history formulated the research project of which the following essays form part. Not all members of the project would necessarily accept such a contextualization, as they belong to a younger generation, whose interests and formation were already critical of economic historiography.

The project, funded generously by the European University Institute between 1984 and 1987, was directed by Stuart Woolf and Carlo Poni. Its purpose was deliberately open-ended: to explore the relationships between social life and institutions in pre-industrial Europe through the perspective of the working practices of the family and group. Our intention was deliberately to reverse the normal approach to the study of the history of work, in which the family appears without autonomy, reactive or responsive to externally imposed authority and conditions. The family at work has formed the focal point of our research, given its role as the base unit of the labour force, as the structure procuring subsistence and as the meeting place where all forms of resources are pooled. Our purpose has not been to ignore the importance of other forms of social organization, such as neighbourhood, community, kinship or friendship, but to study these in relation to the family. At the outset we could not have anticipated the complexity of the conceptual and methodological implications of our approach. But at our regular meetings and annual conferences, to which we invited outside participants, we became ever more conscious of the theoretical ramifications and practical problems of sources and research strategies that resulted from the determination to move away from functionalist or 'vertical' assumptions about social relations by placing families as the main actors in highly specific and closely delimited historical contexts.

Like all research, our concerns were not, of course, without precedents. The choice of theme belongs to a well-established area with distinguished antecedents: the study of the social fabric onto which the successive industrial revolutions were grafted. The social consequences of industrialization, as an object of investigation, are of course far older than the scientific study of the industrial revolution, dating back before Engels to the process itself in its early manifestations. Such consequences coloured and in good part were responsible for the widespread debates of the 1830s and 1840s on pauperism and urban conditions.[13]

---

[13] S. Woolf, 'The Poor and What to Do with Them. The Restoration Debate in Europe and Italy', in J.A. Davis and P. Ginsborg (eds.), *Politics and Society in Nineteenth Century Italy*, Cambridge 1990; J.H. Treble, *Urban Poverty in Britain 1830–1914*, London 1979; H.J. Dyos and M. Wolff (eds.), *The Victorian City*, London 1973.

However, recent historiographical developments have differed from this classic theme in at least two respects. In the first place, there has been a notable shift away from the broad aggregate – the nation-state or the class, anonymous protagonists of impersonal forces of change – towards the study of the component areas of members of such collectivities, such as the local productive region, the inhabitants of the city or the peasant family.

Second, a certain unease about the historical reality, or at least the rapidity, of the breadth of the ruptures and discontinuities imposed by the industrial revolution has encouraged the study of those sectors of the economy or society that would appear to have resisted or, more commonly, to have absorbed the pressures of change. As against the plight of the handloom weavers after mechanization, the prolonged survival of hand technologies in Victorian Britain has returned to the fore.[14] Continuity rather than change, adaptation rather than ruin, have gained or regained attention in recent research. Within this context labour history has acquired a different significance, pushed back chronologically to the centuries before the factory and thematically to the craft and guild before the trade union.[15] A premise for this research project has been the observation that methods of working and earning remained, over a period of centuries, relatively untouched by technological or organizational innovations and constantly structured by institutional and customary practices. This applied not only to the tertiary sector, such as urban consumption trades, porterage or retailing, but to major industries like building and even mining. We concluded from this somewhat unoriginal observation that it would be advantageous to concentrate on the reproduction of work practices, as this could allow us to penetrate the working experiences of the great majority of the labouring families in pre-industrial (and indeed industrializing) Europe, while also highlighting by contrast those processes of production where technical or organizational changes caused real, direct and dramatic effects on the families, as well as gradually transforming the economy of Europe.

The history of the family has attracted considerable attention in

[14] Samuel, 'Workshop of the World'.
[15] W.H. Sewell, *Work and Revolution in France, The Language of Labor from the Old Regime to 1848*, Cambridge 1980; M. Sonenscher, 'Work and Wages in Paris in the Eighteenth Century', in Berg, Hudson and Sonenscher (eds.), *Manufacture in Town and Country*; S.L. Kaplan and C.J. Koepp (eds.), *Work in France. Representations, Meaning, Organization, and Practice*, Ithaca 1986; P. Joyce (ed.), *The Historical Meanings of Work*, Cambridge 1987.

recent years because of the contributions of historical demography and the wave of research on proto-industrialization. At the theoretical level, the conceptualization of the study of the family owes much to both anthropology and sociology. For the anthropologists, the kinship system in primitive societies – of which the family was a constituent, albeit subordinate element – was the key to understanding social organization. For the sociologists, analysis of the functions of the family was of importance in understanding the transition from 'traditional' to 'modern' society. For the former, the family was one more indicator in the decodification of the rules of an essentially unchanging structure; for the latter, it reflected through its composition and comportment impersonal changes of a vaster and omnicomprehensive nature.[16]

Historical demography concentrated attention directly on the family with the methodological innovations of family reconstitution (on the basis of birth, marriage and death registers) and comparisons of family composition, structures and mean household size (on the basis of family listings and *états d'âme*).[17] The reconstruction of family genealogies, of enormous potential for population history, as Schofield and Wrigley have demonstrated,[18] nevertheless tells us little, by itself, of the social relations, internal dynamics and strategies of families. Equally, although the analysis of data on composition and size of household has considerably advanced our knowledge of the family life-cycle, the insistence on statistics derived from household listings produced by authorities for their own multiple purposes has tended to leave the family in a vacuum, insulated as much from the dynamics of its internal relations as from its actions within the wider society.

---

[16] F. Zonabend, 'Regard Ethnologique sur la Parenté et la Famille', in A. Burguière, C. Klapisch-Zuber, M. Segalen and F. Zonabend (eds.), *Histoire de la Famille*, vol. I, Paris 1986, pp. 15–75; R. Rowland, 'Población, Familia, Sociedad', *Gestae*, 1:1, 1989, pp. 15–21; M. Segalen, *Sociologie de la Famille*, 2nd edn, Paris 1988; E. Hammel, 'On the . . . of Studying Household Form and Function', in R.M. Netting, R.R. Wilk and E.J. Arnold (eds.), *Households, Comparative and Historical Studies of the Domestic Group*, Berkeley 1984; D. Sabean and H. Medick (eds.), *Interest and Emotion. Essays on the Study of Family and Kinship*, Cambridge 1984.

[17] E.A. Wrigley (ed.), *An Introduction to English Historical Demography*, London 1966; T.P.R. Laslett (ed.); *Household and Family in Past Time*, London 1972; E.A. Wrigley, *Identifying People in the Past*, London 1973; R. Wall (ed.), *Family Forms in Historic Europe*, Cambridge 1983; M. Barbagli, *Sotto lo Stesso Tetto*, Bologna 1984; L. Stone, 'Family History in the 1980s', *Journal of Interdisciplinary History*, 1981, pp. 51–87; L.A. Tilly and M. Cohen, 'Does the Family Have a History?' *Social Science History*, 1982, pp. 131–79. A major international conference was held at Trieste on 'Strutture e Rapporti Familiari in Età Moderna' (September 1983), whose papers unfortunately have not been published.

[18] R.S. Schofield and E.A. Wrigley, *The Population History of England, 1541–1871. A Reconstruction*, London 1981.

The relevance for the history of the family of the research on proto-industrialization derives primarily from Hans Medick's hypotheses about the effects of such rural industrial development on authority and gender relations within the household. Among the cluster of propositions raised in Mendels' original model, this particular aspect has subsequently attracted relatively little research, although Medick and Sabean developed and expanded the approach into a dialogue with anthropologists on the difficult theme of the nature and role of sentiment in internal family relations.[19] Moreover, the very concentration of research on rural manufacture has led to neglect of other aspects of considerable importance for the history of the family, such as (for example) the relationships between such rural industries and the surrounding agricultural practices, tertiary activities, long-distance migration as an alternative to proto-industry, or urban domestic production.

It is not my purpose to engage in even the sketchiest of historiographical surveys. What our research project shared in common with historical demography and aspects of proto-industrial research was the concentration on the family cycle. This signified a change in dimension from the aggregate to the particular, from macro- towards micro-studies.

Our purpose was not just to test models or hypotheses formulated on the basis of macro-studies, which is the most habitual explanation of case-studies. Our aim was more ambitious. We proposed micro-studies, moving outwards from the family and group, in order to detect what could only be identified at that scale: the changing relations between families and resources, whether economic or institutional. The family was to be studied in its cycle in order to understand its 'strategies' or, as Bourdieu puts it, its *habitus*, ' a system of schemes structuring every decision without ever becoming completely and systematically explicit'.[20] Our common interest was to explore, in the context of the specific theme of the family and work, the relations and connections between

[19] H. Medick, 'The Proto-Industrial Family Economy: the Structural Function of Household and Family during the Transition from Peasant Society to Industrial Capitalism', *Social History*, 3, 1976, pp. 291–315. David Levine, above all, has developed the theme: *Family Formation in an Age of Nascent Capitalism*, London 1976; and D. Levine, 'Industrialization and the Proletarian Family in England', *Past and Present*, 107, 1985, pp. 168–203; A. Dewerpe, *L'Industrie aux Champs*, Rome 1985; A. Cento Bull, 'Proto-industrialization, Small-Scale Capital Accumulation and Diffused Entrepreneurship. The Case of the Brianza in Lombardy', *Social History*, 14, 1989, pp. 177–200; Medick and Sabean (eds.), *Interest and Emotion*.

[20] P. Bourdieu, 'Marriage Strategies as Strategies of Social Reproduction', in R. Forster and O. Ranum (eds.), *Family and Society. Selections from the 'Annales'*, Baltimore–London 1976, p. 119.

families (or their individual members) and the social structuring of access to the labour market and resources. It was through the practices of these families (as distinct from, and sometimes in contrast with, the formal rules) that we hoped to identify relationships that otherwise remain hidden and to understand the mechanisms and functioning of strategies that varied according to the changing needs of individuals and families in their life cycle. In hindsight, it seems to me that, to a greater or lesser extent, we assumed as the conceptual hinterland of such an approach the anthropological idea of exchange as deployed by Sahlins, Bourdieu's sociology of 'practice', Geertz's definition of culture and Elias' insistence on the continuously changing forms of 'interdependence' that condition interpersonal relations.[21] Again, it is essential to add that such concepts served as a stimulus and indirectly. The relationship between the theoretical models of the social scientists and the empirical historical research was never one way. If the concepts encouraged a rethinking of the historical sources, these very sources led to 'a questioning or even rejection of the model as too abstract or historically inaccurate (as, for instance, in the case of Foucault's concept of *renfermement*).

What is common to the essays in this volume is their methodological approach. Our concern for micro-studies goes far beyond a predilection for 'history from below', for justice to be rendered to the forgotten or excluded of history. 'History from below' tends to be written too frequently as the mirror image of history 'from above', institutionally or in sectoral segments. Our aim was to try to understand how institutional forms or rules, theoretically imposed on all society, were appropriated and allocated in different ways by groups and families and transformed in the process.[22] To explore this, the research was deliberately directed towards categories that were not the customary ones: family, guild, charitable institution, the individual life course, relations of vertical interdependence, hierarchies of power or prestige.

Three aspects of this reduction in scale merit attention. First (and most obvious), the change in dimensions acts as an antidote not only to

---

[21] Sahlins, *Stone Age Economics*; Bourdieu, *Outline of a Theory of Practice*; Geertz, *The Interpretation of Cultures*; Geertz, *Local Knowledge*, New York 1983; Elias, *The Court Society*.
[22] Foucault, *Disciplinary Power and Subjection*, pp. 229–42; P. Veyne, 'Foucault révolutionne l'histoire', *Comment on écrit l'histoire*, Paris 1978. Even though one of the main results of our research has been to challenge some of Foucault's conclusions, particularly over the segregation from society of the poor and weak through *renfermement*, it would be ungenerous to deny the significance of his writings for our general approach.

the superficialities, but to the tautologies of many generalizations of the social sciences by exploring the internal dynamics of the object of study, rather than imposing unverified assumptions of behaviour. Second, in order not to reduce the complexity of the reality that emerges from the research, the traditional historical practice of narrative often appears as the most appropriate method of posing questions.[23] Third, placing the family or group at the centre of the study in such closely delimited contexts makes it possible to break down many of the traditional barriers between economic, political and social history. A characteristic of these studies, which derives from the often unexpected linkages that emerged in the course of research, is their integration of themes normally treated as separate.[24]

If the practices of the family at work were the focal point of the research, it was immediately clear that (apart from exceptional cases) the sources rarely allow the family – and even less the family cycle – to be studied directly. The family reconstitution studies of the historical demographers, although they are immediately concerned with the family cycle, are based on sources that throw a little light on the problems of work and subsistence. Only in the case of small communities do the sources permit a direct and concrete historical study of organization within the family and among broader kin, of relationships between families and kin, and between such families and agricultural practices, specific trades, areas or communities.[25] In the cities, it is not normally possible to reconstruct adequately continuous series to identify the structure, alliances and strategies of specific families over a lengthy period, not least because urban populations in modern Europe were so conditioned by migration. Thus, particularly in the urban context, the sources needed to be read not only for the institutional purposes which explained their existence, but even more for what they could be made to yield about family processes, life courses and economic activities. Such an orientation usually necessitated the cross-linking of a range of

[23] This return to narrative remains significantly different from that advocated by Lawrence Stone, primarily in terms of its objectives. L. Stone, 'The Revival of Narrative: Reflections on a New Old History', *Past and Present*, 85, 1979, pp. 3–24; E. Hobsbawm, 'The Revival of Narrative: Some Comments', *Past and Present*, 86, 1980, pp. 3–8. P. Abrams, 'History, Sociology, Historical Sociology', *Past and Present*, 87, 1980, pp. 3–16.

[24] Two excellent studies which reinforce these points are: F. Ramella, *Terra e Telai. Sistemi di Parentela nel Biellese dell'Ottocento*, Turin 1984 and P. Macry, *Ottocento. Famiglia, Elites e Patrimoni a Napoli*, Turin 1988.

[25] An excellent example of such a study in the countryside is D. Sabean, *Power in the Blood, Popular Culture and Village Discourse in Early Modern Germany*, Cambridge 1984.

different records, from the archives of guilds, charitable institutions and judicial bodies to censuses and parochial registers, wills and the vast corpus of notarial acts.

Around these twin axes of work practices and family cycle, the research project has concentrated on three particular themes, ultimately all related to the basic problem of the historical conditions of access to and utilization of the labour market. The first theme assumed the primary importance of the guilds in the urban organization of work, but focussed on the role of the family within these corporations. Hierarchies always existed among urban guilds, and are historically documented in the conflicts over privileges, demarcation lines and ceremonial precedence, as much as over rights of production and distribution of the guild in the 'dominant' city relative to those of the neighbouring towns. Such hierarchies were dependent not just on the economic importance of the corporations, but on the political context within which they operated, on the particular relationship and negotiating power of the oligarchical group of families in control of each guild with local (municipal) and higher (royal) authorities. The relative importance of a specific guild had direct implications in terms of its dimensions, structure and influence in offering employment both to its own members and indirectly, through its production process and the spin-off effect, to a much larger number of individuals and families. Inevitably the sources contain far more about the small group of leading families than about the manipulation by these families of corporate rights and obligations to maintain privileged positions on the market, and hence their own social power.

The second theme of the research project has been the function of charity in the subsistence strategies and employment opportunities of families. It is complementary to the first theme in that it relates to the substantial proportions of urban populations with few or no qualifications, whether in sectors where a dominant guild presence could limit access to the labour market, or in those where the weakness or absence of corporations facilitated exploitation through a normal excess of labour supply, under changing forms of the organization of production. The strategies adopted by families to ensure subsistence correspond to what today is commonly called the 'hidden' or 'informal' sector of the economy. Precisely because it was (and is) an economy of expedients, it is difficult to document. It is primarily at the more formal level of institutionalized charity that the records can be pressed to answer the important question whether such assistance was effective in enabling families to retain their independence, or whether the very methods of assistance tended to confirm the reproduction of the poor, and which poor. The direction of research has been twofold. On the one hand, to enquire what families expected from charitable institutions (such as a professional training, occasional assistance at particular moments of the life-cycle or a refuge for those members they could no longer support) and whether such recourse to poor-relief constituted a normal or exceptional practice. On the other hand, to analyse whether the corpus of charitable institutions in a town adapted to the deskilling in specific industries resulting from the process of economic and organizational change by modifying its choice of clientele and means of assistance.

The third theme in the project relates to the social practices of non-peasant family groups within their rural communities and their wider region of economic activities. In the countryside, where corporations were unusual, specialization of skills in general was not the norm and charitable structures were at best extremely limited, other forms of self-defence explain the success or failure of families. Research has concentrated on the uses of family and kin as forms of solidarity, assuming collective responsibilities and utilizing geographically extended networks. Of specific concern has been the identification of what differentiated non-peasant family groups from the rest of their community, in terms of marriage strategies, transmission of skills or consolidation of extended familial ties by migration.

The essays in this volume offer a partial result of the research project, following on the working papers published in previous years.[26] They are

[26] Stuart J. Woolf, 'Charity and Family Subsistence: Florence in the Early Nineteenth Century', EUI Working Paper No. 85/131, Florence 1985; Massimo Marcolin, 'The Casa d'Industria in Bologna during the Napoleonic Period: Public Relief and Subsistence Strategies', EUI Working Paper No. 85/132, Florence 1985; Osvaldo Raggio, 'Strutture di parentela e controllo delle risorse in un'area di transito: la Val Fontanabuona tra Cinque e Seicento', EUI Working Paper No. 85/133, Florence 1985; Renzo Sabbatini, 'Work and Family in a Lucchese Paper-Making Village at the Beginning of the Nineteenth Century', EUI Working Paper No. 85/134, Florence 1985; Sabine Juratic, 'Solitude féminine et travail des femmes à Paris à la fin du XVIIIème siècle', EUI Working Paper No. 85/135, Florence 1985; Laurence Fontaine, 'Les Effets déséquilibrants du colportage sur les structures de famille et les pratiques économiques dans la vallée de l'Oisans, XVIIIème siècle', EUI Working Paper No. 85/136, Florence 1985; Christopher Johnson, 'Artisans vs. Fabricants: Urban Proto-industrialization and the Evolution of Work Culture in Lodève and Bédarieux, 1740–1830', EUI Working Paper No. 85/137, Florence 1985; Daniela Lombardi, 'La Demande d'assistance et les réponses des autorités urbaines face à une crise conjoncturelle: Florence 1619–1622', EUI Working Paper No. 85/138, Florence 1985; Hans-Ulrich Thamer, 'L'Art du Menuisier. Work practices of French joiners and cabinet-makers in the eighteenth century', EUI Working Paper No. 85/171, Florence 1985; Lucia Ferrante, 'La Sessualità come risorsa. Donne davanti al foro arcivescovile di Bologna (sec.

limited to two geographical areas – south-eastern France and north-central Italy – and to the seventeenth to eighteenth centuries. They illustrate the three main axes of the project: family exploitation of the resources offered by geographical location and regional economies in rural (in this instance mountainous) areas; the role of urban guilds in relation to both the political authorities and the families within the craft they claimed to represent; and the function of charitable institutions in the social relations and life-cycles of the urban poor. Each essay can be read independently of the other contributions, as a micro-study of a particular community, guild or set of urban institutions. But to do so would be to ignore the common concerns in terms of approach and research methodology, aims and results.

As research approach, these essays reverse the tendency to interpret the family in defensive posture against outside economic or institutional impositions. Within social contexts characterized by property relations, working processes and structures of domination,[27] they explore the unwritten norms, mechanisms and structures that conditioned and set the parameters for individuals and families in their working lives. In the rural context, it is through the study of individual families and kin groups that Laurence Fontaine and Osvaldo Raggio have identified those specific characteristics – in terms of family alliances, transmission of property and the exploitation of non-agricultural economic opportunities – that distinguished the pedlars of the Oisans valley and the carriers of Fontanabuona from the subsistence peasantry of their own and nearby communities. In the urban context, Carlo Poni and Simona Cerutti have chosen guilds of apparently middling status – such as Bolognese shoemakers and tanners, or Turin tailors – in order to demonstrate how the institutional authority of such corporations, their rules and regulations, could be appropriated and manipulated by the

Footnote 26 (cont.)

XVII)', EUI Working Paper No. 85/192, Florence 1985; Stuart Woolf, 'The Domestic Economy of the Poor of Florence in the Early Nineteenth Century', EUI Working Paper No. 86/219, Florence 1985; Raul Merzario, 'Il Capitalismo nelle montagne. L'evoluzione delle strutture famigliari nel comasco durante la prima fase di industrializzazione (1746–1811)', EUI Working Paper No. 86/220, Florence 1985; Daniel Roche, 'Paris capitale des pauvres: quelques réflexions sur le paupérisme parisien entre XVII° et XVIII° siècles', EUI Working Paper No. 86/238, Florence 1985; Alain Collomp, 'Les Draps de laine, leur fabrications et leur transport en Haute-Provence, XVII°–XIX° siècle: univers familiaux, de l'ère pré-industrielle à la protoindustrialisation', EUI Working Paper No. 86/239, Florence 1985; Angela Groppi, '"La Classe la plus nombreuse, la plus utile et la plus précieuse". Organizzazione del lavoro e conflitti nella Parigi rivoluzionaria', EUI Working Paper No. 88/325, Florence 1988; Christine Lamarre, 'La Vie des enfants et des vieillards assistés à Dijon au XVIIIème siècle', EUI Working Paper No. 403/89, Florence, 1989.   27 Medick and Sabean, *Interest and Emotion*, pp. 3–4.

leading families in their political negotiations with the urban authorities and in the transmission of their own power within the guild. Sandra Cavallo, through her study of specific charitable institutions at Turin, shows the extremely close relationship between the functioning of urban hospitals, the family life-cycle and the labour market. All the authors discuss institutions, both political and economic, through the eyes of their social 'users', rather than moving from the institutions to (subordinate) society. They emerge with similar conclusions about the capacity of such users to interpret and mediate such institutions in a process of reciprocal appropriation.

The sources employed by the authors are not new, as mostly they derive from institutions characteristic of pre-industrial western Europe, such as guilds or hospitals, or from judicial or notarial acts. But they have been read deliberately in a non-institutional manner, relegating the 'external' history of the institutions to the arena of action chosen by families, whose expectations, ideals and patterns of comportment form the focus of study. Precisely because of the adoption of the family or group and its cycle as the point of departure, the documents were read in an attempt to recover the sense of family time as it affected practices and strategies. The sources needed to be interpreted in terms of why they were produced and what their relationship was to each other: they contained a dialogue between what the 'authorities' thought they were doing and how individuals and families utilized them according to their culture and needs. In some instances this has required a painstakingly minute cross-linking of sources in order to reconstruct individual and especially family biographies, sometimes over generations; in others, it has necessitated a careful assessment of the difficulties and limits of employing fiscal or legal sources (which remain, with notarial acts, the richest mines to quarry for historians of family and work) in order to arrive at conclusions about social hierarchy or group comportment. But in all the contributions there is an explicit preoccupation with the relationship between the sources and what they can be made to reveal, once they cease to be read too literally, about the social use and power of the formal organizational structures within whose framework all individuals and families live. The relationship between the historian and his object of enquiry, in terms of the progressive expansion of the nature of the questions and hence of the sources employed and the information sought from them, is common and central to these essays.

Underlying all the studies is a concern to illustrate the functioning of social relations, both horizontally and vertically (to employ the inelegant terminology of sociology and anthropology). The differentiation was profound between the small oligarchical groups, structured around family and kin in their chosen environment, and the larger numbers working for or dependent upon them; and the evidence would seem to argue against much upward mobility from the lower to the dominant group. The economic realities of social differentiation are explored in these essays in terms of, on the one hand, the mechanisms through which relative levels of wealth and power were transmitted across generations, and, on the other hand, the ties of patronage, dependence and obligation that underlay and conditioned the degree of access to the various and multiple means of survival of the labouring poor. The oligarchy controlling the three Bologna guilds and the Turin merchants taking over the tailors' corporation and creating a religious association, like the tightly regulated families of landowning pedlars in the Alps and the chieftains of the Ligurian clans, all offer examples of the interaction between economic independence and social power in a clearly defined environment (whether institutional or not) utilized by these families to consolidate and transmit their leading position within their communities. In their transactions with higher or more distant authorities – representatives of the state or urban merchants – they would appear to display a broader (and possibly expanding) mental horizon than their apprentices or dependants, whose world was ever more tightly bound by immediate problems of subsistence or debt.[28]

It is more difficult to follow in detail the experiences of these latter families, precisely because their lack of success is reflected negatively in the scarce imprint they have left in the written sources. Hence these essays have relatively little to say about the experiences of journeymen or apprentices, indebted peasants or poor kin. Yet the nature of their relationships with the socially powerful can be glimpsed and at least partially reconstructed through the records of their litigation, as of their debts or requests for assistance. In the rural context, both Fontaine and Raggio point to dependency ties, whether of kin or debt, that operated over long periods, from one generation to another. In the urban context, Cavallo points to a social hierarchy of poverty, with values attached to

[28] This is a theme that would merit study, precisely because it offers another way of exploring the difficult historical question of emotions and prejudices. Is the landless peasant – or English nineteenth-century farm labourer, studied by Keith Snell – more parochial and prejudiced than the landowner? What were the practices towards 'strangers'? K. Snell, *Annals of the Labouring Poor*, Cambridge 1985.

types of employment, which had little to do with any technical distinctions between skilled and unskilled, but need to be explained through the social identification attributed to different forms of work: servants and silk workers at Turin, like building or textile workers in other cities, were favoured by the charitable institutions relative to other poor families, for example in the always heavily populated food trades. But, as Cavallo and Raggio show, access to assistance and employment was also dependent upon the degree of integration into networks of kin or friends who could act as intermediaries. To apply for charity implied an urban knowledge that was only possessed by residents or immigrants who (in Eric Wolf's phrase) were 'plugged in' to some of the modes of urban sociability; what remains to be explored is the role of family ties in such processes of integration.[29]

To reduce the complexity and above all the fluidity of the social structure, of rural village or urban quarter, to rich and poor is to simplify for purely heuristic purposes. Nor can the relations between the elites of these small local worlds and the great majority of their inhabitants be explained merely in terms of direct dependency ties. The social practices of these communities, as of all societies, were far more complicated. As most of these chapters demonstrate, individuals and groups, whether elite or poor, possessed a sophisticated knowledge of rules and regulations, customs and rights, which they appropriated and exploited in their relations with each other, as in their appeals to outside authorities. In conflictual situations, such as over guild prerogatives, the significance of these rules can be assessed, precisely because the conflict itself heightened their perception and written legal expression on the part of the actors. In everyday life, the sense of such unwritten rules remains more opaque, as it can only be inferred from the repetitivity of evidence of what were regarded as normal practices. Even more, the interplay between these norms and the kin networks and ties of protection remains obscure, through paucity of documentation and the methodological difficulties of integrating the two dimensions.

What emerges strongly from all the essays is the vulnerability of these labouring families in pre-industrial Europe, a vulnerability not merely biological (such as lack of heirs, or too many pregnancies and infants), but social in the sense of its exposure to a hostile environment. Family strategies, whether of transmission of wealth and power or of survival,

---

[29] For a later period, but concerned precisely with this problem: M. Gribaudi, *Itinéraires ouvriers. Espaces et groupes sociaux à Turin au début du XX siècle*, Paris 1987.

would seem to have been essentially short term, because of the immensity of the unknown at successive stages of the life-cycle and in the uncertain conjunctures of the world of work. For the Oisans pedlar, the ideal mechanism to transmit his wealth changed as he aged; for the Turin merchants, marriage alliances with tailors and neighbourhood forms of sociability proved temporarily worthwhile because of the particular privileges conserved by the tailors' guild after their loss by other corporations. The charitable institutions were always in direct contact with, and often concerned to correct, the imbalances that characterized specific phases of the family cycle. The evidence of their policies and actions bears witness to a pattern of discontinuities and ruptures within the family cycle, constituted by such traumatic but normal events as the early departure of children, the prolonged absences of the head of household, the abandonment of pregnant women, remarriage of mothers or the solitude of the old.

These structural weaknesses of the families of the labouring classes had immediate and profound repercussions on the possibilities of work and capacities to earn adequately for subsistence. It is in these terms that the highly varied examples of work opportunities presented in these chapters need to be read. For, historically, conditions of work have always implied written or unwritten norms, by no means always related directly to the market, but intimately linked to the social perception of family needs and to community or group customs. The models of work presented by Raggio and Fontaine point to entrepreneurial activities, however closely regulated and based on family solidarities, as a successful alternative to rural subsistence. The restrictive practices so prominent in Poni's and Cerutti's analysis of guilds raise questions not only about their efficacy in the relations between the guild oligarchies and their members (apprentices and journeymen as well as masters), but about the regulation and forms of work where the guilds were weak or non existent. The organization of production within hospitals, discussed by Cavallo, poses a multiplicity of problems about its purposes, in terms of the relationship between institutional production and the collective corporative structuring of the open market; the moral, disciplinary and economic motivations for the complicated and expensive installation of such activities; outside apprenticeship of orphans and the in-house role of private entrepreneurs and artisans; state mercantilist policies and the imparting of practical skills and a work culture utilizable in open labour markets; the interconnections in an urban economy between work opportunities and charitable provision.

In these, as in other instances, the answers to many of the questions about the nature of work in pre-industrial societies can be answered most fruitfully by reference to the organization and developmental cycle of the family. The chapters in this volume, deliberately limited because of their historical specificity as micro-studies of precise and detailed issues, offer some initial responses.

2 ✌ Social relations and control of resources in an area of transit: eastern Liguria, sixteenth to seventeenth centuries

Osvaldo Raggio

One of the main characteristics of the economy and life of Ligurian communities in modern times has been the structural shortage of cereal production. In terms of historical analysis, this reality implies the study of notable problems, such as levels of domestic consumption, forms of subsistence, integration of town and village economies and their dependency on regional and international markets, the nature of the obligations to commercialize and articulate local and extra-local exchanges. In the sixteenth and seventeenth centuries, the products of Ligurian coastal communities which could assure the necessary circuit of exchange and supply of wheat were oil and, to a lesser extent, wine.

Another characteristic of Liguria – shared by many Mediterranean regions and communities – is the interdependence, often within limited ranges, of different ecological areas: a richer coastal strip adjacent to poor valley and mountainous zones, particularly lacking in food products. In these areas the shortage of wheat, compensated only partially by chestnuts and minor cereals, was rendered the more serious by the absence of oil and wine or of the opportunities offered by the sea (fishing and navigation). Because of this, access to necessary integrative resources became particularly dramatic.

The problem of economic integration is one of the critical points of historical and anthropological literature dealing with agricultural societies and with the necessary links between communities and society as a whole.[1] Economic relations with the outside world can derive, in varying degrees, from local initiatives, decisions or pressures of central governments, or from modifications of international markets.[2] The forms they

---

[1] For a review of the studies on Mediterranean communities, see D.D. Gilmore, 'Anthropology of the Mediterranean', *Annual Review of Anthropology*, 11, 1982, pp. 175–205.
[2] See J. Davis, *People of the Mediterranean*, London 1977.

assume, however, are always closely tied to the culture, social organization and local systems of stratification. They can never be separated from the totality of political, administrative and fiscal relations with external centres of power.

Throughout the modern history of the Republic of Genoa, central fiscal pressure on the towns and villages of the territory remained relatively weak. (As we shall see, the only really important exaction was that withheld in kind from the production of oil. It was not accidental that oil, the sole commercializable source of wealth, became one of the main items of the accumulated debt of towns and villages during the seventeenth century.) At the same time the city–capital, which was almost totally dependent on imports transported by sea to supply its urban population, hardly ever fulfilled any redistributive functions towards the towns and villages in crucial food sectors such as that of cereal products.[3] These towns and villages – all characterized by a low rate of domestic consumption – were therefore obliged to obtain their own supplies by establishing a series of relatively autonomous exchange circuits. This lack of economic integration, indicative of a more general weak political integration, determined the polycentric nature of the territory of the Republic and the central role of the coastal towns. In these towns an elite of merchants tried to monopolize supplies through control of the few negotiable local resources, the exchange circuits and the infrastructures for the transformation of food products.

In the following pages I shall study the case of a group of towns and villages in eastern Liguria (Levante), the coastal area around the towns of Rapallo and Chiavari and their hinterlands running into the Apennine mountain range, during the sixteenth and seventeenth centuries. My intention is to illustrate the connections between the ecological and productive system, the social structure, the forms of settlement and the apparatus of economic exchanges. The ethnographical research confirms the central role of towns and merchants. But it also demonstrates that, by virtue of their strategic position and their forms of social organization, even the most marginal and poorest areas in terms of productivity (the mountain villages) were able to play an important role in the activation and control of exchange circuits. These circuits thus became their most important 'resource'.

---

[3] In cases of famine (e.g. in 1630) or plague (e.g. in 1657). In the sixteenth century, as at the beginning of the nineteenth century, the harvest of the majority of the villages was considered sufficient only for two or three months.

Transit of goods and interpersonal relations

In December 1583, two merchants from Rapallo, Lorenzo Boglio and
Gervasio Pessia, were on their way home, by mule, from Parma, where
they had delivered and sold oil and soap. They were crossing the border
area between the valley of Aveto (fief of Prince Doria) and Genoese
territory (*podesteria* of Rapallo), escorted by *messire* Paolo Gerolamo
Della Cella, Antonio Della Cella and by '10 or 12 men belonging to the
Della Cella kin', carrying arquebuses. Thanks to their protection the
two men escaped unharmed from an attack by a gang of nine bandits led
by a leader of the Malatesta family on the Ventarola Pass, and entered
Genoese territory. Along the mule-track which descended towards the
bottom of the valley of Fontanabuona they stopped at the inns of the
Arata family in the *ville* (villages) of Croce, Orero and Pianezza. On the
last part of the same mule-track which led to the town of Rapallo they
were accompanied by 'three young members of the Queirolo kin'. But
between Pianezza and 'Madonna di Monte' they were attacked for the
second time by armed bandits.[4]

This all happened on the last part (about ten miles) of one of the major
routes linking the coastal villages of Levante Liguria to the plain of the
Po. The whole route (sixty to seventy miles) involved a four-to-five day
journey on foot or by mule.[5] It not only crossed the Genoese border, but
also went through the politically fragmented and competitive areas of
the Imperial fiefs. The merchants and muleteers who travelled along the
roads and paths towards the Po plain were constantly exposed to the
danger of attacks by the gangs which operated primarily along the mule-
tracks and their passes, with frequent and rapid moves from Genoese
territory to feudal enclaves where they enjoyed sure refuge and protection.[6] The bandits robbed and extorted money from the merchants and

[4] Archivio di Stato di Genova (henceforth ASG), *Acta Senatus* 524 and *Rota Criminale* 1226.
[5] These indications, drawn from sixteenth and seventeenth-century reports, are confirmed by
studies of the Napoleonic era: ASG, *Prefettura Francese* 1356 and 1357; Archives Nationales
(Paris), F10 353, F11 705, F20 160.
[6] See O. Raggio, 'Parentele, Fazioni e Banditi: la Val Fontanabuona tra Cinque e Seicento', in G.
Ortalli (ed.), *Bande armate, banditi, banditismo e repressione di giustizia negli stati europei di antico regime*,
Rome 1986. The territory of the Imperial fiefs, which belonged to noble Genoese families and
others – Spinola, Fieschi, Doria, Pallavicino, Malaspina – were directly subject to the Emperor.
Their owners had received investiture from him and were able to avoid any interference from
neighbouring states. On the fiefs of the Ligurian Apennines, see A. Sisto, *I Feudi imperiali del
Tortonese (sec. XI–XIX)*, Turin 1956. On feudal organization, see K.O. Von Aretin, 'L'Ordina-
mento Feudale in Italia nel XVI e XVII Secolo e le sue Ripercussioni sulla Politica Europea',
Annali dell'Istituto storico italo–germanico in Trento, 4, 1978, pp. 51–94.

carriers but, as we shall see, their attacks were deliberate and selective. The logic of their violent actions reflected the ties of dependence or collaboration they maintained with feudal lords and local notables. In the absence of reliable institutional guarantees, the normal course of commercial activities required a network of strongly personalized relations of alliance, friendship and collaboration with the villages, kin and feudal lords strategically located along the routes of transit, near the passes and in the valleys.

Let us take a closer look at the protagonists of the story I have sketched. Lorenzo Boglio and Gervasio Pessia were two of the richest merchants of the town of Rapallo. They owned warehouses in which they stocked the oil produced in the hills around the town and imported from western Liguria (Ponente) numerous mules and the products of at least three *savonare* (soap factories).[7] The members of the Della Cella kin lived in the *ville* on the border between the valley of Aveto and Genoese territory. Because of an old feudal investiture by the Malaspina (recognized and renewed by Prince Doria), they enjoyed territorial privileges – they were considered a 'seignory' – and functioned as feudatories and excise-men for the Prince.[8] Their ranks included nobles, notaries, priests, muleteers and *spallaroli* (pack carriers). They received the tolls paid on merchandise in transit. But their primary activities were those of protecting their allies – the merchants of Rapallo and the muleteers who worked for them – of organizing contraband and of discouraging competitors. Between 1500 and 1600 – according to the Genoese authorities, one of the main organizational centres of oil smuggling (and the recycling of stolen goods) was the *villa* of Cabanne, situated at the crossroads of all the mule-tracks leading to the Po plain and in the heart of Della Cella territory. The Arata kin controlled the 'mule routes' in Genoese territory, were owners and managers of six inns, owned the majority of the mules used for transport from Rapallo and had the monopoly of political positions in the Fontanabuona valley. Their most trusted allies in the valley were the Queriolo.[9]

In order to appreciate the importance of this continuous socio-territorial structure which was at the basis of commercial relations, we need to know that these three kin groups were linked by relations of

[7] Archivio Storico del Comune di Rapallo (henceforth ASCR), *Borgo di Rapallo* register 38.
[8] Sisto, *I Feudi imperiali del Tortonese*, and G. Fontana, *Rezzoaglio e Val d'Aveto (Cenni storici ed episodi)*, Rapallo 1940.
[9] See O. Raggio, 'La Politica nella Parentela. Conflitti Locali e Commissari in Liguria Orientale (Secoli XVI–XVII)', *Quaderni Storici* N.S., 63, 1986, pp. 721–57.

reciprocity based on matrimonial alliances, credit and the exchange of favours, friendship and protection, and a political solidarity matured in the course of the factional conflicts which divided the villages.[10]

A kind of reciprocity also characterized the selective relations between these and other kin and the merchants of Rapallo and Chiavari. These relations depended on the infrastructure and services that the men of the inland *ville* could guarantee by virtue of the strategic position they occupied. The commercial circuits of specialized goods produced else-where offered important occupational opportunities not only to innkeepers and mule-owners, but also to a consistent group of muleteers, *spallaroli* (pack-carriers), armed youths and 'bandits', who were rec-ruited by middlemen and *principali* (notables possessing most material wealth, power and prestige) and employed in the transport system along the Apennine paths and in the escorts.

The transit of goods thus signified a structure of interpersonal relations with a complex territorial dimension. The specificity of this system of reciprocity and its geographical expression consisted of the more-than-local dimension of the exchanges, because of the traditional orientation of the towns of eastern Liguria towards the Po valley and the dependence on outside supplies common to the coastal towns and the hinterland.

Oil production and trade

The oil which supplied the exchange circuit was produced on the terraced hills around the two towns, but was also imported in large quantities (partly low-grade oil to be made into soap) from western Liguria, Monaco, Apulia and Spain, in part ordered by Genoese *cittadini* (nobles).[11] Imported oil was added to, or replaced, that of local production and assured the continuity of the flow towards the Po plain even in years when local production barely sufficed for consumption.

Between 1500 and 1600 Rapallo's local production, for example, was estimated at approximately 8,000 barrels in a good year. This was a theoretical quantity because, as is well known, olive production is subject to considerable oscillations due to the normal rest periods of olive

---

[10] Ibid. These relations are documented at the end of the sixteenth century in the notarial acts: Archivio Notarile di Chiavari (henceforth ANC), *Notaio Gio Angelo Della Cella* (1569–76).

[11] See O. Raggio, 'Produzione Olivicola, Prelievo Fiscale e Circuiti di Scambio in una Comunità Ligure del XVII Secolo', *Atti della Società Ligure di Storia Patria* N.S., 22, 1982, pp. 125–62.

trees and their extreme sensitivity to climatic incidents (frost, hail, wind). In any case, in a good year, after subtracting the quantity of oil owed (in kind) to the Republic to supply the city–capital (about a fourth of the production, valued at an administrative price, always lower than the 'market price') and local consumption (estimated, during the first half of the seventeenth century, at 3,600 barrels), the town was left with a negotiable surplus of about 2,500 barrels.[12]

But, as we have said, the flow towards the Po plain was alimented by large quantities of imported oil.[13] This fact signified that the town's merchants were operators in a market of international dimensions, either on their own account or as middlemen working for the Genoese nobility.

In 1572, for example, Antonio Vallebella and Gio Pessia (merchants from Rapallo) declared that they negotiated oil, acting as 'agents' of the nobles Raffaele Spinola and Raffaele Della Torre. At the end of June 1627, the shipowner Michele Cella unloaded at Rapallo ninety-seven barrels of oil ordered by the noble Marc'Antonio Merello at Celle Ligure (Ponente). During the following days the oil was entrusted to seventeen muleteers (twelve from Fontanabuona) who transported it to Lombardy. Between 25 July and 18 August of the same year, 368 barrels of oil purchased by merchants from Rapallo and Genoese nobles in western Liguria crossed the Fontanabuona valley on 152 mules. In 1636–7, 20 per cent of the oil stored in the warehouses of Rapallo was imported. During the same years the town's richest merchant, Marc'Antonio Merello, declared that he purchased oil from Apulia for the Magnificent (Genoese noble) Gio Maria Spinola.[14]

In all cases negotiable oil (whether locally produced or imported) was controlled by the town's merchants and, as we shall see, even the Genoese withholding tax was to the advantage of the 'opulent merchants'.

At Rapallo the merchants managed to appropriate large shares of the production of small landowners of the *ville* through credit and anticipated sales (before harvesting). They granted loans of foodstuffs or money against the promise to hand over 'many oils'. Oil was the

---

[12] During the same period Chiavari had an optimum production of about 15,000 barrels (one barrel = about 66 litres).

[13] Both *fine* (first quality) oil and *coarse* (lower quality) oil. *Coarse* oil supplied the local soap industry, whose product was also exported.

[14] ASG, *Antica Finanza*, 668, 1046 and 1053; Raggio, 'Produzione Olivicola'.

principal resource and the only commercial product of the coastal area and in relations between peasant producers and urban merchants functioned as money. In these asymmetrical relations the exchange rate between oil and money and the ratio between domestic consumption, oil surplus and price of wheat or other cereals was obviously crucial. In fact, the debt certificates in which oil appeared concerned the urban merchants. The loans often have as deadline 'at will' (*ad voluntatem*) and the price of oil is that fixed 'between Rapallo merchants' (*inter mercatores Rapalli*).[15] In some cases an entire village was indebted. In 1573, for example, the heads of household of the *villa* of San Maurizio di Monti requested a moratorium of six months in a petition to the *podestà* of Rapallo. Hail had destroyed the entire olive crop of a year considered exceptional (the oil production of Monti had been estimated at 800 barrels) and the small producers had gone into debt 'above the fruit of the olive-trees' to the *bourgeois* of Rapallo. Similar cases involved the villages near Chiavari at the end of the sixteenth century and, in 1607, the heads of household of Sori who, indebted to the *bourgeois* of Recco, requested a moratorium from the Senate of the Republic.[16]

The same mechanism of credit and advance sales was used by the merchants who controlled the contracts of payments in kind in Genoa. They regulated relations with individual taxpayers, 'paying for oil with wheat, rye, cloth and other goods', or including this particular tax payment in pre-existing credit or customer accounts.

The urban merchants were also the owners, together with some Genoese nobles, of the best olive groves in the villages. They rented these lands to *manenti* (peasant farmers) through share-cropping leases, by which two thirds of the oil (or wine) went to the landlords.[17] In addition, the *bourgeois* owned the majority of the oil-mills.[18]

The central role of the merchants was thus based on an inextricable interlacing between control of production, property, taxation and commerce (import and export). These were the elements which, together with credit and customer ties with the peasants, legitimated their specific social role.

In terms of local production it is obvious that the storing of oil in the

[15] Some examples in ANC, *Notaio Carlo Lencisa* (1577–1621) and *Notaio Gio Batta Borzese* (1578–1603); ASG, *Antica Finanza* 1053.   [16] ASG, *Acta Senatus* 496, 500, 506, 1437, 1688, 1690.

[17] See O. Raggio, 'Mutamenti di Proprietà e Contratti Agrari nel Chiavarese, 1544–1714: l'Espansione dei Domini in Due Famiglie', *Miscellanea Storica Ligure*, 8:2, 1968, pp. 51–81; now in *Atti della Società Economica di Chiavari*, Chiavari 1986.

[18] ASCR, *Caratata del 1647*, registers 12, 23, and 29.

town's warehouses occurred almost entirely outside the market. The harvesting of the product and its successive commercialization were two separate and distinct processes. The 'going price' amongst the town's merchants (and thus the mercantile model) was relatively independent of the transactions between producers and buyers, which involved customer relations of dependency and were often motivated by 'necessity'.

Transit, oil merchants and middlemen

The central role of transit towards the Po valley was a plurisecular constant. Relations between merchants of the two towns and the populations of the valleys of the hinterland were structured around them. In these valleys olive production was practically non existent and other negotiable products were rare. In the hinterlands olive trees did not bear fruit and the wine, sour and insipid, was either destined for domestic use or sold to local innkeepers. The structural deficit of cereal production and the fragility of self-sufficiency were common to the two areas, but hinterland agricultural subsistence activities were organized almost exclusively around chestnut cultivation, exploitation of the woods and sparse pastures. In the Fontanabuona valley, for example, 60 per cent of the land was taken up by chestnut groves and the rest by woods, maquis, meadows and common land. The plots dedicated exclusively to arable were extremely limited, vineyards were only cultivated around the houses and market gardening was restricted to a few plains at the bottom of the valley.[19] Although chestnuts entered local commercial circuits and, along with wood, reached Genoese markets, they constituted an important but insufficient substitute. From an ecological point of view the contrast with the coastal area was therefore sharp. Contemporary sources, such as the later enquiries of the Napoleonic prefects, insist on the extreme poverty of the hinterland valleys, 'all the wealth of the territory lies in the coastal towns'.[20] The secondary importance of land was confirmed by the absence of pressure from outside society to absorb it, in contrast with what happened in the olive-cultivated hills around the two towns. There, during the seventeenth century, both the tax-exempt property of the Genoese nobles and that of the *bourgeois* increased considerably.[21] The ecological constraints, how-

[19] ASG, *Magistrato delle comunità*, registers 768 and 769.   [20] ASG, *Acta Senatus* 515.
[21] Raggio, 'Produzione Olivicola'.

ever, do not explain the exchange mechanism, the economic logic of which was socially based.

In the hinterland valleys, a variety of supplementary, non-agricultural activities was exercised. Livestock raising and small-scale transhumance were practised on the basis of reciprocity and exchange agreements with shepherds of the Imperial fiefs. Domestic silk spinning and weaving were dependent on orders from Genoese silk merchants, as were linen spinning and weaving on those from Lombardy. Mixed woollen cloth, like wooden tools and coal, was produced for local and regional use. Alongside these activities the oil/wheat exchange circuit dominated.

There can be no doubt that most of the oil stored in the warehouses of the merchants from the two towns was destined for export to the Po valley, and in particular to the cities of Parma, Piacenza and Lodi. All the administrative enquiries of the Republic and the visits of the officials of the Genoese oil magistracy confirm this. At Chiavari, at the beginning of February 1575 (while the harvesting and processing of olives was still in course) the entire stock of oil that had so far been produced 'went to Lombardy across the Sturla valley'.[22] In 1623, a state official maintained that the Fontanabuona valley was one of the areas in Liguria where oil smuggling was most commonly practised 'because of its proximity to Lombardy and the facilities the Lombard merchants have had'.[23] This was confirmed by another official in 1640.[24] Then, around 1660, the municipal officials of Rapallo declared that 'all the oil produced in their jurisdiction as well as imported oil is traded by men from Fontanabuona'.[25] In fact during the course of the seventeenth century it appears that the Fontanabuona middlemen increasingly assumed the role of oil merchants oriented towards the Po valley. The number of them who were described as 'oil merchants' (*publice et palam negocians*) and were added to the lists of taxpayers constantly increased during the second half of the century (see table 2.1).

But the Genoese state officials maintained that most of the transit consisted of smuggling. The root cause was the constant worry of avoiding taxes and tolls. Oil was the sole wealth of the territory and the only production which Genoa subjected to territorially wide controls and a withholding tax. The sixteenth-century regulations (*capitoli*), renewed in 1660, 1616 and thereafter every ten years up to the beginning

[22] ASG, *Acta Senatus* 497. At the same date at Rapallo 'no one declared oil produced and sold' (ASG, *Acta Senatus* 500).   [23] ASG, *Antica Finanza* 1053.   [24] ASG, *Antica Finanza* 668.
[25] ASCR, *Foliatium Communitatis Rapalli* 1.

Table 2.1 *Merchants of Rapallo and of the Fontanabuona valley in the seventeenth century*[26]

Years	Rapallo	Fontanabuona
1618	54	7
1652	31	21
1659	51	24
1662	49	39
1664	58	49
1674	42	50

of the eighteenth century (until the great frost of 1709 which destroyed the entire olive groves of Liguria and rendered them unproductive for many years), forbade the export of olives and oil before the payment of the tax in kind. Generally this meant until the beginning of May, sometimes well into June. After payment, licences for *estrazione fuori Dominio* (export beyond the state frontiers) were granted individually for limited periods (for example, fifteen days) but with a tax imposed on every barrel exported.

However, the export prohibitions reinforced the role of the merchant–monopolists, at the expense of the small producers who were obliged to hand over their production levy immediately. Genoa formally forbade merchants from competing in bids for delivery of taxes in kind, but in reality only 'opulent merchants' could ensure deliveries. The merchants who acquired the contracts for delivery to the Genoese magistracy responsible for provisioning the capital were able to negotiate the period and manner of deliveries with Genoa. They could buy oil in western Liguria (an area highly specialized in olive culture and with a consistent surplus) and if necessary pay a 'supplement', divided among those subject to the tax, for each barrel not delivered. They could delay deliveries and, in the meantime, store the entire small local production in their warehouses. Their authority went so far as to enable them to have peasants from the villages imprisoned.[27]

Contraband of oil

Contraband therefore meant non-authorized 'extractions', before or after delivery of the quantity owed in kind to Genoa by the community.

[26] ASCR, *Criminalium* 19 and *Ripartizione tassa dell'olio* 1.   [27] Raggio, 'Produzione Olivicola'.

It was organized by *bourgeois* merchants from the two towns and reinforced the role of the groups and middlemen living in the inland valleys. In fact, a fundamental resource for the success of commercial activities – legal or illegal – based on transporting was, as we have seen, the availability of armed escorts, carriers and strategic structures.

A variety of sources which can be found for the period from the sixteenth century to the Napoleonic years makes it possible to reconstruct the routes and composition of the goods. The mule convoys which started out from the two towns travelled over the mule-tracks towards the three major Apennine passes connecting Genoese territory to that of the Imperial fiefs, and transported almost exclusively oil and soap, though sometimes also citrus fruits. In the other direction, the muleteers from the Po valley transported, along the same routes, wheat, rice, linen, cloth, cheese, hides, salted meat, fuses and gunpowder. The diversification of the merchandise is an important sign of the commercial asymmetry. It is very difficult, and perhaps impossible due to the absence of tolls, to obtain quantitative data concerning the legal flow of goods; just as it is obviously impossible to quantify the illegal traffic. But the central role of transit and the contraband phenomenon are well documented by numerous indirect sources, particularly criminal ones.

The *spallaroli*-smugglers and the 'bandits', recruited by middlemen from the hinterland valleys, used paths in the woods next to the mule-tracks, travelled armed, and could rely upon a dense network of protectors and informers. Let us look at a few examples. In the summer of 1572, the *bargello* (the law-enforcing officer) of the Court of Rapallo surprised, at Isolana (Fontanabuona valley), three muleteers from the Arata kin 'with no certificates' and with three mules carrying seven wineskins full of oil. The muleteers, using arquebuses, resisted the attempt to sequester their goods, helped by 'many people who showed up with stones in their hands'.[28] In May of the same year, Gio Pessa, on being stopped while leaving the town of Rapallo with three bales of soap and eight loads (*some*) of oil on the backs of seven mules and with an escort of four youths, declared that he was on his way to Pianezza in Fontanabuona and was transporting 'foreign' oil for the nobles Raffaele Della Torre and Raffaele Spinola and their Rapallese merchant–middlemen.[29] In 1575 Battino Arata, Marco Arata and Batta Queirolo were convicted of trading oil without a licence.[30] Again in 1575 the

---

[28] ASG, *Notai Giudiziari* 596/2.   [29] Ibid.   [30] ASG, *Acta Senatus* 503 and 1412.

captain of Chiavari proposed the institution of particular licences for the transport of oil even within his jurisdiction ('from one place to another'). Merchants and muleteers declared in fact that they transported oil to Fontanabuona or to the Sturla valley, but illegal 'extraction' was then organized in these valleys.[31] In 1576, Ercolino and Paoletino Della Cella were stopped by the *bargello* in Fontanabuona with three mules loaded with oil which they said were being transported by order and with the permission of Prince Doria.[32] In 1579, at Carasco, just a few miles from Chiavari, the *bargello* was forced to flee 'by nine or ten armed youths' who were escorting two muleteers and had been informed of his arrival by a valley innkeeper.[33] (Inn and tavernkeepers represented authentic pivots of a series of social networks and were often directly involved in contraband activities. The taverns also had a fundamental logistic function.) In 1593, Batta Cademartori, when stopped at Calvari in the Lavagna valley (four miles from the town of Chiavari), offered the *bargello* five or six ducats in exchange for his impunity. The same *bargello* was confronted and threatened a few hours later by a group of men, armed with arquebuses, who were escorting nine mules carrying oil.[34]

Threats, corruption and ties with the elite of Chiavari allowed the Bacigalupo of Carasco to organize smuggling together with the 'merchants engaged in wholesale trading'.[35] In 1608, the *bargello* of Chiavari succeeded in confiscating five *some* of oil in Fontanabuona.[36] The same year the muleteers transporting Paolo Pessia's oil to Piacenza tried to bribe the *bargello* of Rapallo by offering him money.[37] In 1624, among those accused of illegal 'extraction' we find the captain of Rapallo himself, who authorized exports in exchange for 'money, butter, cheese and sausages'.[38] On 6 June 1625, on the Rapallo hills, the *bargello* stopped a party of muleteers and merchants escorted by armed men from Fontanabuona. The intervention of the latter allowed the muleteers to go on towards Piacenza. At the subsequent trial the following were summoned as suspects: Aurelio Arata, who declared himself to be a merchant of wheat, rice and wine and owner of mules used in trading with Lombardy, Bobbio and Piacenza; Gio Andrea and Rolandino Arata, merchants from Fontanabuona; Teramo Cagnone, from Rapallo, who said he was a merchant and trader of rice, wheat, cheese and linen and owner of three mules; Ambrosio Cagnone and Venturino

[31] ASG, *Acta Senatus* 500.   [32] ASG, *Acta Senatus* 499.   [33] ASG, *Acta Senatus* 507.
[34] ASG, *Acta Senatus* 555.   [35] Ibid.   [36] ASG, *Acta Senatus* 1693.
[37] ASCR, *Extraordinariorum* 1.   [38] ASG, *Sindicato Riviera Levante* 931.

Canessa who said they were *camalli* (manual porters).[39] A month later, along the stream of Rapallo, the same *bargello* stopped another *camallo* who was working for the same Teramo Cagnone and Pelegro Arata.[40] On 22 August of the same year came the turn of three muleteers from Rapallo who were transporting oil and soap to Fontanabuona, where they said they were to exchange these goods for wheat flour, on behalf of three merchants from the town: Pantalino Merello, Giovanni Cagnone and Simone Pessia.[41] In 1628, among those accused of smuggling we again find Aurelio Arata, who confirmed that he was a trader in oil, wheat, rice, linen and cheese, and owner of six mules.[42] In 1632, two other smugglers – Felino and Ambrosio Arata – declared that they were muleteers for Gio Pessia.[43]

The common and constant elements in the cases I have studied are the direction of the transit (the Po plain via the hinterland valleys, and in particular via Fontanabuona); the presence of armed escorts; the close collaboration between the Rapallese merchants and the merchant– muleteers from the Fontanabuona valley; the continuity of the same surnames (Pessia, Cagnone, Arata . . .); and lastly a partial combination, through the same persons, of the oil/wheat circuit. A further element, confirmed by other sources, is the increase in contraband (and probably an intensification of controls) after the 1620s. We shall return to this aspect later.

The problem of soldering together the oil and wheat circuits obliges us to explain the selective partnership ties which united the towns' merchants to those of the internal valleys and the social logic of the exchanges.

Wheat transit and middlemen

As opposed to other towns in Liguria whose privileged wheat supply route was the sea,[44] the populations of Rapallo and Chiavari depended almost entirely on trading with the Po plain. But Lombard wheat did not reach the two towns directly. Its flow towards the coast stopped in the hinterland valleys, sites of important weekly markets and annual fairs.

Behind the coastal towns, from west to east, the *ville* of Roccatagliata

---

[39] ASCR, *Extraordinariorum* 20.   [40] Ibid.   [41] Ibid.   [42] ASCR, *Extraordinariorum* 21.
[43] ASCR, *Extraordinariorum* 26.
[44] For example, some villages in the extreme eastern part of Liguria exchanged their wine for wheat transported by shippers (ASG, *Camera del Governo, Finanze* 47).

(upper Fontanabuona), Monleone and Pianezza (Fontanabuona valley), Borzonasca (Sturla valley), Carasco (Lavagna valley) and Varese Ligure (Vara valley) were the major market-places filtering the supplies of the coastal area, particularly to the towns of Recco, Camogli, Santa Margherita, Rapallo, Chiavari, Lavagna, Sestri Levante and Moneglia. The *ville*-markets were all situated in the hinterlands near or at the crossroads of the mule-tracks which connected the coastal area to the Po plain. Roccatagliata was the site of a weekly market frequented by Lombard muleteers (from Lodi, Voghera and Varzi), travelling from the Torriglia market (an autonomous Imperial fief) on their way to Genoese territory.[45] Two weekly markets were held at Monleone and Pianezza, where, at the end of the sixteenth and throughout the seventeenth century, two hundred mules arrived from Lombardy carrying wheat and other cereals.[46] The muleteers from Bobbio and Santo Stefano d'Aveto met at Borzonasca and went on to Carasco, a *villa* situated four miles from Chiavari at the junction of two muleteers.[47] Varese was the site of a weekly market (on Saturdays) and of an annual three-day fair (1–3 September) attended by merchants and muleteers from Parma and Piacenza and those from Bardi and Compiano (territories of the Imperial Count, Conte Landi).[48] All these *ville*, located in a fifty-kilometre semi-circle were recognized 'institutionally' both as trading places and as grain markets. The importance of these *ville* as market-places can be partly explained by their strategic position and by the strong potential offered by the coastal towns' dependency for food. However, the means of control of and intervention in the circulation of wheat varied considerably and illustrated the role of social groups and often violent local entrepreneurs.

The existence of the Roccatagliata market, for example, was the cause of constant conflict – including reprisals and retaliations – with Torriglia and with Prince Doria's excisemen who controlled the passes between the feudal area and Genoese territory. The existence of the Borzonasca market depended on kin, friendship and reciprocity relations among the 'principal personages of the place', the Della Cella and Prince Doria. The war of 1575, the revolt of the feudatories in 1591, as well as the frequent feuds among the kin of the valley provoked the closing of passes and the interruption of transits, thus creating immediate problems of

[45] ASG, *Acta Senatus* 505, 508 and 1412.
[46] ASG, *Acta Senatus* 512 and *Antica Finanza* 668; ASCR, *Foliatium Communitatis Rapalli* 1.
[47] ASG, *Acta Senatus* 512 and 1448.   [48] ASG, *Acta Senatus* 512.

supplies for the *ville* and Chiavari. One of the reasons for the good fortune of the Bacigalupo of Carasco as oil and wheat merchants was that they owned a mobile bridge over the river which separated the Lavagna valley from the town of Chiavari. In 1578, the town officials accused them of obliging Lombard muleteers to stop at Carasco for several days, especially during the winter when the river was swollen, 'spending a lot of money in the taverns and selling their goods at prices negotiated with two or three wealthy men from the *villa*'.[49] The wheat arrived at the Chiavari market only after this intervention. In 1604, a project of the town council of Chiavari for the construction of a bridge at Carasco and of a new 'road to Lombardy' provoked violent opposition from the Bacigalupo and from representatives of the *ville* near Carasco, and sparked off internal conflicts among the populations of the Lavagna valley and the Sturla valley, who controlled two alternative routes towards the plain. The various positions were supported by contrasting petitions from *bourgeois*, merchants, local notables, muleteers, *spallaroli*, and political or administrative representatives of the *ville*.[50] The highest level of strife was thus found in relation to control of the transit routes and the territories crossed by the circulation of goods.

In general, however, markets and fairs were areas and times of peace and were open to all, whether 'foreigners' or populations of the *ville* and towns. The tradition of free and direct supplies for all, of whatever 'status, rank and condition', before the intervention of local wholesalers, seems to be confirmed.[51] The practice of participating in the markets of the internal valleys, which were held, at least in neighbouring valleys, on different days, was widespread among the population of the coastal area, retailers and merchants. It is easy to find people from Chiavari and Rapallo at Santo Stefano d'Aveto or in the Taro valley in the records contained in judicial sources. The market and fairs of Varese Ligure were frequented by merchants from Parma, sellers from Compiano, *granatini* (wheat merchants) from Chiavari and Sestri Levante, the inhabitants of the *ville*, millers, bakers and their helpers. At the Torriglia market, Lombard merchants and muleteers sold wheat and other victuals to the inhabitants of the *ville* of Recco and the upper Fontanabuona valley. The wheat and rice transported by the muleteers of the Po

[49] ASG, *Acta Senatus* 535.   [50] ASG, *Acta Senatus* 589.

[51] See E. Grendi, 'Annona e Annone nella Liguria del Seicento', communication at the conference *Cultura e storia dell'alimentazione*, Imperia, 8–12 March 1983. See, for example, the *capitoli* for the market of the *Università* of Sarzana (ASG, *Acta Senatus* 1437).

plain were obviously the goods most in demand, but among the products both bought and sold from other places were also oil, wine, cheese and cattle. At some markets and at particular times of the year there were direct oil/wheat exchanges. This was the case at the Monleone market in Fontanabuona, which was most intensely active during the months following the olive harvest in the coastal area.[52]

These market places were only one aspect of the complex forms of exchange and trading that went on in this intermediate area between the coast and the Po valley. They illustrate the weight and role of 'suburban' communities which suffered from serious food shortages but were situated at the borders of sovereign jurisdictions and in 'route areas'. The other, and more important, strong points of these communities were, as we have seen, their activities as protectors of transits and organizers of contraband. Their active intervention in commercial flows was then complemented by the availability on the spot of a good infrastructure of mills for the transformation into flour of wheat and the other cereals from the Po valley.[53] We shall see later those aspects that made the hinterlands of the more important coastal towns of eastern Liguria an influential route. For the present I shall limit my study to the valleys situated directly behind the towns of Chiavari and Rapallo, and particularly to the Fontanabuona valley.

Kin, friendship and transit

The conflict to which I have referred between the *ville* of the Lavagna valley and the Sturla valley, set off by the project of constructing a new road, demonstrates that without transit (and contraband) some villages would perhaps not have been able to play the role they did. (It is not accidental that some local historians have explained the breakdown of the valley communities and the overseas emigration of the later nineteenth century in terms of the end of mule transits towards the Po valley.)[54] The 'border' communities of eastern Liguria were in fact extremely sensitive to political conflicts along the border of the Imperial fiefs and to the evolution of relations between these fiefs and the state of Genoa, which involved closing passes and changing jurisdictions.

The relations of cooperation and competition which were established

---

[52] ASG, *Antica Finanza* 668.   [53] See below, pp. 69–70.
[54] See R. Leveroni, *Cicagna, Appunti di storia sociale e religiosa*, Chiavari 1912 and G. Fontana, *Rezzoaglio e Val d'Aveto*.

between local groups and merchants from the towns illustrate their common dependence on the opportunities offered by transits and external resources. But the language of these relations – always described as 'friendship' or 'enmity'[55] – demonstrates that the social effects of economic and practical interests were dependent upon the forms of social and political organization and upon local culture.

The social context of the inland valleys was extremely coercive. Local society was organized according to a system of relations of a political, juridical, fiscal and ritual nature classified as 'kinship' relations. The entire universe of social relations was conceptualized in terms of kin. The 'kin' aggregated all those with the same surname and who considered themselves 'relatives' and therefore 'friends', regardless of blood ties and biological realities, in a territory of varying dimensions. The territories consisted of one or two *ville* or parishes, sometimes situated in different jurisdictions, within and without Genoese dominion. Those individuals whose kinship relation was distant or undefined referred to themselves as 'surname kin'. Endogamy, the rules of 'patrilocality' which governed the means of access to land and to local resources, the provision of dowries for daughters and their exclusion from the paternal heritage, contributed to the formation of dense local groups of 'relatives' and accounted for the fact that the concepts of local groups and 'kinship' were never completely separable. Surname and place of residence were thus the fundamental principles of organization of the social sphere.[56]

This cultural logic organized the relations among the various kin and within each kin, as well as economic activities and relations with society as a whole. This is why the story of the two merchants from Rapallo (Lorenzo Boglio and Gervasio Pessia) cited at the beginning constantly refer to 'kin'.

The recruitment of young employees as carriers or armed escort groups generally occurred within 'kin' which could be very wide. In some cases a hundred heads of household bore the same surname. In a context in which the emancipation of children occurred very late (at twenty-five to twenty-seven years of age) and in which paternal property could remain undivided amongst siblings for a long time, the possibilities of employment offered by transport traffic and smuggling were the prerogatives of the youngest sons and young bachelors. The most powerful noble-

---

[55] The relations between the town merchants and the hinterland kin suggest the trade partnership model described by M. Sahlins, *Stone Age Economics*, Chicago 1972.

[56] Raggio, 'La Politica nella Parentela'.

middlemen of the hinterland valleys always resided along the mule-tracks, above all those with a 'large kin' or those who controlled vast coalitions of relatives, allies and dependants. Their success and effective leadership depended upon their capacity to coordinate the coalition, variegated and stratified according to the levels of status and fortune of the nuclear family groups making up the 'kin'.[57] The notables or chieftains (*principali*) offered a meeting point for diversified activities and professions exercised by vast kin groups situated in contiguous localities. Their major function was to coordinate these activities, to ensure the exchange of goods, services and information – and thus of reciprocity, to guarantee protection to the least privileged members of the kin, to control the internal tensions and centrifugal pressures, and to manage the social relations with neighbours, other kin and the outside world.[58]

The enmities and feuds characterizing the human and territorial borders of kin groups in the hinterlands were responsible for the orientation of relations with the coastal towns as well. The merchants of the towns needed logistic structures (the inns), carriers and above all escorts and armed protection. They therefore maintained privileged relationships with a few kin and their chieftains. They 'had to have open roads for their trading'.[59] 'Friendship' was expressed by behaviour based on reciprocity: the exchange of favours and gifts and the sharing of advantages and profits.

The case of the two most important merchant families of the town of Rapallo – the Pessia and the Cagnone – illustrates this point. At the end of the sixteenth century, these two Rapallo families based their success in trading with the Po valley on relations of collaboration and goodwill with families of the Fontanabuona valley (the Queirolo and the Arata) and of the Aveto valley (the Della Cella). The Della Cella in particular, as we have seen, ensured armed escorts against 'bandits' on the Apennine passes. The 'bandits' may be considered a specific social group generated by illegal activities and conflicts between kin. A majority of them were members of the largest and most powerful kin and played a central role in feuds and in activities linked to transits. (Genoese sources frequently underline the practical equation between smuggler and bandit.) Their role, however, was ambiguous. The bandits were often youths and boys, but they belonged to all levels of the social hierarchy. They maintained close relations with their relatives and with the local

[57] This analytical perspective is developed by G. Levi, *L'Eredità immateriale*, Turin 1985.
[58] See Raggio, 'La Politica nella Parentela'.   [59] ASG, *Rota Criminale* 182.

elites, but they were organized in *compagnie* (bands which also aggre-gated individuals from smaller and poorer kin networks and from other communities). They were extremely mobile and so were partly released from the stricter territorial ties and from parental and community social control. Lastly, they were involved in extra-local and diversified networks of relations. They were therefore able to negotiate their position within the kin and the community and to obtain, at least in some situations, relative autonomy and contractual power with the middle-men from the hinterland valleys and with the merchants of the coastal area. In 1584, for example, Giovanni Pessia left in Belletto Della Cella's tavern money and gifts (including a pair of green socks) for the 'young' Della Cella and for the 'bandits' so that they would not disturb the passage of his mules directed towards Piacenza.[60] During the following years Giovanni Pessia and Bernardo and Pietro Cagnone complained that, 'despite the gifts', money was extorted from their muleteers. They accused the Della Cella of playing both sides. A bandit captured by the *bargello* and interrogated by a Genoese official confirmed their suspi-cions. The oil stolen from the Rapallo merchants' muleteers with the complicity of the Della Cella had been resold to Rolandino Arata.[61] An entire network of relations was thus torn by mistrust. During the following decades these relations deteriorated still further and in the mid seventeenth century the Pessia affirmed that they had been obliged to interrupt their commercial dealings with Piacenza and Parma because of their 'enmity' with the Della Cella.[62]

Commercial relations were regulated by ties of 'kin' and 'friendship' and by local culture.[63] 'Friendship' and 'enmity' defined the success or the exclusion of merchants, and explained the routes and directions of commercial flows. All the reports we have agree that the bandits, before robbing the muleteers, asked: 'What kin are you from?' or 'Who are you working for?' Economic and commercial transactions were above all social relations. The conflictual use of resources and transit routes was an aspect of the complex relations existing among kin. The merchants had to take these kin relations into account as a whole if they wanted 'free routes'. The merchants, who often held public offices in the two towns, constantly took sides in inter-kin conflicts and in factions. The conflicts

[60] ASG, *Rota Criminale* 1226.   [61] Ibid. and *Acta Senatus* 526 and 542.
[62] ASG, *Antica Finanza* 668.
[63] My interpretation owes much to K. Polanyi, *Primitive, Archaic and Modern Economics*, edited by G. Dalton, Garden City, NY 1968, and *The Livelihood of Man*, New York 1972.

illustrated complex extra-local networks of political alliances which always went beyond the restricted horizon of the single *villa* or parish and involved both the notables of the coastal towns and the lords of the Imperial fiefs.

During the first half of the seventeenth century, the increased fiscal and administrative pressure of the Republic – made concrete by more systematic controls of oil production and exports and by the introduction of new taxes, direct and indirect, ordinary and extraordinary[64] – reinforced the role of the merchant–middlemen, smugglers and 'bandits' of the hinterland valleys.

It was not mere chance that during the same decades the Genoese officials worked against banditry in both the communities of Chiavari and Rapallo, and in others also situated in transit areas (for example, the Bisagno and Polcevera valleys).[65] It is quite clear from the sources that the bandits were for the most part youths who constantly moved between Genoese territory and the feudal enclaves. They had solid ties with the local elites and were employed in contraband, in armed escorts, in feuds and in factional conflicts.

On the whole, during the seventeenth century, the inland villages evaded direct tax, withholding payments, and always maintained a strong bargaining power with respect to the political–administrative elites of the two towns, headquarters of local government. In terms of the present research, an explanatory element of this situation, besides the management of smuggling, was the active intervention of notables in the flow of cereal products from the Po plain.

The villages which I have considered, in the valleys crossed by mule-tracks, and sites of markets and fairs, all possessed a good system of water mills, partly used for milling chestnuts but functioning particularly for the wheat which arrived from the Po valley in exchange for oil. The upper Recco valley had 37 mills, the Fontanabuona valley 48, the Lavagna valley 32, the Sturla valley 61, the Graveglia valley 45, and so on.[66] The coastal area, on the contrary, had just a few mills, which were inactive for four to six months a year because of lack of water.

Ecological conditions, logistic structures and mills for processing cereal products were the same in Fontanabuona and the contiguous

---

[64] See G. Felloni, 'Distribuzione Territoriale della Ricchezza e dei Carichi Fiscali nella Repubblica di Genova (Secc. XVI–XVIII)', *Ottava Settimana di Studio Datini*, Prato 1976 (typed paper).

[65] ASG, *Rota Criminale passim*.

[66] ASG, *Acta Senatus* 514 and *Magistrato delle Comunità* 768 and 769.

valleys and villages. The particular example of the Fontanabuona valley illustrates how the possibility of exploiting all the employment opportunities offered by the exchange circuits, and in general by relations with external society, was closely linked to the existence of local entrepreneurs.

The 48 mills in the Fontanabuona valley belonged to 45 owners from 23 kin, but the four most numerous and powerful kin of the valley possessed a third of all the mills concentrated around the *villa*-market of Monleone in the parish of Cicagna. The kin of Cicagna possessed, besides the monopoly of milling Lombard grain, that of the baking and retail sales of bread in a vast area including the major coastal towns of Levante. 'The men of the villa of San Giovanni Battista di Cicagna . . . make bread to sell, which they bring to Sestri, Lavagna, Chiavari, Rapallo, Santa Margherita, Portofino, Camogli, Recco, and all these villages abound in it every morning.'[67]

At the beginning of the seventeenth century the area, including these towns (where 20 per cent of the population lived), had a population of 48,418 inhabitants (*anime*), divided into 8,592 households (*fuochi*).[68] The bread baked at Cicagna was sold above all to Chiavari and Rapallo and it is significant that these two towns had very few bakers. At Rapallo at the end of the seventeenth century there were numerous *fidelari* (makers of 'pasta') but only one baker.[69] The Chiavari 'charter' of 1607, which set up a Provisioning Office and rigidly regulated the baking and sale of bread in the town, left untouched the freedom to sell 'white bread baked in Cicagna'.[70] In 1622, the officials of Rapallo, who were asking the Senate of the Republic to set up a Provisioning Office, denounced the town's dependence for food supplies on the Monleone market and the miller–bakers of Cicagna.[71] During the following years, the same officials tried in vain to make the wheat arrive in town and to prevent 'foreigners' from having access to the Monleone market.[72]

The miller–bakers of Cicagne derived extraordinary power from this crucial function of supplying the two towns and the greater coastal area. The internal bases of their power were the kin and clientele networks involved in the activities of milling cereals and baking and distributing bread. They operated in fact as a clique capable of imposing its leadership over all the Fontanabuona valley. When in 1624 Genoa

---

[67] ASG, *Acta Senatus* 1828.   [68] ASG, *Manoscritto* 218 and *Acta Senatus* 600 (1607 Census).
[69] ASCR, *Actorum Communitatis Rapalli* 4 and *Censoria* 1.   [70] ASG, *Acta Senatus* 1691.
[71] ASCR, *Criminalium* 19.   [72] ASCR, *Actorum Communitatis Rapalli passim.*

imposed a tax on the millstones, the millers succeeded in making 'all men and the whole community' pay 'to avoid supporting the burden', although only they reap the benefits', as the heads of households in the parishes excluded from milling and baking complained.[73] The strategy of the miller–bakers was supported by the *panetere* (bread-carriers) and the *rivendaroli* (sellers), men and women who left Cicagna every day at dawn, their baskets full of 'white bread', to go to the coastal towns.[74]

While the ties with the Rapallo oil merchants were probably crucial as regards relations with the outside world – albeit difficult to document and to reconstruct – in the valley the social framework within which the miller–bakers operated was the kin, as in the case of protection of transits and organisation of contraband. Mills and ovens were managed and used by enlarged domestic groups, and the sale of bread was coordinated by the extended kin. The mills often belonged jointly to several heads of household and were enjoyed in turn on a yearly basis, or by the week when there was a shortage of water in the locks. In 1631 numerous witnesses from Cicagna and the neighbouring *ville* declared that this was normal practice in the valley.[75] The territorial organization of the sale of bread reflected exactly the settlement of the kin and the state of their relationships (of alliance or of conflict). The result was a division of the areas of sale (although the logic of this also needs to be reconstructed in the light of the function of credit in *ville*/town relations). In any case, each kin had a relatively stable clientele in the various coastal towns and was in constant competition with the other kin organized around the miller–bakers for the defence or the conquest of new areas of sale. At the end of the sixteenth century, for example, the Leverone, 'who baked bread to sell at Chiavari', were afraid of attacks and reprisals by other kin (the Fopiani and the Barbazelata with whom they were feuding) and so employed numerous armed escorts or used children to transport bread.[76] The sale of bread – after its baking, which was done during the night in common ovens and by both men and women – was generally women's work,[77] even though the *panetere* (like the muleteers and oil merchants) were almost always accompanied by armed youths.

[73] ASG, *Acta Senatus* 1828.
[74] On Wednesdays and Saturdays, market days at Rapallo, the departure from Cicagna was brought forward to 4–5 o'clock 'at night, to sell bread to the innkeepers' (ASCR, *Extraordinariorum* 9). In 1618 the *bargello* of the court of Rapallo, back from Cicagna, said: 'it was barely dawn and the bread-carriers were already on their way' (ASCR, *Extraordinariorum* 8).
[75] ANC, *Notaio Lorenzo Leverone* (1631).   [76] ASG, *Acta Senatus* 1427.
[77] ASG, *Antica Finanza* 822. On the role of women in distribution activities, see S.W. Mintz, 'Men, Women, and Trade', *Comparative Studies in Society and History*, 13, 1971, pp. 247–69.

This specific business initiative did not exclude the participation of the millers' kin in other activities linked with the exchange circuits and in transports. The pre-eminence of certain kin can in fact be explained by the vast range of activities they controlled or coordinated. Even the wealthiest kin were always characterized by strong internal stratification based on status and fortune. The poorer and less fortunate members of the kin were recruited by the entrepreneurs and the chieftains for the humblest or most dangerous jobs. In addition, relative forms of specialization favoured collaborative relationships, reinforced by marriage alliances between the kin of the upper and lower valleys. This was the case, for example, of the Leverone from Cicagna (millers and bakers) and of the Malatesta (carriers) who were settled along one of the mule-tracks which went from the bottom of the valley towards the Apennine passes. In general, however, the entrepreneur roles were multiform. The activities of merchant, innkeeper and miller could co-exist in the same kin and in some cases in the same people.

The rich millers, the middlemen and the local entrepreneurs gave work especially to 'poor relatives', young bachelors and women. But the recruitment of sellers, carriers and 'bandits' took place outside kin networks as well. This offer of employment was an important element in the formation of more extensive networks of alliance, clientele and dependence, which in turn constituted the bases of the prestige and power of the local chieftains. The activities of mediation – supported by a particular form of social organization – between two different external societies thus allowed for the existence of a wealthy elite in an ecologically poor context.[78]

The forms of social organization, control of resources and articulation of channels of exchange which have been described in this article as particular to one area of eastern Liguria were probably characteristic of the entire politically fragmented Apennine region between Piedmont and Lucca.[79]

[78] See the notes for the imposition of a tax on 'businesses' in 1626, in ASG, *Finanza Pubblica* 2604. The general framework for Liguria is reconstructed by E. Grendi, 'La Distribuzione della Ricchezza Privata nel Territorio della Repubblica dei Genovesi attorno al 1630', *Miscellanea Storica Ligure*, 15:1, 1983, pp. 301–13.
[79] See, for example, M. Berengo, *Nobili e mercanti nella Lucca del Cinquecento*, Turin 1965; A. Torre, 'Elites Locali e Potere Centrale tra Sei e Settecento: Problemi di Metodo e Ipotesi di Lavoro sui Feudi Imperiali delle Langhe', *Bollettino della Società per gli Studi Storici. Archeologici ed Artistici della Provincia di Cuneo*, 89, 1983, pp. 41–63; S. Lombardini, 'Appunti per un'Ecologia Politica dell'Area Monregalese nell'Età Moderna', in *Valli monregalesi: arte, società, devozioni*, Vicoforte 1985; G. Tocci, *Le Terre traverse. Poteri e territori nei ducati di Parma e Piacenza tra Sei e Settecento*, Bologna 1985.

3 ✼ Family cycles, peddling and society in upper Alpine valleys in the eighteenth century

Laurence Fontaine

Introduction

Within the framework of questions raised by our collective research on the family and work in pre-industrial societies, the aspect chosen for particular investigation here is one particular activity, peddling, which it is difficult to describe as a trade in the strict sense of the word. Peddling provided country dwellers with contact with towns, but only temporarily, during the actual journey, differentiated their practices from those belonging to the community as a whole. We need to ask whether peddling marked off those engaged in it with regard to allocation of social roles or domestic tasks and ways of envisaging marriage and the transmission of patrimonies; and whether, given the fact that it brought some country dwellers into contact with urban markets, it modified the whole set of social relationships within village communities.

A working hypothesis involving a special consideration of family histories aims both to fill in certain gaps in the kind of statistical and macroscopic social history that ignores the variations connected with family cycles, and to stress the processes of change and social dynamics not usually covered by ethnographical studies of older peasant societies. The object of the approach adopted here is to discover the ways in which family groups created links and networks to ensure continuity and to show how the history of groups was shaped by the confluence of the histories of individuals.

To do this we need to work at two levels, that of the family, studied in the unfolding pattern of family cycles, and that of village groups as they developed. This twofold approach has meant using the traditional tools of the historian of the family and rural societies (such as tax rolls or

Translation from French by John C. Whitehouse.

marriage contracts) in a rather different way, and rethinking the models normally proposed for societies in upper Alpine valleys.[1]

Since they were sharply divided in two ways – with a split between Catholics and Protestants on the one hand and migrants and settled population on the other – the high mountain valleys of the Oisans alpine massif in Dauphiné were selected as the area to be investigated. In theory, the Catholic/Protestant division was eradicated by the Revocation of the Edict of Nantes, but the consequences of royal policy on village family and economic structures were still felt at least until the end of the eighteenth century. The division between the migrant and settled populations was a highly distinctive feature of the areas in question until the First World War. The valleys belonged to a region subject to land-tax (taille réelle),[2] and no noble or ecclesiastic, apart from the parish priest with a tiny living, was resident within their bounds. The lord was the Duke of Lesdiguière, whose seat was at Vizille.

We can examine Clavans, a village at an altitude of 1,400 metres, as described in the tax registers. Since the poll-tax rolls (the best source of information, since they include every head of a family) are only partly extant,[3] it has proved necessary to use others in conjunction with them, particularly the land-tax rolls. A comparison between the two sources for two years in close proximity, 1733 and 1735, shows that an undifferentiated use of them does not significantly modify the hierarchies that emerge. Within both the poll-tax and the land-tax rolls (which show the size of the holdings on which they are based) there is a strict correlation between land owned and taxation, with two livres and sixteen sols of poll-tax demanded for every sétérée of land owned.[4] In

[1] R. Blanchard, 'Le Haut-Dauphiné à la fin du dix-huitième siècle, d'après les procès-verbaux de la Révision des feux de 1700', *Revue de Géographie Alpine*, 3, 1915, pp. 317–419 (p. 402) establishes in connection with the agro-pastoral system characterizing the Alps in the nineteenth century, the 'law of transhumance': 'Basically it is no more than one expression of the great law pertaining in mountain regions and governing all the facts of human geography, which we could call the law of transhumance, and which entails the use of successive zones of altitude according to annual variations in temperature.' According to André Allix, 'Man is no doubt not the slave of nature, but in all the political variations helping or hindering his success, he always makes use of nature according to the same principles, namely those imposed on him by physical reality' (A. Allix, *L'Oisans au Moyen-Age, étude de géographie historique en haute montagne d'après des documents inédits suivie de la transcription des textes*, Paris 1929, p. 157).
[2] Taxes were fixed for all the twenty-one communities of the Oisans area and imposed on each of them according to the number of households it contained. L. Cortes, *L'Oisans, recherches historiques, tourisme*, Grenoble 1926, pp. 96–112.
[3] Some between 1695 and 1702 and a complete series between 1733 and 1745.
[4] The *sétérée* (about 3,800 m²) was worth 576 Dauphiné toises and was divided into 4 quarterelles, each made up of 4 civérées (Cortes, *L'Oisans*, p. 122).

addition, since the measurement of each individual plot in the mid eighteenth century, land was always expressed in terms of sétérées of 'good land' and valued on that basis.[5] A graphical distribution of the individuals figuring in both rolls also shows a very similar pattern, in which only the landowners in the poll-tax rolls are taken into consideration, as they are the only ones to be affected by size. The differences observable in the hierarchies are attributable to the fact that for poll-tax purposes the number of male and female servants was added to the value of the land owned. The great gap in our knowledge arises from the fact that landless peasants were not included, which means that we cannot know what became of families who moved out of the world of ownership. Did they emigrate? Were they reduced to beggary in their own community? A final point is that the socio-professional nomenclature in the registers is very vague. Inhabitants are described as day-labourers, ploughmen or traders, but any particular trader might, in a given roll, be classed under any of those headings, which makes it impossible to isolate traders as such on the basis of these sources alone.

Table 3.1 gives the percentage of heads of families below and above the average for each roll examined and the number of people involved. Table 3.2, following Jacques Dupâquier's method, groups individuals in terms of their position with regard to the average,[6] showing on the one hand those between half the average and the average and on the other those between the average and one and a half times the average, then between one and a half times and twice the average, then between twice and three times the average, and so on.

With regard to the number of heads of families, there is a very early break. In 1676, the roll listed 171 heads of families, whereas by 1695 there were only 64. In the intervening years, the Revocation of the Edict of Nantes had savagely drained the village of its population, which took a century and a half to climb back to figures close to those of 1676, since the highest level (that of 1851) was 93 houses, 101 households and 427 inhabitants.[7] The general pattern of development showed an increasing gap between the richest and poorest in the second half of the century, with a movement from 60 per cent to 70 per cent of the population below

[5] *Archives Départementales* (*AD*), Isère, IIC 312, *Procès verbaux de la Révision des feux*, pp. 1121, 1125–9 and 1135, and B. Bonnin, *La Terre et les paysans en Dauphiné au 17e siècle. 1580–1730*, University of Lyons II, typescript thesis, 1982, p. 412.

[6] For the methodological aspects, see J. Dupâquier, 'Problèmes de mesure et de représentation en matière d'histoire sociale', *Actes du 89e congrès national des sociétés savantes, Lyon 1964*, Paris 1965, pp. 77–86.   [7] *AD* Isère, 123M 20 to 27.

Table 3.1 *Distribution of heads of household in relation to the average valuation for tax purposes*

	Below average %	Above average %	Number of assessments	Type of roll
1676	59.0	41.0	171	Local-tax (*négotiale*)
1695	77.0	23.0	64	Poll-tax[a] (*capitation*)
1702	62.0	38.0	65	Poll-tax
1717	60.0	40.0	74	Land-tax (*taille*)
1717[b]	60.5	39.5	71	Poll-tax
1733[c]	66.0	34.0	82	Poll-tax
1735	62.0	38.0	86	Land-tax
1735[b]	61.0	39.0	80	Poll-tax
1745[c]	67.0	33.0	95	Poll-tax
1773	71.0	29.0	120	Twentieth-part (*vingtième*)
1787	69.5	30.5	92	Land-tax
1803	71.5	28.5	112	Land-tax

Notes:
[a] Very crude (most assessments being 1, 3 or 10 livres).
[b] Excluding beggars.
[c] Including beggars.

Table 3.2 *Spread of taxation assessments, Clavans, 1676–1803*

Year	Below 0.5 %	0.5–1 %	1–1.5 %	1.5–2 %	2–3 %	3–4 %	4–5 %	Above 5 %
1676	44.0	15.0	10.0	18.0	8.0	4.0	1.0	—
1695	25.0	52.0	5.0	1.0	17.0	—	—	—
1702	25.0	37.0	13.5	11.0	13.5	—	—	—
1717	32.0	28.0	15.0	18.0	5.0	1.0	—	—
1717[a]	45.0	15.5	14.0	8.5	13.0	3.0	1.0	—
1733[b]	39.5 + 13.0	13.5	12.0	7.0	11.0	2.5	1.0	—
1735	38.0	23.0	17.0	5.0	12.0	3.0	1.0	—
1735[a]	35.0	26.0	24.0	5.0	6.0	—	2.0	1.0
1745[b]	30.0 + 16.0	22.0	20.0	4.0	5.0	—	2.0	1.0
1773	40.0	31.0	6.0	4.0	10.0	7.5	—	2.0
1787	45.5	24.0	5.5	9.0	13.0	1.0	1.0	1.0
1803	59.0	12.5	9.0	4.5	12.5	1.0	1.0	1.0

Notes:
Average = 1
[a] Excluding beggars.
[b] Including beggars (the second percentage shown).

In 1773, the richest (above 5) paid between 6 and 7 times the average. This increased to between 7 and 8 times in 1787 and between 9 and 10 times in 1803.

the average and a swelling of the numbers of extreme groups, accompanied on the one hand by an increase in those individuals with incomes below half the average, and on the other by the appearance of one or two solid fortunes.

This methodology, which was developed with regard to non-mountainous country areas,[8] is based on several postulates. These are that family and fiscal unity are one and the same thing; that the patrimony is not shared out amongst several heirs; and that land, if not the only form of wealth, is at least a pertinent reference in the make-up of the wealth of all the inhabitants.

In mountain areas, there are many exceptions to those postulates. In the first place, although the wife's goods are entered under the husband's name with a note 'by dowry', the members of the same household may be included in several assessments. In such cases, only a knowledge of the families involved makes it possible to reunite husbands and their wives who may figure elsewhere, widowers and widows whose children are mentioned separately, or children of a first marriage, or daughters receiving a dowry under their father's will but not yet married and living in the family home. Second, an analysis of notarial documents and inventories compiled after death shows that land played a marginal part in the patrimony of 'elites'. Third, the registers presuppose that land was owned solely in the village, or that a distinction was made between villagers and outside merchants, which was not always the case. In fact, trading families owned property in several communities. Fourth, a knowledge of the families shows a further distortion in those particular sources that emphasize the succession of generations, with both emancipated and married sons at the bottom of the scale on which their father is one of the largest landowners. The low rates of tax paid by these sons does not reflect their true position, and certainly shows no more than their youth, since they were the future heirs of men who really counted in the village. For instance, the Eymard family, the richest in 1735 – Claude being the most highly taxed inhabitant, at twenty livres – is shown as broken up in the 1745 rolls (Claude had died in 1740), with his widow paying four livres, his (now married) son Jean paying seven, and his two other sons Pierre and Claude four each, in a year when the average rate of poll tax was 4.9 livres. The decline in the wealth of the family might be seen as reflecting the struggle each of the survivors had

[8] J. Dupâquier, 'Des Rôles des tailles à la démographie historique. L'Exemple du vexin français', *Annales de Démographie Historique*, 1965, pp. 31–42.

to engage in to retrieve their social position, but that was certainly not the case, since the registers take no account of what every villager knew, namely that the sons were the heirs of the leading creditor in the village.[9]

Judged solely on tax and parish registers, Alpine society certainly gives the impression of being a society of small landowners of equally lowly status and of giving credence to the commonly presented picture of mountain communities.[10] Nevertheless, its particular features – which mean that tax rolls have to be used with considerable care – cannot therefore be neglected, since they make it possible to use the sequence of deaths and marriages to follow the ups and downs of each individual family over several generations.

Family cycles and the transmission of property

The statistical facts show the Oisans area – and a large part of the Alpine valleys – as a region with a dowry system in which daughters with dowries were excluded from succession and from inheriting the paternal home; it was a virilocal area in which sons inherited the house and from the father.[11] But such facts hide the process of adaptation in play at times of major family, biological and economic occasions and obscure the complexity and dynamism of the societies in question. On the other hand, an approach which sees every family document as part of an overall strategy permits us to understand the processes of change and perceive the logic proper to the various family groups making up the society. If, for example, we take marriage contracts, put them in the context of the developing family cycle and compare them with parental wills, we can see that there is no single model of the devolution of property, but rather an *ideal* one, which is to keep a son who will inherit

[9] The discrepancy between the real financial situation of the peasants – given the circulation of credit and debts – and the amount of tax they paid brought others in its wake. Some paid it on fields they had temporarily given to a creditor in repayment of monies due, whereas the person cultivating them was not taxed in proportion to the size of his landholding. Tenant farmers were also ignored, and taxed only on what they actually owned.

[10] A. Poitrineau, *Remues d'hommes: Les migrations montagnardes en France. 17e–18e siècles*, Paris 1983, pp. 6–24; H.G. Rosenberg, *A Negotiated World. Three Centuries of Change in a French Alpine Community*, Toronto 1988, takes up the same thesis with regard to the modern period in the history of the Queyras valleys.

[11] H. Pecaut, *Etudes sur le droit privé des hautes vallées de Provence et de Dauphiné au moyen-âge. Documents inédits*, Paris 1907; J. Tivollier, *Le Queyras*, 2 vols., Gap 1938; R.K. Burns, Jr, 'The Circum-Alpine Culture: a Preliminary View', *Anthropological Quarterly*, 36, winter 1961, pp. 130–55; A. Collomp, *La Maison du père. Famille et village en Haute-Provence au XVIIe et XVIIIe siècles*, Paris 1983. Rosenberg, *Negotiated World*, pp. 26–8, shows that practices were a great deal more complex than the rule.

the house and to exclude all the other male and female children from the succession once they have been provided with sums of money. The actual arrangements that appear in notaries' archives prove that the ideal was not always achieved and that there were other models representing a compromise between what was desired and the biological constraints involved (the essential data being the age of the father and the children at the time the will was made). Such arrangements also show that the father making provision for his children during his own lifetime was making a bet on the future, based on a great deal of uncertainty and involving kin, with all the lack of sure knowledge that that also implied. Marriage contracts can then be seen as one stage in a flexible overall strategy, a point at which those making gifts attempt to negotiate several possible futures for the family.

A generation-by-generation study of families makes it possible to trace the development of customs and responses to various historical situations. It provides a means of grasping, in terms of the solutions the family thinks of in order to preserve its continuity, the tensions that arise, shift, decrease or disappear within it; it shows the possible room for manoeuvre that families and individuals have within economic and mental constraints that rigidly condition the ways in which they can adapt and change.

We shall present these various incompletely achieved models through the example of one family, the Gourands, since it offers an illustration of the whole pattern of development of trading families in the eighteenth century (see figures 3.1 and 3.2).[12] The family can be briefly situated in the context of the varying levels of wealth in the village. In 1676, six Gourands figured in the local tax rolls (*tax négotiale*), and Pierre, the son of Thomas, was amongst the fifteen richest families, paying two and a half times the average in a year when the richest paid five times the average. In 1702, he was the only Gourand, and his was one of the ten wealthiest families, paying twice the average tax in comparison with the three times the average paid by the richest. In 1717, he moved into the group of the five richest families. Noé, his only living son, succeeded him in 1721.

By 1733, he was the wealthiest man in the village, paying four times the average poll tax. On his death in 1758, the patrimony was split up

---

[12] Here we are solely concerned with merchants, who were the only people with sufficient resources to take time into consideration. See Collomp, *Maison du père*, pp. 211–75, on the specific features of merchants and muleteers in the villages of Haute-Provence.

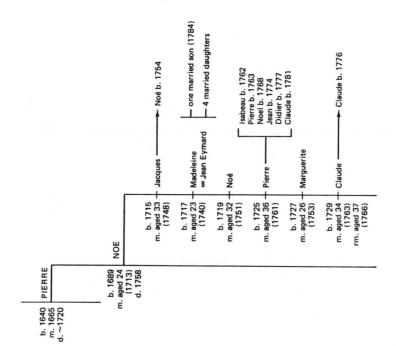

Figure 3.1 The Gourand: genealogical table. 1789: 7 living Gourand grandchildren: none married, aged 34 to 8 years (b. = born; m. = married; rm. = remarried; d. = deceased).

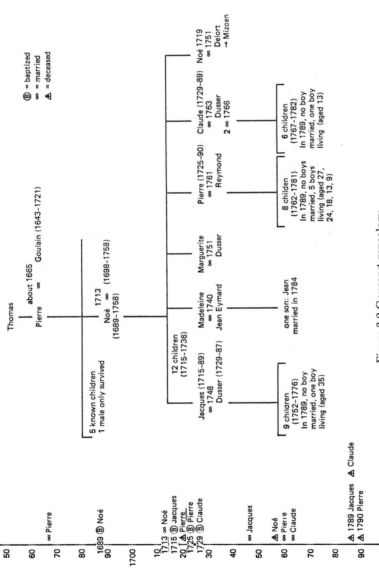

Figure 3.2 Gourand genealogy.

among his three heirs Jacques, Pierre and Claude. In 1733 all three were
in the group of largish landowners, each paying between twice and three
times as much as the average, for 19, 13 and 14 sétérées of land
respectively. At the time, there were two inhabitants with the distinction
of paying six times the average. Their ranks remained stable until the
Revolution.

The main situations in which the desired model was not achieved are
as follows. If one of the spouses died intestate and without issue, his
property reverted to his family and his wife returned to her own family.
Such a case was sufficiently rare to make the Gourand family appeal to
the Parlement of Grenoble for a ruling when it occurred in 1763. In other
cases, the spouse left a will, which sometimes did not authorize the
reversion of the property to his or her family until after the death of the
surviving spouse and sometimes offered the latter a part, or – if there was
no close family – the whole of his patrimony.

If the father died when his children were still young and he had not
had time to express his last wishes, his property was divided equally
amongst all his sons and daughters, and his widow's male next-of-kin
(her father or brother) was given the responsibility for administering the
children's property until they reached the age of fourteen. Alternatively,
trustees were appointed. If he did have time to make a will, however, he
charged his 'beloved wife' to raise the children until they ceased to be
infants and reached the age of trusteeship, and always made provision
for her accommodation and income, whether she remained in the family
home or not.[13]

As a general rule, the older the children at the time of the father's
death, the easier it was to ensure that the succession be arranged to follow
the pattern of the ideal model. In 1748, Noé married off his eldest son
Jacques, who was thirty-three at the time, to Dominique Dusser, the
daughter of a merchant whose wealth was almost as great as his own (see
figure 3.3).

Jacques continued to live in the family home, and his wife brought a
dowry of 1,200 livres, half in money and half in land and moveable
goods. At the time of his marriage, Noé gave his son one sixth of his
property – no further details are given – to be available for him 'at the

---

[13] On the fate of orphans, see L. Fontaine, 'Migrations d'etablissement et migrations d'exclusion au
XVIIe Siècle: une Mesure des Solidarités Villageoises', *European University Institute Colloquium
Papers*', 'Work and Family in Pre-Industrial Europe', 10–12 December 1987, no. 380/87 (col.
92), 19 pp.

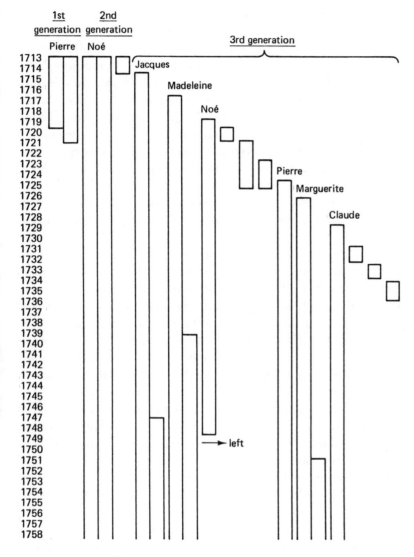

Figure 3.3 The heirs of Noé Gourand, 1713–58.

1st generation (1650–1720)
Pierre m. Elisabeth Goulain (1643–1721)
2nd generation
Pierre (1670?)
Suzanne (1676–1731) died without issue
Anne (1680–1720) left
Noé (1689–1758)
   m. Catherine Bathier (1698–1758)

3rd generation
Jacques (b. 1715) m. Dominique Dusser, 1748
Madeleine (b. 1717) m. Jean Eymard, 1740
Noé (b. 1719) m. into Delort family and left, 1751
Pierre (b. 1725) m. 1761
Marguerite (b. 1727) m. into Dusser family, 1753
Claude (b. 1729) m.
   (i) Marie-Madeleine Eymard, 1763
   (ii) Anne Dusser, 1766

(b. = born; m. = married).

time of their separation . . . whereas they intend to live together in common'. The proportion offered relates to the situation in the household at the time, when only one daughter out of Noé's six children was married. Ten years later, when he drew up his will, his other daughter was married and his youngest son, Noé, was established in another parish. The situation in the household at the end of his life shows how far he remained from the ideal model of the devolution of possessions, for he was obliged to cancel the gift he had made to Jacques at the time of the marriage contract, to ask him to return to the body of the property what he had already received and to share out his property among the three sons, namely Jacques, whom he would have liked to be his only heir, Pierre and Claude, whom he had not yet established. He cut out those who had left the family home and set up on their own, giving them only a few goods.

A system as flexible as this does, however, include an element of rigidity, which no doubt explains why fathers hesitated to set up their children during their own lifetime. Although property made over to the future heir could be revised right up to the final codicil and did not generally feature in marriage contracts,[14] the dowry was not modifiable even if it might not be fully payable until the death of the wife. In times of crisis, the state of affairs in which the dowry could not be touched could mean that children with a dowry became their father's sole heir – since they had a claim on the inheritance – whereas sons, who had received nothing, simply inherited debts. These unintended consequences of the custom did not escape Fr Col, the parish priest of Clavans at the beginning of the nineteenth century, who entered them in his notebook with other problems raised by his pastoral practice, intending to seek authoritative opinions on them. He wondered whether, when the proper progression of the inheritance was being reversed, daughters with dowries should not be asked to collaborate with heirs in wiping out the liabilities of the estate.[15] It is understandable that a father should be tempted to wait until death was imminent before marrying off his children and deciding on ways and means of dividing up his property.

We can have some idea of the tensions that these customary patterns of

---

[14] Maurice Garden makes the same observation with regard to marriage contracts in Lyons: M. Garden, *Lyon et les Lyonnais au XVIIIe siècle*, Lyon 1970 (abridged edition Paris 1975); the same observation in Rosenberg, *Negotiated World*, p. 24.

[15] *AD* Isère, 27J3/47, papers of Fr Nicolas Col. His exclusive concern with the dowries of daughters shows in its own way how practices of inheritance had developed. At that time, which was a period of economic crisis following those of the Revolution and the Empire, the tendency was to provide dowries only for daughters and to leave the undivided inheritance to sons.

inheritance exerted on the economic equilibrium of families at times of population growth or economic crisis. By the mid eighteenth century, population growth was forcing families to change their behaviour.[16] They acted at two levels: family organization and occupation. In the first area, the risk of marrying off children while they were still young was taken less and less frequently.[17] Pierre Gourand and Elisabeth Goulain, who had married at an early age themselves,[18] married off their son Noé in 1713, when he was twenty-four (figures 3.1 and 3.2). All his sons, however, married when they were over thirty (Jacques at thirty-three, Noé at thirty-two, Pierre at thirty-six and Claude at thirty-four). On his death in 1790, Pierre had made provision for a dowry for his eldest daughter, aged twenty-eight, and named his five sons, all of whom were single, as his heirs. Jacques married off his eldest daughter Catherine when she was thirty, his second was still a spinster when he died in 1789 and only Jeanne-Marie had married younger, at twenty-four (being, however, six months pregnant at the time). Noé's son was thirty-five in 1789 and still unmarried. Few of the grandchildren of Noé senior were married in 1789; and Claude's were still young, the eldest being only twenty.

Prolonged celibacy as a device for keeping the family patrimony together was not an easy matter, as the early marriage of Jeanne-Marie and the conflicts between the settled son and his unmarried brothers indicate. Upon the death of their father in 1758, Pierre and Claude called for the inheritance to be divided, which Jacques refused to countenance until 1761, when his brothers went to law and forced him to do so. Both then took advantage of the new situation to get married during the next year.[19] Jacques' unwillingness is understandable, since for him setting up his brothers meant losing the leading place in the

---

[16] The lack of firm data before the nineteenth century makes it difficult to know whether there was growth or stagnation in Alpine regions in the eighteenth century. The case of Oisans confirms R. Blanchard's intuition. He suggests that the marked increase in the early nineteenth century was simply a reproductive reaction to the very high mortality rates of the 1790s and the inroads made by the Napoleonic wars (*Les Alpes Occidentales*, vol. VII, Grenoble 1956, p. 530). An analysis of the migratory systems of the villages in question shows upsurges of cyclical overpopulation taking place since the fifteenth century (L. Fontaine, 'Les Réseaux de colportage des Alpes françaises entre 16e et 19e Siècles', *Bollettino Storico della Svizzera Italiana* (forthcoming, 1989).

[17] P.P. Viazzo and D. Albera, 'Population Resources and Homeostatic Regulation in the Alps: the Role of Nuptiality', *Itinera*, fasc 5/6, 1986, pp. 182–231, suggest that late marriage and the high level of celibacy in the Alps from the nineteenth century was perhaps a recent phenomenon (pp. 188–90).

[18] We know neither the date of his birth nor that of his marriage, but his wife was born in the mid seventeenth century and died in 1721 at the age of seventy-eight (he had died during the preceding four years), and in 1685 they had a son who was perfectly capable of signing.

[19] Gourand family records.

village. The movement from late marriage to permanent celibacy can also be observed, providing as it did a means of maintaining one's position in the village without dividing up the patrimony and coping with economic situations in which an increase in wealth continuous and rapid enough to justify sharing out the property amongst the children without excessive impoverishment was not possible.

Two final examples, the marriages of the children of Noé senior (son of Pierre), Madeleine and Noé, show the need to visualize marriage contracts as one element of a family 'policy' for the future, constantly adjusted and reformulated to restore lost equilibrium or grasp the opportunities provided by the fate of other families in the marriage market or other members of the kin group.[20] Thus Madeleine married at twenty-three, ten years earlier than her brothers, since the father of the family into which she was to move had just died without having installed an heir in his house, which meant that one of the sons had to take over. That event, which broke a family equilibrium, meant that Noé senior had to choose between marrying off his daughter earlier than he would have liked or losing the chance of a marriage alliance with the other big family in the village. In the gamble between sudden and disturbing opportunities and the caution urging him to wait until the end of his natural life before setting up his children, Noé took the risk and opted for his daughter's marriage. Events proved him right, for he was able to continue increasing the wealth of his family.

Noé, the youngest son, married in 1751 into the household of his maternal uncle, who lived in the neighbouring village of Mizoen – literally nepotism, one might say. His wife brought a dowry of 2,100 livres, principally in the form of land. Noé senior gave 1,000 livres which he promised 'to pay at first request, free of interest'. At his death in 1758, the money still had not been paid. At the time of the marriage, he gave a few animals, a little linen, two pewter plates and some meadows, to a total value of eighty livres. It was Noé junior's mother's brother, Pierre Batier, an innkeeper and merchant, married but with no surviving children, who brought the house and land, 'all that he owns, in one of the hamlets of Mizoen, in goods, land and buildings'. These properties were quite obviously brought together for one of his own sons (who failed to

20 On this approach to the marriage market and the strategies blurring what the rules provided for, see P. Bourdieu, 'Les Stratégies Matrimoniales dans le Système de Reproduction', *Annales ESC*, 1972, pp. 1105–25, and 'De la Règle aux Stratégies', *Terrain, Carnets du Patrimoine Ethnologique*, 4, 1985, pp. 93–100.

survive), with the logic underlying (as we shall see) the majority of acquisitions of land. As was always the case, the contract provided for a life pension should they part, 'whereas they intend to live together in common'. In fact, such oft-repeated clauses were not exclusively connected with possible incompatibilities of temperament, as has often been assumed, but were part of the range of scenarios imagined in an attempt to make it possible to adapt the future life of the family to whatever fate might have in store. This is shown by the fact that, contrary to the wording of the contract, Pierre Batier lived in another hamlet near Mizoen, where his dwelling house and business premises were situated. By means of that clause and device, he made sure that he and/or his wife would have a refuge in their old age should they need one, insurance against the possibility of being unable to work through illness and, for the present, a tenant farmer to work the land brought together for his own descendants which he had not time to cultivate. The pension he asked for was in fact not really a pension, since no mention was made of either wood for heating or the occasional joint of meat: Batier asked for four setiers of rye and two of wheat, these quantities to be halved if his wife was left a widow. It should also be noted that the future husband would not be able to ask anything from them connected with their work. Batier's will also shows that he never lived with Noé and that his wife never moved into the latter's house. His heir was the son of his other sister, who went to live with his widow.[21]

Sorting out the details of such contracts from the point of view of the family cycle thus changes their scope and shows them in a new light. The same is true for other types of documents, such as legal obligations and farm leases. They reflect attempts to direct the future in the face of a limited control of what was to come, the ever-present threat of illness and death and the ability of the men of the time to imagine various scenarios in order to make the best possible provision for safeguarding their own existence and that of their families. They illustrate one of the fundamental discontinuities between pre-industrial societies and those of our own days. What Arlette Farge so tellingly called 'the fragile life' is less precarious today,[22] and family continuity less of a pitting of wits against the ups and downs of biological life. The struggle for family continuity and security, despite the death and illness that could destroy it at any time, takes us back to the methodological problems forming the basis of our

[21] *AD* Isère, 3E 898, 24 August 1754.
[22] A. Farge, *La Vie fragile, Violence, Pouvoirs et solidarites à Paris au XVIIIe siècle*, Paris 1986.

practice as historians. What meaning can we ascribe to the establishment of a model of devolving property if it is rarely achieved and
conceals the behaviour of a group of villagers who, although they were a
minority, were nevertheless an essential part of the society we are
examining? And do we not come closer to the cultures we are studying if
we turn our perspective round and try to understand situations in which
the social groups failed to achieve their aims in terms of the parameters
controlling them rather than to define a norm subject to too many
exceptions?

Specific features of trading families

In the milieu we are describing, endogamy was very marked and the
levels of wealth circumscribed the range of possible marriages, since
within the merchant group the small core of the four or five wealthiest
families intermarried. The geography of village marriage was therefore
very restricted, and the rich merchants increased the area of possibilities
by moving out into the same small group that dominated the surrounding communities. The three generations of the Gourand family of
Clavans all married into the mercantile elite of the mountain area.
Although some married innkeepers or notaries, this was not an exception
to the rule, since in the eighteenth century the distinction between such
occupations was not hard and fast. All were also merchants, and took
part in itinerant trading.

Here as elsewhere, trading also encouraged fathers to emancipate
their sons, even if they were unmarried and lived under the paternal
roof.[23] Emancipation met the demands of family organization and the
necessary allocation of tasks arising from a family structure based on the
obligatory absence of the father. Business, whether conducted in markets
and dealing with the sale of animals or before a judge or a notary, was not
a matter for women, and whether a man was there to see to it determined
when he could leave to engage in his trading. Thus, when his sons were
too young to act in the place of his own father, Noé senior did not leave
for the plain until after the Bourg d'Oisans fair in mid November,

---

[23] Pierre 'emancipates Noé' – who is twenty-three years old – 'from paternal authority so that he
may be able to negotiate and make contracts without his father's presence', *AD* Isère, 3E 887, 29
May 1713. Noé did the same for his own sons, Jacques and Noé, who married in his lifetime at
thirty-three and thirty-two respectively, Jacques on 25 November 1748 (family records) and Noé
on 28 June 1751 (*AD* Isère, 3E 889).

arranging for power of attorney for a brother-in-law to enable him to settle particular deals. As soon as his sons were old enough to engage in business, he left the valleys at the end of September, leaving the responsibility for family matters in their hands.[24]

The reason for choosing the Gourands is that it enables us to bring together mercantile migration and details of religious denomination. In the seventeenth century the villages in the high Oisans all had a Protestant component. Some, like Mizoen, were completely Protestant, others like Clavans and Besse were almost equally divided between the two denominations or, like La Grave, Villard d'Arène, le Freney and le Mont-de-Lans, had a large Protestant minority.[25] The Revocation of the Edict of Nantes had dramatic effects: the emigration beginning in the 1680s and continuing until the early years of the eighteenth century, or the death of a group of 250 people trying to reach Switzerland together in 1686, broke Protestantism in these valleys.[26]

The Gourand family abjured Protestantism on 4 October 1684 and did not take part in the great exodus of 1686. On the other hand, Pierre, his wife, their two children, his in-laws and a dozen other inhabitants of Clavans tried to flee the following summer. After their arrest and imprisonment, they obtained a verdict of clemency, found the money needed to get out of prison and returned to their village permanently. They offer an exemplary illustration of the fact that, by the second generation, belonging to a society was more important than the earlier religious affiliation. Indeed, although Pierre's children married into families of recent converts, two daughters and two sons of Noé senior married into two old and not insignificant Catholic families, one of them in fact, the Eymard, being that of the parish priest who was the architect of the Revocation in the village and the other, the Dusser, the one that was most insistent in pressing for the application of the edict of the Revocation against the most powerful Protestant families (see figure 3.4).[27]

---

[24] *AD* Isère, 3E 896, 4 October 1744 and 26 September 1745.

[25] *AD* Isère, 4G 272/1 and 4G 277, pastoral visits of Mgr Le Camus in 1672 and 1686.

[26] *AD* Isère, B 2513, 22 June 1686; H. Blet, E. Esmonin and G. Letonnelier, *Le Dauphiné, recueil de textes historiques choisis et commentés*, Grenoble 1938, pp. 181–4; *Recueil de documents relatifs à l'histoire politique, littéraire, scientifique, à la bibliographie, à la statistique... du Dauphiné*, 2e fascicule, 'Emigrés Protestants Dauphinois Secourus par la Bourse française de Genève, 1680–1700', a list published for the first time by E. Arnaud, Grenoble 1885; M. Sauvan-Michou, 'La Révocation de l'Edit de Nantes à Grenoble 1685–1700', *Cahiers d'Histoire*, no. 2, 1956, pp. 147–51.

[27] *AD* Isère, B2154, 22 August 1687. L. Fontaine, 'Affari di stato, affari di famiglie. Politica antiprotestante, strategie private e vita comunitaria in una valle alpina del XVIImo secolo', *Quaderni Storici*, no. 72, 1989.

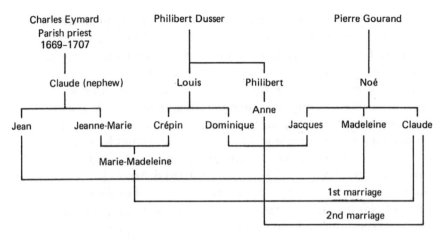

Figure 3.4 Marriage alliances: Gourand, Eymard, Dusser families.

Family cycle, land and credit

The use by the group of merchants of village resources in the wider sense (that is both agricultural and human resources) created an unusual society, which is obscured by the habit of seeing land as the basic form of wealth in rural communities. In fact in the Alpine valleys, the wealthiest barely owned the five hectares needed to support a family,[28] and the study of notarial archives and of the development of one or two merchant families shows a quite different society, completely structured around credit networks, strongly inegalitarian and hierarchical, in which land, beyond the function of meeting the needs of kin, played a marginal part.

A systematic analysis of the sales of land and loans has shown that notaries recorded roughly the same number of each and that their distribution by number shows a relative polarization of sales around tiny lots of between 25 and 50 livres or large ones of over 100 livres in value, while loans were concentrated around the 50 to 100 livres' level; the records also show that an inheritance in the form of land was worth between 100 and 500 livres.[29]

However, such documents only reflect part of the circulation of debts,

[28] Bonnin, La Terre, p. 748; M. Aymard, 'Autoconsommation et Marchés: Chayanov, Labrousse ou Le Roy Ladurie?' Annales ESC, 1985, p. 1384.

[29] L. Fontaine, 'Le Marché Contraint, La Terre et la Révocation dans une vallée Alpine', Revue d'Histoire moderne et contemporaine, forthcoming, 1990.

credits and goods, since most deals were conducted verbally between the parties or in the form of notes kept by the creditor until the debt was settled, at which time he would return them to the debtor or mark the dates of part-settlement. Transactions thus mounted up in the form of verbal or written promises to pay that the debtor committed himself to keeping within a short time limit, generally of between six months and a year. The deadlines were never met, however, and from time to time – depending roughly on family factors such as an approaching death or the need to establish a child, or economic ones such as hard times or the fear that the debtor would not be able to honour his debts – the creditor would 'insure' the loans. Both parties would then produce a joint statement of account before a notary, with the debtor signing a bond or handing over one or two pieces of land. This device provided an official recognition of the sum loaned. Then once again there would be delays in the repayment of the capital, and once again the interest would be more or less regularly paid. But new deals would add to the original debts and lender and borrower would go back to the notary to register a new bond in which the capital and hence the arrears in interest would be increased.[30] The formulas the notary used give us an insight into the nature of the transaction: 'previously paid' refers to the settlement of debts; 'now paid' indicates that there had been an earlier private transaction and that the matter had now been settled, although there had been no previous exchange of money in the presence of the notary. When there had been a real payment, the notary would write 'paid really and in coin of the realm in the presence of myself, notary, and witnessed and accepted by the vendor in complete settlement and to his satisfaction', or the money was described as 'counted' or 'numbered'. In land sales, since it was mostly a question of credit transactions, the notary recorded that the money had been paid 'previously' or would be paid to the creditor 'in settlement'. To this would be added the list of

---

[30] In November 1699 for example, 'Sieur Pierre Garnier, parish clerk . . . amongst other debts acknowledges that he owes to Sieur Pierre Gourand, merchant, the sum of 77 livres, to wit 19 livres 10 sols both for interest and labour and settlement of a bond passed by maître Bard the twenty-seventh day of July 1695, 33 livres promised on the nineteenth day of June 1697, 24 sols remaining for supplying victuals, which sum is agreed by both parties, . . . and promises to pay the debt in a year with interest' (*AD* Isère, 3E 884, November 1699). In June 1713 Pierre Garnier signed a further bond, this time for 240 livres, which included the bond for 78 livres dated 1695, the work and costs of the 1699 document, '20 livres promised in the undertaking of the twentieth day of July 1703 which has now been returned to him' and 82 livres for the 'interest on the two earlier capital sums which the aforesaid Gourand has kindly reduced' (*AD* Isère, 3E 887, 11 June 1713).

creditors the buyer was committed to reimburse. It is therefore difficult
to make a purely statistical use of such registers in order to work out the
circulation of debts and property, as the date on the documents can refer
to transactions that had taken place much earlier, a number of land
purchases obscure simple exchanges between several individuals and
some of the money circulating was not known to the notary, in some
cases permanently and in others for several decades.

The way in which the Gourand family managed its patrimony
introduced loans and sales into the factors producing this distribution
and provides information about social relationships in the village. In
1695 Pierre Gourand moved into the group of the eleven most heavily
taxed men as a result of the way in which he benefited from the desertion
of his co-religionists, much of whose property was assigned to him as next
of kin.[31] This multiple inheritance was to help him settle his own
borrowings, which amounted to 620 livres in three lots.[32] His first act, in
1697, was to repay 75 livres to Jacques Bernard, a merchant in Besse, for
taxes the latter had paid for land owned by Pierre in that village. He then
used the sum of 365 livres he had received to pay Sieur Pierre Garnier
and Jean Aubert for 'work and other items supplied over several years', a
reference to work from tradesmen (Aubert was a shoemaker) and to
dealings within the village in animals and cereals. The last sum went into
settling migrant activity, since he owed four bonds dated 1665, 1668,
1670 and 1672 respectively to 'the Sieurs Jean and Daniel Horard
brothers, merchants in Mizoen'.[33]

At that time itinerant trading was part of the huge networks around
which village migrations were organized. As their debts have shown the
Gourands worked in Burgundy for the Horard brothers. The latter, who
had set up shops both in Burgundy and in Lyons,[34] were themselves part
of the network built around the Delor family, another important family
of merchants, partly settled in Lyons where Thobie Delor had acquired
burgess rights,[35] and to whom the Horards were related by marriage.[36]

[31] Royal declaration of 1689 giving property to the next of kin to ensure that it would be cultivated.
[32] *AD* Isère, 3E 849, 8 July 1697, 4 February 1699, 5 February 1699. These reckonings are of course
not exhaustive, since some of the transactions were not conducted through notaries or were
recorded by notaries in the places where the pedlars went to trade.
[33] *AD* Isère, 3E 884, 4 May 1700; 3E 885, 29 July 1703.
[34] P.H. Chaix, 'Les Grandes Familles nobles de Bourgogne au XVIIe siècle', *1090e Congrès national
des Sociétés savantes–Dijon 1984*, Paris 1986, Section d'Histoire moderne et contemporaine, vol. II,
pp. 23–40 (p. 28).
[35] O. Martin, *La Conversion protestante à Lyon (1659–1687)*, Geneva–Paris 1986, p. 34.
[36] *AD* Isère, 5E 238/1.

This network shaped by the most important families of the neighbouring village, Mizoen, spread into France, Switzerland, Germany and Italy.[37] Migrations were interlinked, and merchants who had emigrated were dependent on those still trading in the villages, even if most of their time was devoted to their business in the town,[38] for recruiting relatives and villagers to carry the pack and spread their trade throughout the surrounding country areas. These were pedlars in our sense of the word, and their migrant trading was carried out exclusively in the six winter months. The Gourands were members of this group, being on the one hand debtors and obligees to the more powerful merchant families and on the other traders and handlers of money in the village, forming the final link in the trading networks.[39]

In the first place they sold livestock and cereals on credit and lent cash. Pierre had bonds worth 868 and Noé 839 livres.[40] All were payable within periods varying from one to ten years, but only two merchants met their commitments to Noé within the prescribed time limits (a total of 134 livres). The interest on bonds was specified ('at 4%'; 'at 5%'; 'at 20 deniers'; 'at the legal rate'), but this does not mean that the rate shown was the real one, since the documents could not show more than 5 per cent, and interest was periodically incorporated into the capital. By virtue of the rights thus acquired over their debtors' harvests they controlled access to the urban market.

Second, they controlled the internal labour market in the village for the same reasons. In the valleys, agricultural work concentrated over short periods of time had to be carried out alongside and in the same season as pastoral activities. There were also the vagaries of the climate, which periodically entailed extra work to harvest and get in as quickly as

---

[37] Besides the Delor and Horard families, the network also included the Vieux, Bérard and Coing families (to mention only the most important ones). *AD* Hautes-Alpes, 1E 7214 to 7219, Registers of the notary Rome at La Grave; E. Arnaud, *Histoire des protestants du Dauphiné aux XVIe, XVIIe et XVIIIe siècles*, 3 vols., Paris, 1875, vol. I, pp. 499–510; Chaix, 'Les grandes familles', p. 28.

[38] As Mgr Le Camus noted with regard to most villages during his pastoral visit to the Oisans area. In July 1678, at the harvest season, the bishop was staying at the house of a merchant who was 'at Nevers, where he trades', and remarked that 'some of the inhabitants of Huez with families there spend almost the whole year in the place where they have their shops and goods and leave their wives and children at home'. At Venosc he observed that 'this parish is one of the richest in the Oisans area. There are several pedlars who trade, some in France and others in Italy or Germany, leaving their families at Venosc, whither they return from time to time' (*AD* Isère, 4G 273).

[39] L. Fontaine, 'Le Reti del Credito, la Montagna, la Città, la Pianura: Merrcanti dell'Oisans tra XVII e XIX Secolo', *Quaderni Storici*, 68, 1988, pp. 573–93.

[40] *AD* Isère, 3E 089, 3 November 1723; 3E 8890, 23 September 1724; 3E 893, 6 April 1729; 3E 895, 26 February 1740.

possible crops threatened by an early snowfall. At such vital times in the cycle of agricultural work, the merchant families took advantage of the rights that their lending activities gave them over human resources. They were also the only regular providers of work, the only ones to employ male and female servants in order to carry out their winter trading freely, and hired labour according to the needs of the family at the various stages of its cycle, at some points sending out their livestock for winter stabling and at others using the children of their debtors as shepherds.[41]

Third, alongside the use of the labour force within the community, there was part of the income earned by migrants, who offered their outside work to pay off debts contracted within the village. From the 1760s, when the word 'pedlar' began to appear in notarial documents, the traders who already engaged in peddling acted as intermediaries between town merchants and those taking up the activity for the first time. Thus the Gourand family, who always bought their stock for their winter textile selling from the same suppliers, sponsored young pedlars with them and in exchange settled any outstanding business such suppliers had with other pedlars in the village. Indeed, in the eighteenth century, the activity was no longer merely a part of the network of shops set up by people who had emigrated from the mountain area, and town merchants were increasingly making use of the pedlars from the mountains, so long as their property and debts were guaranteed by other families.[42] In September 1745, for example, Jean Aubert signed a bond for 253 livres for Jacques Gourand, 'for one similar to which the parties concerned have amicably settled the balance of the aforesaid amount that Martin his brother, with Antoine his other brother, may owe to the sieurs Gallant and Parrain, merchants at Lyons', and promised to repay Gourand half during the course of that year and the balance during the following year, at 5 per cent interest.[43] Unlike Pierre Garnier (note 30), Jean Aubert freed himself from debt very quickly and by 1773 was a member of the group of the richest men in the village, which he had not been in 1745, and was twice as rich as the richest merchant (who owned four times the average compared to Aubert's seven times and more). In 1803–4 (Year XII) he was by far the biggest landowner, with holdings of over ten times the average.

[41] In 1753, when his children were old enough to take care of the harvests, Noé entrusted his flock to the daughter of François Moullaret and the girl's wages were deducted from her father's debt.

[42] L. Fontaine, *Le Voyage et la mémoire, colporteurs de l'Oisans au 19e siècle*, Lyon 1984.

[43] *AD* Isère, 3E 896, 26 September 1745.

What was the part played by land in relation to these credits? The Gourand family used the inheritances received as the next of kin of fleeing Protestant relatives to pay off their debts, and never had a policy of acquiring land in the village. Pierre bought nothing on the two major occasions when Protestant land was sold – that is before their flight – but he himself was then considering emigrating; and in August 1691, when many vacant inheritances were put up for auction, he bought only one building with loft space and a garden valued at 90 livres[44] and the equivalent of two sétérées of fields and two journaux of meadowland, a total of 125 livres, which he received in settlement of debts owed him.

Like his father, Noé senior benefited from property left behind by Protestant refugees. After lengthy litigation, he forced those occupying the land, which they thought was their own, to buy it back from him, which brought him in property worth almost 600 livres, for which the families cultivating the land had to agree either to pay a sum of money for the privilege of doing so or accept deductions from their crops until the purchase price had been met. In the meantime, the former owners had to pay taxes and land charges on the property.[45] Noé also acquired many more properties than his father, but he had more children to set up. His acquisitions amounted to 1,133 livres, all coming from the settlement of debts owed to him. From the middle of the century, the growing population meant that access to land was increasingly difficult, and the means of acquiring it were almost wholly connected with debt or unequal exchange. Noé's sons made more use of this than he had himself.[46]

The inventory carried out after the death of a merchant from Besse shows the unequal division between land and monies due in trading families. The 1685 land roll shows Jean Bernard as owning just under 15 sétérées of land, which was around average for the twenty-four wealthiest inhabitants of the village. Calculated at the best prices, the land element of the patrimony was worth at most 1,500 livres. On the other hand, he owned a flock valued at 520 livres by the notaries, the

[44] *AD* Isère, 3E 885, 29 May 1702.
[45] *AD* Isère, 3E 980, 12 November 1725; 3E 890, 9 December 1725; 3E 891, 10 December 1727 and 5 April 1728. These examples also demonstrate the critical care and reservations with which tax rolls must be treated.
[46] Jacques did business in this way by complementing an exchange of arable for meadow land with 'his savings' gained from his migrant trading (*AD* Isère, 3E 889, 22 October 1749). Two years after his marriage, Pierre exchanged his house, valued at 150 livres, for that of Firmin Charbonnel, valued at 586 livres, undertaking to pay the difference in price to various creditors of Firmin and his late father. Among them was Pierre himself, to the sum of 22 livres in tax he had paid for Firmin (*AD* Isère, 3E 5414, 9 January 1765).

equivalent of 2,950 livres in 'louis d'or, Spanish pistoles and other currencies', goods (oil, shoes, cloths, silks, haberdashery, spices, knives and a gun) worth 415 livres and, most importantly, notes for debts worth 10,387 livres (erroneously entered as 10,907 by the notary), including four from the community (in total 3,776 livres), 43 from individual villagers (in total 3,665 livres), 6 from pedlars (in total 2,063 livres), 800 livres from his son-in-law for the dowry of his deceased daughter, and (recorded in a special notebook) non-recuperable loans to the poor (83 livres).

Although in theory monies due were expressed in terms of land, they were in fact based on a network of personal relationships and human work both inside and outside the community. The latter, because it could generate surplus wealth or increased debt, was at the heart of the mobility of village groups.

The great length of time (at least a generation) over which indebtedness persisted both strengthened the authority of the merchant and his family by creating lasting networks of debtors and also enabled them to plan the future of their families. The limited marriage market encouraged families to acquire properties outside their immediate area as possible places to set up their sons, and all of them had holdings in other parishes. Land acquired in settlement of debts provided a possible means of arranging marriages, and in the meantime brought in an income from tenant farmers. The 240 livres that Pierre Garnier owed Pierre Gourand in 1713 had grown to 578 in 1744 as a result of interest and court costs, for Noé had had to take Pierre Garnier's heirs to law. Julien, Pierre's heir, therefore sold to Noé 'each and all of the real estate, buildings, meadows, lands and woods he has and holds in the community of Clavans'.[47] This was not the end of Julien, however, even if he no longer figured in the land rolls, and he turns up again first as a tenant farmer on the same holding and twenty years later as one of the debtors of Jacques, the son of the late Noé. The ruin of the family is apparent from the tax rolls: in 1717, four years after signing his bond to Pierre Gourand, Pierre Garnier (son of the late Thomas) was one of the middling landowners with 40 per cent above the average tax, as well as parish clerk. By 1733, his children were amongst those paying 60 per cent less than the average poll-tax, and in 1738 they were receiving their share of the dole of wheat for the poor. One sister married in 1743, a year before the above arrangement

[47] *AD* Isère, 3E 896, 28 September 1744.

was made, with a dowry valued at 60 livres, as compared with the 1,000 livres or so Noé's daughters had each received.

This landed policy brought together the interests of both the father and the merchant. In the first role, a man could plan to set up one or more of his children in the future; in the second, he could gain access to parish pasture land, develop his activities as a stock raiser and widen his 'credit' and the land basis on which the loans his suppliers gave him for his winter trading depended.

The mechanics of credit and debt at the heart of village hierarchies and power struggles also influenced Catholic/Protestant relations in the seventeenth century. We have seen that there was little circulation of money in the villages, where settlement was almost entirely a matter of credit. It found its way into dowries and passed from merchant to merchant like paper money. Alongside this circulation of debts there was also a circulation of power over human work and a blurring of religious divisions. The land-tax collector (the *mistral*) was one of the essential poles of the redistribution of power relationships between the religious denominations. By accepting the post, in fact, he committed himself to paying the tax to the king at a given date and recuperating the total amount from the heads of families. This made him the village's chief creditor, and the records of the Clavans *mistral* show eighty-three families to have been in debt to him in 1700. Since he was a member of only one of the denominations, his activities meant that he was an essential agent in the welding together of the two religious communities through the medium of credit.[48]

The merchants thus enjoyed total authority over village life. This was connected to the many parts they played and the many kinds of income they received, and was based on a clientele of people bound to them by legal agreements and networks of dependence. Such clienteles came together, merged or were juxtaposed according to the rivalries or agreements between the most powerful families. They were likewise affected by economic circumstances that disrupted strategies and, when money was short, necessitated the redistribution of credit and power among the major families on bases other than those of membership of a village community or a religious denomination. Sometimes the 'elites' would agree amongst themselves to establish and control well-defined

---

[48] On his visit to Clavans in 1672, Mgr Le Camus pointed to the good relationship between the two denominations, and the attitude of the parish priest who 'behaved in just the same way with both Huguenots and Catholics' (*AD* Isère, 4G 272/1, pastoral visits of Mgr Le Camus, 1672).

clienteles, sometimes they would fight for power over families by supporting the strategies of debtors trying to decrease their dependence, to borrow from more than one source and to change notaries in order to try to keep their patrimony secret with the aim of creating a margin of independence from the power of the merchants.

Even though they were largely peasants like the other members of their community, the men described in the archives as 'merchants' and then as 'pedlars' constructed the cycle of their family destinies. By skilful manipulation of the links forged by their occupations as traders, by time, and in several different places, they tried to handle prudently various strategies for ensuring that their families would survive and become established despite the powerful biological hazards of human life. Notwithstanding the slender and fragile agricultural resources of their high Alpine valleys, they built up an idiosyncratic society which enabled an infinitely greater number of people to live in them than nature alone could have supported, and their mastery of local conditions, based on full use of the village's own resources and the penetration of more distant external markets, lies at the heart of the 'overpopulation' of this area of rock and ice.[49]

[49] In fact, when merchants left the village and there were no other families able to take over from them, winter migration dried up and the community very rapidly became impoverished. This was the case in, for example, Saint-Christophe at the end of the seventeenth century, as the bishop of Grenoble noted on his pastoral visit: 'In the past there were rich merchants', but now 'the parish is one of the poorest in the diocese, with many families who eat no bread for three months of the year, living for the rest of the time only on herbs cooked with whey without salt, and live on the dried leaves of root crops during the winter' (*AD* Isère, 4G 271/283).

4 ❧ Local market rules and practices. Three guilds in the same line of production in early modern Bologna

Carlo Poni

This study proposes to reconstruct the relations between butchers, tanners and shoemakers (three trades which were also guilds) in Bologna, a relatively large city of around 60,000 inhabitants.[1] The three guilds were linked together by the trading of skins. The tanners bought the already flayed ox, cow and calf hides from the butchers and tanned them before selling them to the shoemakers. The leathers so produced were then used to make shoes.

While the flayed hides deteriorated rapidly in quality, the leathers lasted longer, although they too lost their value quickly once they became too dry. Both the hides and the leathers were intermediate products in the same line of production. This peculiarity, common to many goods, creates special relationships between individual firms in the

This chapter was first presented and discussed at the workshop on 'Work and Family in Pre-industrial Europe' at the European University Institute of Florence (1984), and later during a seminar at the University of Pisa (1985), at the Wissenschaftkolleg zu Berlin (1986) and at the Department of Economics of the University of Bologna (1988). I have benefited from the stimulating comments and suggestions of Wolfram Fischer, Vivian Gruder, Abdellah Hammoudi, Christopher H. Johnson, Patrick Leech, Mario Mirri, Massimo Riccottilli, Michael Sonenscher, Heinrich A. Winkler, Stefano Zamagni. Special thanks are due to Gunther Teubner, Philippe C. Schmitter and Terence Daintith who first introduced me to the idea of long-term contracts and negotiations; to Wolf Lepenies for making difficult but fruitful criticisms, and to Patrizio Bianchi for suggesting useful tools of economic analysis. I am also in debt to Stuart Woolf who has read carefully and provided many improvements to this article.

Weights and measures: the Bolognese libbra was equal to 0.369 kg. The Bolognese lira was made up of 20 soldi, each of 12 denari; or 20 bolognini of 7 quattrini each. Soldi and bolognini were equal in value, the denaro being valued at only 58 per cent of the quattrino.

[1] In 1569, the population of Bologna reached over 60,000 and in the 1581–7 period levelled out at between 70,000 and 72,000. It then dropped in the years of scarcity from 1591 to 1594 and fell in 1595 to 58,900, to rise again above the 60,000 mark in 1597. It then maintained this level until the plague year of 1630 when it collapsed to around 45,000. It was only in 1660 that it recovered again to 60,000. In the course of the eighteenth century, the population rose slowly to reach 70,000 to 71,000 inhabitants and remained at this level from 1771 to 1791, to fall again during the years of French domination (A. Bellettini, *La Popolazione di Bologna dal secolo XV all'unificazione italiana*, Bologna 1961, pp. 24–32).

different phases of the productive process. These production relationships are essentially mediated by the market: semi-manufactured goods
are bought, transformed and resold, and are then subject to other
transformations and transactions before finally reaching the consumer
market. Such an organization of production can be replaced by the
verticalization of several phases in the productive process within a single
firm or conglomerate (internal organization).

Both these organizational modes of production have specific costs, as
has been pointed out in the work of some economists.[2] There are, for
example, the costs of internal management – the monitoring and
assessment of the performance of the sectors and phases operating within
a single firm. Choosing a spot market also has costs, those of market
research and the negotiation of prices, quality and the desired flow of
goods. These potentially high costs can be reduced by recourse to long-
term contracts with clauses guaranteeing quality, quantity, price and
delivery times, to be negotiated periodically. If the goods are perishable,
there is all the more reason to make use of such contracts in order to
decrease risks and costs, the alternative being the internalization of
production within a single firm. With the help of these analytical tools,
rather summarily outlined above, I will attempt to examine the market
relationships between the three guilds in seventeenth- and eighteenth-
century Bologna, in the light of certain questions which the neo-
constitutional economists have raised with regard to the dilemmas and
strategic choices facing the business world of the present day.[3]

Obviously the attempt to apply such notions in a context very
different from that in which they were produced must be viewed with
some caution. I have used them with discretion and only when I have
wanted to provide particular conceptual precision. But the final text
offers the reader ample scope to point out deformations and improper

[2] Studies on the different forms of production organization ('new institutional economics') are
closely tied to the work of O.E. Williamson. See *Market and Hierarchies: Analysis and Antitrust
Implications*, New York 1975; *The Economic Institutions of Capitalism: Firms, Markets, Relational
Contracting*, New York 1985; *Economic Organization: Firms, Markets and Policy Control*, Brighton
1986. See also A. Francis, J. Turk and P. Willman (eds.), *Power, Efficiency and Institutions. A Critical
Appraisal of the Markets and Hierarchies Paradigm*, London 1983; R. Clarke and T. McGuinness
(eds.), *The Economics of the Firm*, Oxford 1987. A good review of this literature is provided by E.
Rullani, 'Economia delle Transazioni e Informazioni: Saggio sulla Nuova Teoria Economica
dell'Organizzazione', *Annali dell'Impresa*, no. 2, 1986, pp. 9–17.
[3] A similar operation, although with large interpretative ambitions, was carried out by D.C. North
in his *Structure and Change in Economic History*, New York 1981. See also by the same author,
'Markets and Other Allocation Systems in History: the Challenge of Karl Polanyi', in *Journal of
European Economic History*, 6, 1977, pp. 703–16, and 'Transaction Costs in History', in *Journal of
European Economic History*, 14, 1985, pp. 557–76.

uses. Nevertheless, words are not stones, and these too are conditioned by the context in which they appear. In my case, the initial inspiration for this research came from a long and passionate familiarity with the work of Marcel Mauss and Karl Polanyi, and in particular with concepts such as 'reciprocal obligations' and 'market embedded in society'.[4] The archival sources which I have examined would have remained silent had it not been for their insights and hypotheses. The final text is thus a compromise between different methodologies. This has resulted in some ambiguities and imbalances – but perhaps also in a certain creative tension. Other debts are to colleagues who are beginning to study the history of trades and guilds in the early modern period, a subject which has been neglected for far too long.[5] Our efforts are only at the very beginning, but they promise well. Studies of the trades and the guilds of

[4] M. Mauss, 'Essai sur le Don', in *L'Année Sociologique*, Paris 1924–5 (reprinted in M. Mauss, *Sociologie et anthropologie*, Paris 1960); K. Polanyi, *The Great Transformation*, New York 1957; K. Polanyi, C.M. Arensberg and H.W. Pearson (eds.), *Trade and Market in the Early Empires*, Glencoe 1957. It is almost superfluous to refer to E.P. Thompson's seminal article, 'The Moral Economy of the English Crowd in the Eighteenth Century', *Past and Present*, 50, 1971, pp. 76–136.

[5] S. Kaplan, 'Réflexions sur la Police du Monde du Travail, 1700–1815', *Revue Historique*, 263, 1979, pp. 17–77; W.H. Sewell, *Work and Revolution in France*, Cambridge 1980; A. Griessinger, *Das symbolische Kapital der Ehre: Streikbewegungen und Kollektives Bewusstsein deutscher Handwerksgesellen im 18. Jahrhundert*, Frankfurt-on-Main, Berlin and Vienna 1981; Rainer S. Elkar (ed.), *Deutsches Handwerk in Spätmittelalter und Früher Neuzeit*, Göttingen 1983; A. Black, *Guilds and Civil Society in European Political Thought from the Twelfth Century to the Present*, Ithaca 1984; M. Sonenscher, 'Journeymen, the Courts and the French Trades, 1781–1791', *Past and Present*, 114, 1987, pp. 77–109; C.Mozzarelli (ed.), *Economia e corporazioni. Il governo degli interessi nella storia d'Italia dal Medioevo all'età contemporanea*, Milan 1988; 'Corps et Communautés d'Ancien Régime', a collection of articles introduced by J. Rvel, in *Annales E.S.C.*, no. 2, 1988, pp. 295–451; R. Reith, 'Zur beruflichen Sozialisation im Handwerk vom 18. bis ins frühe 20. Jahrhundert', *Vierteljahrschrift für Social- und Wirtschaftsgeschichte*, 76 (1), 1989, pp. 1–27, and the important German bibliography listed here. On the Bolognese guild in the early modern period see L. Gheza Fabbri, 'Le Adunanze Segrete dei Carpentieri Bolognesi (1573–1574)', *Atti della Accademia delle Scienze dell'Istituto di Bologna. Classe di scienze morali. Rendiconti*, 1978–9, pp. 32–44, 'Drappieri, Strazzaroli e Zavagli: una Compagnia Bolognese tra il XVI e il XVIII Secolo', *Il Carrobbio*, 4, 1980, pp. 163–80 and *L'Organizzazione del lavoro in una economia urbana. Le Società d'Arti a Bologna nei secoli XVI e XVII*, Bologna 1988; M. Fanti, *I Macellai bolognesi. Mestiere, politica e vita civile nella storia di una categoria attraverso i secoli*, Bologna 1980; C. Poni, 'Misura contro Misura: come il Filo di Seta divenne Sottile e Rotondo', *Quaderni storici*, 47, 1981 and 'Norms and Disputes: the Shoemakers' Guild in Eighteenth Century Bologna', *Past and Present*, 123, 1989, pp. 80–108; G. Tamba, 'Da Socio a Obbediente. La Società dei Muratori dall'Età Comunale al 1796', in *Muratori a Bologna. Arte e società dalle origini al secolo XVIII*, Bologna 1981, pp. 43–156; A. Guenzi, *Pane e fornai a Bologna in età moderna*, Venice 1982, 'La Carne Bovina: Consumi, Prezzi e Controllo Sociale nella Città di Bologna (Sec. XVII e XVIII)' in *Popolazione ed economia dei territori bolognesi durante il Settecento*, Bologna 1985, pp. 537–51, *La Fabbrica delle tele tra città e campagna. Gruppi professionali e governo dell'economia a Bologna nel secolo XVIII*, Ancona 1988 and *La Tessitura femminile tra città e campagna a Bologna nei secoli XVII e XVIII*, Bologna 1988; F. Giusberti, 'La 'Ruga delle Pescherie' de Bologne au XVIIIeme Siècle: Conflits et Transactions', *Annales E.S.C.*, no. 2, 1983, pp. 401–8; M. Fornasari, 'Il Padre della Fame è la Fatica: l'Ascesa Sociale di un Notaio Bolognese nel '500', *Il Carrobbio*, 13, 1976.

the Ancien Regime may become the key to understanding whole sets of institutions, rules and behaviour which have not yet made an appearance on the stage of history.

Transactions between tanners and shoemakers

Shoemakers in Bologna did not have the right to tan the leather they needed. The leather that they cut and sewed could be tanned only by members of the tanners' guild.[6] The tanners, in turn, did not have the right to make shoes.[7] While the tanners' guild possessed a monopoly of the preparation and sale of hides, the shoemakers had no absolute monopoly over demand to match the tanners' monopoly of supply. Yet they were the most significant buyers of tanned hides (the other buyers being the coach makers, glove makers and saddlers) and were able to make use of certain juridical devices in order to control the market and thus guarantee the supply of raw material that they required. In principle at least, each shoemaker had to limit his purchases, calculating them on the basis of his shop's requirements. All the leather he purchased had to be used for the making of shoes. He did not have the right to resell leather, a measure which prevented the speculative resale of the finest leather, the poorest quality leathers remaining for shoe production.[8]

This network of dependence and compensation guaranteed a system of reciprocal obligation, although it neither set nor indicated the prices at which goods were to be sold. The prices of tanned hides and leather were negotiated from time to time according to procedures established during the sixteenth century, if not earlier. In principle, the rates for tanned hides were negotiated by representatives of the two guilds. If no

---

[6] The Bolognese tanners were divided into three guilds: the *pellacani*, the *callegari* and the *cartolai*. In principle, only the *pellacani* – the richest guild with most members – had the right to tan ox, cow and calf hides, and I use the word 'tanners' to refer to this group alone. The *callegari* had the right to tan the hides of small animals (goats, sheep, etc.) and on request also a small number of calf hides. The *cartolai* also only had the right to finish those hides which were the monopoly of the *callegari*. There were frequent conflicts between these three guilds, despite the fact that some of the members of the *pellacani* guild were also members of that of the *callegari* and/or that of the *cartolai*. This conflict will not be considered here. At the end of the eighteenth century the three guilds were combined, after protracted negotiations, to form a single guild of *callegari*. Unless otherwise specified, I use the word 'tanners' to indicate the master-shopkeepers and not journeymen; and 'leathers' to indicate both types of leather produced: sole leather made from ox and cow hides and upper leather made from calf hides.

[7] See the *Statuti dei Pellacani*, in the Archivio di Stato di Bologna (hereafter ASB), Assunteria Arti (hereafter Arti), *Notizie attinenti a l'Arte dei Pellacani*, vol. I. The reciprocal exclusion, already present in the statutes of the sixteenth century, was confirmed in the statutes of the shoemakers' guild. See *Statuti et Ordini della onoranda Compagnia et Arte de' Calzolai della città di Bologna*, Bologna 1721, p. 64.   [8] Ibid.

agreement could be reached, as in 1612, 1654 and 1659, the two sides requested the intervention of the authorities.[9] They appealed directly to the Cardinal Legate, the representative of the papal government, who would then appoint one of the judges of his court to act as arbitrator.[10] The talks between the representatives of tanners and shoemakers would be granted a hearing before the judge. After listening to both sides, cross-examining the consulting experts and accountants, the judge would close the debate with a decree fixing the new price list. This decision, although it took the form of a decree, was not final. If one of the parties was not satisfied with the decision, it had the right to appeal and to present new arguments in its favour.

In February to March 1659, for example, the representatives of the shoemakers' guild called for a reduction in the price of leathers in the light of the decrease in the 'price of materials [principally gall] used to tan and perfect leather'.[11] The tanners opposed this demand, claiming that 'the prices of hides from which leather is made' had risen greatly and outweighed the reduction in the price of the materials. The judge, Giuliano Laureti, appointed by the Cardinal Legate to arbitrate in the dispute, presented his decision on 15 March 1659 in favour of the shoemakers. He rejected the arguments of the tanners on the grounds that all previous decisions on the matter had been based on the price of the materials used for tanning, and that the price of leather must increase or decrease in relation to fluctuations in the price of the materials.[12]

---

[9] *Decretum differentiarum in causa et materia pretii coraminum facta per Excellentiss. Dom. Herculem Rangonem Judicem, die 14 januarii 1612*, Bologna 1634; A. Papinio, *Decreto in data 19 ottobre 1654 che stabilisce li prezzi dei corami in sequito di lite insorta fra le Società dei Pellacani e quella dei Calzolai*, Bologna n.d.; G. Laureti, *Decreto in data 17 marzo 1659 che stabilisce li prezzi dei corami in sequito di vertenza insorta fra la Compagnia de' Calzolai e l'altra dei Pellacani*, Bologna n.d.; G. Laureti, *Decreto in data 15 maggio 1659 che modifica l'altro del 17 marzo . . . del prezzo dei corami e in ciò ad istanza della Compagnia dei Pellacani contro quella dei Calzolari*, Bologna n.d. The decree of Ercole Rangone can be found in ASB, Arti, *Notizie attinente Pellacani*, vol. I. The other three decrees are preserved in the Biblioteca Comunale dell'Archiginnasio (hereafter BCAB) and are cited with the title indicated in the catalogue of the library. Between 1600 and 1660, the price of leather had been fixed by decree on at least two other occasions, once by Judge Scipione Beneduccio (sometime before 1612 according to Judge G. Rangone), and once by Judge Francesco Panighi on 14 September 1634 (cited by G. Laureti).

[10] The Cardinal Degate represented the sovereign, the pope. The head of the diocese was the archbishop. On the institutional structure of the *governo misto* of Bologna, see 'L'Ordinamento Bolognese dei secoli XVI–XVII: lo stato, il governo e i magistrati di Bologna del Cavalier Ciro Spontone, edizione del MS. B. 1114 della Biblioteca dell'Archiginnasio', ed. S. Verardi Ventura, 2 vols., *Archiginnasio*, nos. 74, 1979 and 75, 1981.

[11] The story which follows comes from G. Laureti, *Decreto in data 17 marzo 1659. . .* (no page numbers).

[12] This principle was reaffirmed in an agreement signed by the two guilds in 1647, mentioned in ASB, Tribuni della Plebe e Collegio delle Arti (hereafter Tribuni), Atti, Libro Giallo, IV, 1647–70, 6 May 1648, fo. 76.

Because the price of the materials had fallen from '110 lire per thousand libbre' to '80 lire per thousand libbre' since the price of leather had been set in 1654, the judge ordered a reduction in the price of various types of leather by nine quattrini per libbra. This decrease applied to all the fourteen different types of skins and leather, regardless of variations in the quantity of materials used and their incidence on the costs of production, the assumption being that the prices (and thus the gains and losses) would balance out. The decree not only fixed the new prices, it also reproduced, almost to the letter, the regulations governing relations between shoemakers and tanners that had been incorporated into the 1612 price agreement (decreed by Judge Ercole Rangone). These regulations stipulated the quality of the product and set out punctilious procedures for ensuring the supply of leather, something which naturally favoured the interests of the shoemakers.

In particular, the tanners were required to produce leather that was 'dry, seasoned and properly conditioned . . . experience having shown that leather is often sold damp and sodden to the detriment of shoemakers and of the public'. The head of the tanners' guild had to supply the head of the shoemakers' guild with a precise list of 'all the quantities of fresh hides' that the tanners had bought from the butchers, as well as of all the leathers 'heated up' (that is, prepared) daily, with the name of the tanner who had processed the skins. The tanners could cut only half of each tanned hide, leaving the other half intact throughout 'the whole of the following day', so that it might be sold 'in one piece at the pleasure of the shoemakers and distributed in accordance with the orders of the heads of the said shoemakers'. Lastly, tanners were prohibited from hoarding skins 'in a way prejudicial to the shoemakers' guild'.

The tanners' guild, dissatisfied with the decree, immediately appealed to the Cardinal Legate, arguing that the decrease of nine quattrini was out of proportion to the drop in the price of the materials. They asked for a 'revised calculation'. The Cardinal Legate accepted their request because, he declared, everyone is entitled to have 'his just due'.[13] Judge Laureti then reconvened the representatives of the two guilds and together with them appointed two accountants. The calculations were reviewed and after several meetings 'a common consensus' was reached on 15 May 1659: the price would be lowered by eight quattrini instead of nine. The reduction of one quattrino was a minuscule gain for the

[13] G. Laureti, *Decreto in data 15 maggio che modifica l'altro del 17 marzo* (no page numbers).

tanners. More important for them was the elimination of all the punctilious rules in favour of the shoemakers, leaving only the one that guaranteed the quality of leather.

This brief sequence of events highlights the existence of a decision-making process aimed at obtaining the agreement of the parties concerned. In principle the corporate interests set the price of leather, and the political authorities intervened to arbitrate only when the two sides failed to reach agreement.

Another body which in some cases acted as arbitrator between the shoemakers and the tanners was the Tribuni della Plebe e Collegio della Arti, a magistrates' court whose responsibility was to check the quality and prices of foodstuffs and other consumer goods such as leathers and shoes.[14] One such intervention took place in 1648 when, with the two guilds in conflict, the magistrates advised them to nominate two experts who would be responsible for fixing the price of the leathers.[15] In 1671, these same Tribuni, adopting a decision which was better suited to their institutional role, claimed, apparently for the first time, the right to fix the price of leather in the name of a political and moral principle: the 'public good' and the 'benefit of the poor'.[16] According to the Tribuni, those judges charged by the Cardinal Legate with the settling of disputes 'between shoemakers and tanners with regard to the price of leather' had to conform to earlier procedures. But the Tribuni could intervene on their own initiative to lower the price of leather, and consequently of shoes, in favour of the poor (a concept not openly expressed in the preceding negotiations). Neither Judge Laureti, nor any other judge could impose rules on the Tribuni, who had to act according to their own norms. The Tribuni alone, free from outside interference, could decide whether or not to examine production costs before fixing new prices, and whether or not to accept objections from a contesting guild.

With these assertions the Tribuni intended to introduce new norms that contrasted with traditional practices and that would justify their

---

[14] The Tribuni were made up of representatives of the twenty-one official guilds and eight citizens representing the four sections of the city nominated every two months and serving on a rotating basis. They were secondary courts attended only by one judge and a notary. See V. Sacco, *Istruzione per li Signori Gonfalonieri del Popolo o Tribuni della Plebe ed onorandi Massari delle Arti*, Bologna 1740.   [15] ASB, Tribuni, Atti, Libro Giallo.

[16] For the arguments used by the Tribuni to justify their interventions, see ASB, Tribuni, Atti, Libro Rosso, v, 21 July 1671, fo. 39v and 21 August 1671, fos. 40–1. According to the jurist Vincenzo Sacco, the Tribuni should not have 'only the relief of the poor at heart' but also the 'earnings of the artisan–shopkeeper which must serve to maintain his . . . family' (V. Sacco, *Istruzione*', p. 48).

intervention, unsolicited by either the tanners or the shoemakers. In practice, however, they applied rules similar to those used by previous arbitrators, which Judge Laureti had reaffirmed. In the first few months of 1671, the price of gall fell from eighty to sixty-two lire per thousand libbre. In consequence of this decrease in price, the Tribuni authorized new rates that reduced the price of leather by eight quattrini per libbra. The price of 'black lustrous leather' alone was left unchanged in response to the tanners' request. Why was the shoemakers' guild silent on this occasion? According to Giacomo de Cavalariis, a former tanner turned informant for the Tribuni against his own guild, 'the reason the shoemakers don't appeal to the magistracy to lower the price of leather ... is that, if they did, the tanners would stop giving them credit'.[17] This information sheds light on the economic relations between the tanners and the shoemakers. The procedures to set quality and prices may be looked upon as devices for defending a weak and poor craft against one that was richer and more powerful. The tanners, not more than twenty in number, also enjoyed a strong oligopolistic position in supplying the market in comparison to the demand that arose from several hundred shoemakers and cobblers.[18]

How the tanners responded to this second price reduction is not known. They may have lowered the quality of the materials they used, and hence of the end product, in order to reduce production costs, as some sources seem to indicate. On 12 April 1703, the Tribuni gave their support to the 'many complaints and protests of the poor purchasers [the shoemakers] who buy ... leather that is of such low quality that before long it is worn out, and this is because the tanners have been processing the fresh hides with bark and not with the gall that has been used since time immemorial, bark being very harmful'. The Tribuni seemed inclined to prohibit, 'in the name of the public good and for the benefit of the poor', the production of 'similar goods that are harmful to all persons and of profit only to those who make them'. They appointed a commission of enquiry that included representatives of the tanners' and shoemakers' guilds. Its task was to gather information about the 'quality

[17] J. de Cavalariis' testimony was given on 13 August 1671 (ASB, Tribuni fos. 42–42v). De Cavalariis also gave the Tribuni calculations on the production costs of tanning, which were unfavourable to the tanners but which could not be used as they were inconclusive.

[18] It could hardly be said, however, that the tanners were in a flourishing condition in 1671. They were just beginning to climb out of a deep crisis which had begun in 1637 when they lost their near-exclusive monopoly of the right to tan the coarse hides. According to the Tribuni, in 1671 'numerous butchers' were also tanning hides (ASB, Tribuni, Atti, Libro Rosso, V, 21 August 1671, fo. 41).

of . . . leathers tanned with bark and of that tanned using gall, and the differences between them'. But the commission not only enquired into the quality of goods but also paid particular attention to the cost of production.[19]

The cost of bark, the commission found out, was twenty lire per thousand libbre, barely a third of that of gall, so that bark had in part replaced gall and lowered the cost of the materials used in tanning by approximately 50 per cent. On 4 May, after hearing the tanners' representatives and considering their calculations, the Tribuni were granted an audience with the Cardinal Legate who praised the 'vigilance and zeal' with which they had worked for the 'poor and the public'. In his presence and with his consent a new price list was issued set out in two tables. The first of these confirmed the prices fixed in 1671 for skins tanned with gall alone; the second set lower prices for the majority of the leathers, treated with a mixture of bark and gall.[20]

The tanners' guild protested against this decision, claiming that their representatives had not been adequately heard. To dramatize the conflict they addressed their pleas to the Cardinal Legate and the Assunteria del Pavaglione, a committee of the city Senate. The hand of their legal advisor may be seen in the language of their petition, which drew on the principles the Tribuni themselves had previously expressed. The tanners argued that the new price rates 'rested on causes that were groundless, far removed from justice or equity, and very prejudicial to the public and to private persons'. The tanners' guild did not deny that bark cost less than gall, but stated that 'when you work with bark and gall, over twice as much is required . . . and so there is little difference in cost between the two kinds of materials. Furthermore, since more than twice as much time is needed to treat leather with bark and gall combined than with gall alone, more money is spent on wages for more journeymen and on rent for larger workshops, and capital is left idle for a longer time.' They argued that the two ways of treating hides incurred the same costs and also resulted in 'the same quality, so that they could scarcely be distinguished, having the same appearance, the same colour, the same excellence . . . the same degree of perfection, as is well known to the shoemakers, whose job it is to have a proper knowledge of the intrinsic quality of different kinds of leather'. Having demonstrated the inconsistency of what they called the 'prime causes' for the new rates, they demanded, in conclusion, that the two types of leather should be

[19] ASB, Tribuni, Atti, Libro Bianco, VII, fo. 78v.   [20] Ibid., 4 May 1703, fos. 85v–86v.

sold at the same price (that of 1671). The tanners not only highlighted what they saw as the incompetence of the Tribuni; they further charged the court with subordinating the public to the private interest. According to the petition, the magistrates had been deceived by some of the Tribuni 'who favoured the rates in question, but who themselves are interested parties because they hoard and speculate in foreign gall [gall was imported from the Levant], and are suspect of promoting their particular interests'. The tanners in contrast identified themselves with the public interest. By using bark, the tanners brought profit 'to the economy of this city, because those monies that would have been transferred to foreign countries for the purchase of Levantine gall are spent in the territory of Bologna on bark that accumulates in the woods of the region, benefiting the owners of the woods and the workers thus employed.[21]

The tanners' statement, a copy of which the Tribuni obtained from Abbot Buzzetti, 'a hearer of the Chamber' of Cardinal Legate d'Adda, struck a hard blow at the honour of the Tribuni. They had good reason to fear that the prices set on 4 May would be withdrawn without their knowledge. They felt they were under accusation when Abbot Buzzetti asked them to reply to the tanners' criticisms and to state 'their reasons and motives so that the most appropriate and needful resolutions might be reached'.[22] But they were reassured by the solidarity of the Assunteria del Pavaglione and the Gonfaloniere (the head of the Senate). Some backstage mediation must have led the tanners to send a conciliatory letter to the Tribuni on 30 May 1703, which entreated them 'reverently. . . to deign to listen' to their arguments, so that the price of leather might 'be lowered by an equitable degree . . . without harming the trade'.[23] Representatives of the two sides resumed talks, and after a few minor disputes they reached an agreement – with the help of the Cardinal Legate and the Assunteria del Pavaglione. A formal public investigation (*scandaglio*) would be made of the process of production to determine the costs of producing skins tanned with different materials.[24]

[21] The tanners' protest is recorded in the registers of the Tribuni (vii, 24 May 1703, fos. 93v–94). They had apparently already presented a protest to the Assunteria del Pavaglione, although I have not yet been able to find it. The Assunteria del Pavaglione superintended the silk-worm cocoon market (called *Pavaglione*), but also had some degree of jurisdiction over the tanners.
[22] ASB, Tribuni, VII, 22 May 1703, fo. 92v.   [23] Ibid., 30 May 1703, fo. 95v.
[24] During the first meeting with the Tribuni (1 June 1703) the tanners' representatives had promised that they would not use bark in the future so long as they were allowed, as a transitory measure, to sell the leathers already prepared with bark and gall. This request was implicitly refused, however, by the Gonfaloniere and by the Assunti del Pavaglione (ibid. fos. 97–97v). On 3 July 1703, the 4 May tariffs were suspended.

These operations began on 18 August 1703, with a solemn ritual designed to install trust in public authority among the participants. In the presence of five members of the Tribuni, representatives of the tanners and the shoemakers, and a notary who recorded the event, six hides (two of good quality, two of medium and two of low quality) were weighed, washed, cleaned, stamped and cut into two parts. The twelve pieces of hide were then passed to three tanners. Six pieces (two of each quality) were given to the tanner Francesco Carlini, who swore on the Bible to process the skins 'faithfully and honestly' with gall and bark. The same ritual was repeated on the same day with two other tanners, Tadeo Corticelli and Francesco Pignoni, each of whom was given three pieces of the same qualities as those worked by Carlini. Both took an oath on the Bible that they would process the pieces faithfully, Corticelli with gall alone and Pignoni with gall and myrtle leaves. The investigation ended in March 1704 with a conclusion in favour of the tanners. Several weeks earlier the Tribuni had anticipated this outcome and abolished the rates they had previously introduced.[25]

Some time later, with the creation in the 1730s of the Assunteria al sollievo delle Arti – a new Senate committee that was granted wide powers of control over the guilds and industrial activities – the Tribuni had to give up a part at least of their right to intervene. On 18 September 1747 the Assunteria al sollievo delle Arti took the decision to raise the price of leathers, at that time in short supply, because, 'having examined the issue . . . we think that since leathers are sold in the neighbouring towns and villages at higher prices than in Bologna, it is impossible that all the leathers produced in the city remain here, or that one should place hopes in foreign imports'.[26]

In the cases examined so far, the interventions made by public bodies to fix the price of leather appear to have been motivated by three factors: the desire to solve the conflicts between the two guilds; the wish to defend the needs of the poor; and the need to match the prices of neighbouring

[25] The 'soundings' ritual (*scandaglio*) is described in ibid., fos. 113–113v. From this source it appears that the *scandaglio* was suspended after six months. From other sources we know that the tanning process lasted a longer period, from twelve to twenty-four months. After being treated with chalk, the hides were unhaired, fleshed and stretched. After this, the real work of tanning began, which ended with the hides being laid in ditches in distinct layers, each layer separated from the others by gall and tanning bark. See F. Griselini, *Dizionario delle Arti e dei Mestieri*, vol. V, Venice, 1769, pp. 179–92. The 'soundings' were normal practice in Bologna and were frequently used to decide upon the cost of making bread and thus the price of bread on sale. See Guenzi, *Pane e fornai a Bologna*, pp. 77–136 and 'La Carne Bovina', pp. 537–51.

[26] ASB, Arti, Atti, VII, 18 September 1747, fo. 64. This Assunteria was presided over by the Gonfaloniere.

markets, the reason behind the variations in price being, in at least three cases, a decrease in the price of the materials.

But the shifts in the price scale of leather were also connected to changes in the price of fresh hides, something which is clear from the negotiations that took place from 1771 to 1772, when shoemakers and tanners were initially allied against the butchers.

In late 1770 a rise in the cost of livestock had forced the butchers to demand from the Tribuni a sharp increase in meat prices. Instead, they had to put up with what the Tribuni described as 'a very modest' (*discretissimo*) price increase. To make up for their loss, at least to some extent, the butchers had no alternative but to ask for an increase in the price of hides. They faced opposition on this issue from the tanners and shoemakers, but were supported by the Tribuni and by the authorities in general. In the course of the discussions between butchers, tanners and shoemakers, the latter were in the weakest position. At first the shoemakers sided with the tanners in an attempt to prevent or limit, in the name of the 'just price', the increase requested by the butchers. Once the higher price came into effect, however, the shoemakers were abandoned by the tanners, who tried to pass the increase on to the shoemakers by raising the price of the leathers. The Tribuni conceded this second increase, justifying it with an even-handed argument that sought to take account of the interests of both guilds. In their decision of 26 March 1771 the Tribuni declared: 'If the price of leather was fair when the hides cost less, an increase in the price of the said hides, in the absence of a decrease in the other costs involved in tanning, must have as a consequence an increase in the price of leather, provided that it is kept within narrow limits and that it constitutes as slight a burden as possible on the shoemakers and the public, and that the shoemakers obtain satisfaction for their complaints about the poor quality of the leather.'[27]

The shoemakers were the only guild that did not accept either price increase. On the day of the decision, the Council of the shoemakers' guild informed the Tribuni that they had further arguments to present, a

---

[27] ASB, Tribuni, Atti, Libro Rosso, XVIII, 26 March 1771, fos. 132–132v. The opposition to raising the price of hides which began on 6 October 1770 continued on 14 and 26 March 1771, when a rise was decided. In short, the prices of the hides could also vary in relation to the price of meat. If meat prices rose, guaranteeing the butchers high earnings, then the price of hides could decrease, as the income of the butchers was based above all on the sale of meat. But if meat prices did not rise to offset increases in the price of livestock, the butchers would attempt to compensate for their loss of earnings (although this compensation could not be adequate) by raising the price of the hides.

statement that at least served to postpone the immediate approval of the decision. Invited on several occasions to present their arguments, the shoemakers' guild resorted to delaying tactics.[28] Meanwhile, with a further increase in the cost of materials, the current prices fixed in March could no longer be maintained. In December 1771, the Tribuni conceded a new 'tacit' increase of six quattrini per libbra on the price of leather (a 'tacit' increase did not require the publication of a new list, but only that the written permission be displayed in the shop).[29] On 4 May 1772 the Tribuni set the new rates, explicitly sanctioning the previous increase. The minutes of this final meeting indicate that the shoemakers' arguments were heard several times, but that they had 'nothing relevant to add', except to make a request 'for the lowest price increase possible'.[30] During these complex negotiations the authorities, it appears, tended to arbitrate patiently between the conflicting parties rather than to impose their own solutions.

I am fairly certain that I have recorded all or nearly all the negotiations and price alterations prompted or decided by the authorities, at least as regards the eighteenth century. According to a 1772 report by the tanners, after 1671 there were neither 'increases nor decreases in the price of leathers, either gross or retail, as the price of the materials and the other costs involved varied only slightly'.[31]

The sources consulted contain few but distinctive traces of direct negotiations between tanners and shoemakers, although the random soundings carried out in the notarial archives (on the reasonable assumption that the contracts were registered by notaries) have not yet borne any fruit.[32] The (hopefully) temporary absence of these sources makes it impossible to complete the analysis of the negotiations between the tanners and the shoemakers. But this absence should not affect our understanding of the framework within which the two guilds operated. This, I believe, can be defined as an institutional bilateral monopoly with a barrier to entrance constituted by the rules and practices of guild membership (the necessary requisites being Bolognese citizenship, a

[28] Ibid., 19 April 1771 (fo. 138); 8 June 1771 (fo. 145); 21 June 1771 (fo. 150).
[29] Ibid., 23 Dec. 1771, fo. 191v–192.
[30] Ibid., 4 May 1772, fos. 221. In 1775, the shoemakers tried again to obtain a price reduction (ibid., 23 and 30 March 1775, fos. 440 and 443).
[31] ASB, Arti, Misc. Arti, XXIII, no. 60, 20 January 1772.
[32] All the decrees issued between 1612 and 1659 (see note 9) referred back, more or less explicitly, to direct negotiations which had failed. The notaries had an important role in the life of the guilds, writing and signing the minutes of the councils, as well as all official documents and contracts.

three-to-five-year apprenticeship, adulthood, the passing of the entrance examination and the paying of a subscription).[33] Only the tanners had the right to tan ox and cow hides; only the shoemakers (and a few other small groups) had the right to buy the leathers. The price and quality of the goods, on the other hand, were periodically negotiated by the representatives of the two guilds, often in the presence of the authorities, or directly by the authorities themselves who were *substitutes*, in certain situations, for the transactional autonomy of the guilds.

Transactions between butchers and tanners

From 1581, the negotiations between the tanners and the butchers over the price and quality of the flayed skins took place according to the same principle of reciprocal exclusion.

The contracts between the tanners and the butchers also included precise regulations regarding sales procedures. After flaying the skins, the butchers had to put them 'on show' without wetting them, 'in a dry place and not rolled up together', which in practice meant not in the shop but in an open space, which could be nearby. It was here that the tanners had to come to buy the hides, either the day they were flayed or the following morning (if this was not a holiday, in which case they had to come a day later).[34] This regulation gave a guarantee to the tanners that they would not be buying water-sodden hides. The butchers, in turn, were sure of the sale of their hides before they lost all their natural humidity. If the buyer had not paid for the hides, the tanners' guild had to take responsibility for the debt. Later, a ban was issued by which no tanner could be admitted to the market unless he had provided adequate financial guarantee.[35] In principle, these contracts were renewed every three to five years, either during Easter or immediately afterwards, and were valid from Good Friday, when (after Lent) the 'butcher's year' restarted.

[33] On the difficulties bilateral monopolies may have in operating smoothly, see O.E. Williamson, *Economic Organization*, pp. 106–7.

[34] These contracts also established that the hides should be free from bone, noses, lips and pieces of meat and that the butchers should not wash the hides until they had been flayed. These clauses and those cited in the text were found in the contract registered by the notary Giovan Battista Taccone on 28 February 1581 (ASB, Notarile, vol. 1574–1608, fos. 55v–57). The same clauses are present in all the contracts I have found from the end of the sixteenth and throughout the seventeenth century. In the eighteenth century, they were replaced by a more general expression which obliged the butchers to sell the hides 'in a good condition'.

[35] ASB, Arti, *Notizie attinenti l'Arte dei Pellacani*, vol. I, *Statutorum Artis Pellacanarum*, 15 April 1600, fo. 27.

Unlike the direct agreements between the shoemakers and the tanners, I have found a considerable number of long-term contracts between the tanners and the butchers. Up to now, in the notarial archive and in some files of the Senate, I have found three contracts for the 1582–1600 period, three for the period from 1601–1700 and three for the years between 1701 and 1731.[36]

If direct negotiations failed, then the authorities intervened, either on request or on their own initiative. Thus on 23 April 1604, 5 June 1604, 27 March 1619 and 14 September 1634, the prices of the hides were fixed by the Cardinal Legate and a Senatorial commission working together.[37] In 1587 and 1637, with no agreement between the two parties, the same authorities conceded to the butchers – despite opposition from the tanners – the right to tan the hides themselves, or to sell the skins at whatever price they wished. On 6 April 1709, on 4 May 1715 and during the period from 1770 to 1772, it was the Tribuni who arbitrated between the representatives of the two guilds.[38] To these seven interventions we may add nine others, between 1610 and 1725, which confirmed decisions already taken or which affected other important aspects of the negotiations.[39]

We need not enter into the details of all these interventions. But the unsuccessful negotiations of 1637 are worth looking at briefly, as they throw light on the negotiating strategies of the two guilds.[40] In this year, the tanners, whose warehouses were full of unsold leathers due to competition from imported leathers (which were cheaper, although of lower quality), refused to grant the butchers the rise in the price of hides they were requesting. But the failure to reach an agreement was also due to the intransigence of the butchers, who in fact wanted to break with the

[36] The first four contracts I have found were registered by the notary Giovan Battista Taccone on 28 February 1581, 23 March 1584, 13 April 1594 and 17 April 1601 (ASB, Notarile, vol. 1571–1608). The next two were registered on 14 April 1609 by the notary Stefano Tacconi (ibid., Notarile, vol. 1596–1610) and on 20 March 1624 by Vincenzo Vaselli (ibid., Notarile, vol. 1621–4). The three contracts stipulated in the eighteenth century were registered by Camillo Bartolotti on 10 June 1720 and on 21 March 1721 (ibid., Notarile, vol. 1719–22) and by Casimiro N. Minelli on 28 March 1731 (ibid., Notarile, vol. 1730–2). I was able to trace these documents with the help of a *Sommario delle scritture ritrovate nelli libri dell'Archivio dell'Arte dei Pellacani* of 19 July 1732 (ibid.), generously pointed out to me by Maria Gioia Tavoni.
[37] *Statutorum Artis Pellacanarum*, fos. 32v–33, 33v–34, 47v–48 and 58–58v. But see also *Sommario delle scritture . . . dell'Arte dei Pellacani*.
[38] For the decisions of 6 April 1709 and 4 May 1715, see *Sommario delle scritture . . . dell'Arte dei Pellacani*.   [39] Ibid.
[40] What follows can be found in the dossier *Beccai contro Pellacani*, in ASB, Arti, *Notizie attinenti l'Arte . . . dei Pellacani*, vol. II. See also the printed pamphlet *Informatione ai Signori di Reggimento per il Massaro et huomini della Compagnia dei Pellacani*, Bologna 1637, in ibid.

tanners, having already bought some workshops in which hides could be tanned. The tanners, not having immediate access to the information as to the butchers' intentions, put up what they saw as a sufficient defence of their interests by agreeing that the butchers should have the right to sell the hides at whatever price they wished, as long as they sold them only to the authorized buyers (that is, only to the members of the tanners' guild). But the butchers cleverly sidestepped this restrictive clause by taking up the problem of the market size directly with the authorities. After obtaining the agreement of the Cardinal Legate and the Senate, they offered their hides, by means of a 'printed edict', to all who wished to buy them, even if they were not members of the tanners' guild.[41] To those who proposed to buy 'in large numbers', the butchers granted the use of tanning workshops. But they were also prepared to sell small quantities to tanners' journeymen, a provocative move aimed at opening up a breach in the solidarity of their adversary. Once confusion and disagreement reigned in the ranks of the tanners, it would be easier for them to enlist the deserters and fugitives needed in order to set up their own tanning workshops, intended to internalize and verticalize production.

In effect, the butchers broke with the bilateral institutional monopoly over at least two strategic issues. They bought the right to tan hides (recognized by the Cardinal Legate with the concession of patents indicating names and not specifying time limits) and they drastically lowered the barriers to entry and exit, thus transforming a monopolistic market controlled institutionally into a 'contestable market'.[42] Both these breaks were bound to put the tanners in an impossible position, as in fact happened. But what advantage did the butchers draw from this?

If we start from the hypothesis that the fixed prices were too low with respect to production costs, the butchers were right in working towards and obtaining the concession of the right to tan the hides. Their aim was to capture in the medium term, if not all, at least a part of the income that the tanners earned from the low price of the raw materials. By putting themselves on the demand side as well as that of supply, they would have gained as tanners what they lost as butchers. In addition, by expanding

[41] The 'printed edict' is in *Notizie attinenti l'Arte dei Pellacani*, vol. I.

[42] On contestable markets, multiproduct firms and economies of scope, see W.J. Baumol, J.C. Panzer and R. Willig, *Contestable Markets and the Theory of Industry Structure*, with foreword by E.E. Bayley, New York 1982.

the multiproduct aspect of their firms (producing meat and hides for two different markets: one for consumption and one for intermediate products), they would have been able to obtain economies of scale and also economies of scope, adding another sector to those in which they traditionally worked. In particular, operating within a multiproduct firm (or seventeenth-century 'conglomerate') they would have been able to shorten the transaction times relating to the transfer of the hides to the tanners, avoiding one of the burdens of transaction costs.[43]

The second move – the offer of tanning workshops to those who wished to enter the market – had the aim of raising demand and thus the price of the hides. But it would have had another, unintended effect. It would have reduced the sunk costs and thus created conditions which were favourable also to pirate entry ('eat and run entry'), damaging both the guilds in conflict.[44] In short, at least on paper, the two measures were contradictory, although it is not known how this contradiction was managed in practice.

Having lost their monopoly over the hides and facing defeat in the leathers market, the tanners were hit and nearly wiped out by a severe and long-lasting crisis. The decision of the Legate, in 1656, to force the butchers to sell the hides only to tanners with their own workshops does not seem to have had any lasting effects.[45] It was only in 1665 that the tanners began to win back their monopolistic privileges. By around 1690, when the traditional negotiations over price, quality and transaction procedures began again regularly, they appear to have been regained in their entirety. Not even the butchers were able to gain sufficient advantage from the difficulties of their adversary. According to the tanners, in order to run their new tanning workshops the butchers had to employ artisans who lacked the necessary skills, with consequent losses in quality, price and earnings.[46]

After this episode, a bitter experience particularly for the tanners, the antagonistic cooperation between the two guilds was kept at acceptable levels of conflict with no further outbreaks of head-on warfare. The

[43] The joint production of beef and leathers is considered by the authors of *Contestable Markets* pp. 75–6) as an intuitive case of a multiproduct firm.

[44] *Contestable Markets*, pp. 6–7, 349–51.

[45] This ban has not been found, but it is summarized very briefly in *Sommario delle scritture ... dell'Arte dei Pellacani*.

[46] See an undated letter (post 1637) sent by the tanners' guild to the Gonfaloniere in the dossier *Beccai contro Pellacani*.

tradition of long-term contracts was resumed and with it the negotiations over prices, quality and selling procedures.

Rules and practices

What was the real effect of the prices and of the levels of quality that were
legally set? Were the agreements actually respected and carried out by
all the members of the guilds involved? And were the guilds able to
convince or compel their members to adhere to the settlements?
Analogous problems have been examined by students of contemporary
industrial relations. Agreements between the representatives of labour
and business lose credibility if either side fails to gain the full consent of its
members. 'Obligation of influence' is the term currently in use in Italy to
designate the practice of conferring responsibility on representatives of
labour and business in order to ensure the consent of their members to
agreements they have negotiated.[47] The same problem exists with the
long-term contracts we are dealing with here, contracts which are full of
clauses aiming to avoid or limit damage resulting from 'opportunistic'
behaviour. How, then, was this problem resolved in eighteenth-century
Bologna? How were those who violated the rules punished and to which
tribunal were appeals made? We know that the guilds themselves could,
on certain occasions and within certain limits, act as tribunals (as was the
case with a considerable number of the Bolognese guilds). Unfortunately, however, the archives of these guilds have been lost. Yet evidence
does indicate that when the guilds failed to enforce the agreements, the
authorities – the Tribuni and the Assunteria Arti – intervened.

In 1752, the Tribuni imposed harsh punishments on those tanners
who refused to pay the butchers the agreed price, suspending their right
to buy hides. In the magistrates' view, there could be no individual
deviation from the price agreed by the guilds. If the tanners believed that
the price of the hides was too high, they had to present written objections
to the magistrates and, following an enquiry, 'if they were held to be
right, justice would take its due course'.[48]

The year after, in February 1753, the butchers tried to sell the hides at

[47] G. Ghezzi, *La Responsabilità contrattuale delle associazioni sindacali*, Milano, 1963, pp. 65–76.
[48] ASB, Tribuni, Atti, Libro Bianco-Rosso, vol. XV, 14 June 1752, fo. 165. Most of the tanners
considered that the price fixed (14 lire 5 soldi for a hundred libbre of hides) was too high and
should be lowered.

a price higher than the legal rate. The Tribuni requested that the butchers also follow the appropriate procedures, 'if they have a complaint against the price'.[49] The real price, as these examples indicate, had to conform to the legally established rates.

Nevertheless, the prices that the artisans paid were pegged to the quality of the goods, and could vary somewhat from the official rates. Fresh hides that were not of equal weight were not considered to be of equal quality. From a Senatorial source of 1730, we learn that the agreed prices were applied to hides weighing over eighty libbre, while the prices of lighter hides tended to be lower (see table 4.1).

But the price of the hides did not depend on their weight alone. It was calculated that 'dry' hides – above all those arriving from slaughter-houses in the countryside – might lose up to 60 to 70 per cent of their original weight. A fresh hide weighing 80 libbre, once it had been dried would weigh only 30 libbre; a hide weighing 75 libbre when fresh would weigh only 25 libbre when dry; and one weighing 65 libbre when fresh would weigh a mere 20 libbre when dry. Graduated prices were drawn up, taking account of such variations and establishing proportions between different weights of fresh and dry (but not dessicated) hides.

The larger, dry (but flexible) skins tended to rise in price, while fresh skins saturated with water or damp tended to decrease in price. In 1746, the tanners obtained from the city government an order that recognized their right to obtain a reduction in the price of hides that had been excessively soaked by the butchers or damaged by cuts when the animals were skinned.[50] In 1770, this right was confirmed but at the same time limited: the tanners could only contest the excessive dampness or poor quality of a hide at the moment of purchase.[51] Again, in 1783, the tanners complained that they had to pay for 'water, blood, and filth' at the same price as the skins. These complaints, which on occasions

---

[49] Ibid., fo. 250. In 1742, the Assunteria al sollievo delle Arti, 'in view of the continuing controversy between tanners and butchers over the price of hides', decided to leave 'each side in liberty this year to act in the way that best suits its business' (ASB Arti, Atti, VI, 9 April 1742, fo. 277v).

[50] See the Order, *Bando sopra le pelli delle macellerie*, Bologna, 21 April 1746 (ASB, Archivio del Legato, Bandi).

[51] See the Order, *Bando sopra le pelli si grosse che minute che cadono in comparto*, Bologna, 22 August 1770 (ASB, Archivio del Legato, Bandi). In 1771 the butchers complained that the tanners, instead of fetching the hides on the days agreed upon, left them 'in the butchers' shops for two or three days to the grave damage and prejudice of the butchers' (ASB, Tribuni, Atti, Libro Rosso, 24 July 1771, fo. 163). When the hides became dry, they could be refreshed by certain procedures which, however, were incapable of restoring their original pliability.

Table 4.1 *Weight and price variations of fresh and dry hides*

Fresh hides		Dry hides	
Weight libbre	Price per 100 libbre	Weight libbre	Price per 100 libbre
80	12.15	30	30.0
75	11.15	25	28.0
65	11.0	20	20.0

The graduated prices were mainly applied to hides from rural areas.

Source: Seconda parte d'informazione al Legato sopra il regolamento delle tre Arti pellacani, caliegari e cartolari, attached to the *Relazioni, riflessi, memorie . . . sopra il regolamento per le tre Arti* (ASB, Arti, Misc. I, no. 88, probably 1737).

developed into real disputes, were only kept within limits by the fear the tanners had of the butchers, 'intractable and blood-thirsty people'.[52] The butchers had a long-standing tradition in Bologna of being the most militant of the guilds and of playing leading roles in political agitations.[53]

The tanners, then, complained that the fresh hides were excessively damp, but the shoemakers, in turn, protested that the leathers were too oily. In other words, the tanners – in spite of the technical regulations laid down in the statutes of their guild and confirmed by judicial decrees – apparently behaved in the same 'opportunistic' way as the butchers. Having soaked the hides in tallow, they saturated them 'craftily' in chalk powder 'in order to dry out and conceal the tallow and the excess oiliness'. The shoemakers therefore paid for 'tallow and skin chalk' and made shoes that were of poor quality, 'thus incurring the complaints of the general public'.[54] In August 1745, the Assunteria al sollievo delle Arti ordered that the 'shoemakers who had bought material of poor quality' from the tanners should bring it to the Assunteria so that appropriate steps might be taken.[55] According to the shoemakers, the

[52] See the report, *Sentimento del Consultore Gavazzi sopra l'instanza dell'Arte delle tre Arti dei conciapelli,* 10 September 1783 (ASB, Arti, Misc. XXXIV, no. 50) and *Risposta dei Tribuni . . . per ovviare li abusi che si commettono dai macellai* (ibid. no. 65, 17 November 1783).

[53] M. Fanti, *I macellai bolognesi . . .*

[54] See the report, *Riflessioni sopra i capi di ricorsi avanzati dai pellacani, callegari e cartolari,* attached to the *Memoriale delli pellacani, callegari e cartolari all'Assunteria d'Arti* (ASB, Arti, Misc. II, no 64, years uncertain). See also *Ricorso e ragioni dell'Arte dei calzolari al Vicelegato contro l'Arte dei pellacani e calegari . . . per gli abusi introdotti,* 23 November 1768 (ASB, Arti, Misc. XXI, no. 36).

[55] ASB, Arti, Atti, VII, 17 August 1745, fo. 23.

tanners obliged those who wished to purchase 'good-quality leathers' to buy a certain percentage of third-rate leathers as well. New negotiations ensued, against the wishes of the tanners, in an attempt to bring prices into line with the actual quality of the leathers.[56] In short, the prices legally declared and agreed to were not the same as the prices which were actually paid. The legal rates were a reference point, a yardstick, alongside which a series of 'private' transactions took place.

As has already been mentioned, a large percentage of the leathers the tanners produced were sold to the shoemakers. But they were not obliged to buy all the leathers they were offered. This situation gave rise to considerable tensions between the two guilds, especially when the unsold leathers began to dry out and to lose weight and quality. At such times, when local demand was weak, the tanners tried to export at least some part of their unsold leathers. But they could not do so without the permission of the shoemakers' guild, which had to indicate its consent by stamping the leathers to be exported from the city, even those sold in the countryside around Bologna. The shoemakers' guild, fearing that its members might be left without sufficient supplies of leather, would not agree easily to apply the stamp, and would do so only for small amounts not exceeding fifty libbre.[57]

When tanned hides and leathers were in poor supply, the shoemakers' guild would request the right to import. They too first had to obtain the permission of the tanners' guild, which then stamped the imported leathers (a permission equally difficult to obtain).[58] This perfect reciprocity of control over import and export (at least in principle) forced the conflicting parties to turn once again in the second half of the eighteenth century to the authorities (the Assunteria al sollievo delle Arti), who had the final say. A decision in favour of one of the parties was reached after careful consultations and thorough investigations of the quantity and

---

[56] ASB, Arti, Atti, VI, 9 May 1737, fo. 99. See also *Promemoria dell'Assunteria d'Arti al legato sopra li qui annessi ricorsi dell'Arte dei calzolari contro li calegari*, 4 November 1793 (ASB, Arti, Misc. LIV).

[57] Control of exports was provided for by the *Statuti et ordini della onoranda Compagnia*.

[58] In 1756 the tanners were ready to supply the city with a constant flow of leather, just to obtain the right to export their goods. But the proposal was not accepted. See the report, *Informazione dell'Assunteria d'Arti, . . . sopra il memoriale dei pellacani e callegari dove dimostrano che l'incaglio che hanno dei corami da essi fabbricati deriva per colpa dei calzolai*, 6 December 1756 (ASB, Arti, Misc. XVIII, no. 60). The shoemakers in the second half of the eighteenth century, in order to lower the price of leathers, produced a printed manifesto to start up a cooperative which would look after the sale of imported hides on their behalf. The shop was actually opened and operated for a few years, but with little success. The Assunteria Arti considered ordering its closure, but in the end decided to let sleeping dogs lie; the shop was never made legal.

quality of the leathers on sale, stored in the warehouses, or in the process of being tanned. The records of these investigations, although not preserved in their entirety, are a precious source for reconstructing the scale of artisan activities as well as tanning techniques.[59]

Not all the export and import trade, however, was open and above-board. Whenever prices of leathers were higher in Bologna than in neighbouring areas, a clandestine import business sprang up. The effect of this was to depress legal prices. On 27 July 1730, for example, the head of the shoemakers' guild stated that 'good quality leather' could be purchased 'at 11 soldi per libbra', even though the official price was 'higher, that is to say 14 soldi per libbra'.[60] A few weeks later the head of the tanners' guild explained that they had been obliged to reduce prices 'below those fixed by the official list' in order to combat the 'continual import . . . at lower prices of leathers produced in the countryside'.[61] The tanners then made the characteristic move of requesting more stringent controls on imports, so that they might raise the prices once again instead of undercutting official prices. As previously noted, on 18 September 1747, the Assunteria al sollievo delle Arti granted a price increase for those leathers in short supply, so as to balance the prices of such goods produced in Bologna with those of the surrounding areas.

The attempt to make use of the market as a means of sustaining the whole elaborate system of corporatist relations seems evident. However, the exchanges between butchers and tanners and between tanners and shoemakers cannot be accounted for by market forces alone. On the contrary, they were founded on the rights and duties that derived from guild membership. The rules and regulations of the corporate bodies provided a sense of security. The fixing of price guidelines protected the interested parties from sudden, uncontrolled leaps in price levels caused by monopolistic practices and short-term disturbances in the market. Through the daily exchanges, the butchers, tanners and shoemakers experienced the freedom of negotiating quality and prices while buffered against excess risk. The political authorities intervened from time to time to mediate between the interests involved or to defend the 'common good' (as they perceived it).

---

[59] See for example, *Visita dei Tribuni . . . col massaro dell'Arte dei calzolari a varie pellacanerie e botteghe*, 23 July 1738 (ASB, Arti, Misc. X, no 24); *Relazione dei Tribuni . . . sopra la visita fatta alle Pellacanerie*, 16 January 1769 (ibid., Misc. XXI, no. 41).
[60] ASB, Tribuni, Atti, Libro Bianco-Rossi, XI, 27 July 1730, fo. 20v.
[61] Ibid., 26 August 1730, fo. 33v.

Selling by quota

Butchers and tanners were also linked by relations which went deeper
than those indicated in the price list. The tanners, in accordance with a
practice called *comparto* (quota), were obliged by law as well as by custom
to buy all the hides provided by the butchers at the agreed price, and to
buy them only from designated butchers. When the price was negotiated, the head of the tanners' guild established the number of hides
each tanner had the right to buy. Another operation followed (of which
only few traces survive), giving precise indications as to the particular
tanners to whom each butcher or group of butchers had to sell their hides
in order that each buyer received the correct quota assigned to him.

In principle, these personalized reciprocal obligations, if they were
formulated by the guild officials, had to be approved by the Senate and/
or the Cardinal Legate. But we should remember that in the early stages
(the long period between 1577 and 1629), during which these obligations were established, it was the Legate and/or the Gonfaloniere who
decided these quotas (at least formally).

This form of social obligation was constructed according to specific
rules. Neither the officials of the tanners' guild nor the authorities could
establish equal or arbitrary quotas. The hides were divided amongst the
tanners according to their wealth and their hierarchical rank within the
guild.

What were the origins of these transactional constraints set up around
the middle of the sixteenth century? They can be considered as a delayed
response to certain monopolistic practices of the 'richer and more
powerful' of the tanners, accused by the guild itself in a report to the
Vice-Legate (14 December 1510) of buying all or nearly all the hides
from the butchers, to the detriment of the 'poor' tanners, who were
virtually forced out of business. Once all or nearly all the hides had been
bought up, the richer tanners sold the leathers to the shoemakers at
inflated prices and on credit, thus capitalizing on their advantage.[62]

These harmful practices could only take place by going flatly against
fundamental transactional norms. According to the old statute, if a
tanner was engaged in negotiations concerning more than ten hides, he
would have to concede a part of the sale to any other tanner who arrived
subsequently. The same statute, in order to prevent secret agreements

---

[62] Letter to the Vice-Legate (14 December 1510) reported in *Statuti Pellacani*, pages unnumbered, in
Notizie attinenti l'Arte dei Pellacani, vol. I.

between monopolists, forbade the tanners to buy hides until they had been flayed and put on display in a place open to the public.[63] The report sent to the Vice-Legate accused the rich tanners of buying in a covert manner, inside the butchers' workshops in private rooms, in order to get around the ten-skin rule and to negotiate the price of the hides 'by weight' (*a peso*), as if they had already agreed upon 'a certain price per libbra', rather than coming to an agreement based on an evaluation of their value carried out 'by sight' (*a occhio*), as was the tradition.[64] According to the tanners' guild, these two new practices had to be severely forbidden, and liable to a fine of ten gold scudi. This proposal was given immediate effect in a ban issued by the Vice-Legate. We do not know, however, how the ban was applied in practice and with what success. Thirty years later, on 1 December 1541, the ban was abolished and replaced by a new set of regulations, according to which each tanner could buy hides from the same butcher only in alternate weeks and as long as he bought them 'publicly and openly', the penalty being a fine of ten gold scudi and exclusion from the guild.[65]

These procedures had the conscious and explicit objective of preventing hoarding and offering reasonable access to the market to the poorer tanners. At that time (1541) the price of the hides was left to private negotiations. However, if agreement could not be reached by making an on the 'spot' evaluation, negotiations could be continued on the basis of weight.[66]

On 7 August 1554, these regulations were replaced by new norms set down by the Gonfaloniere and imposed on the guilds. For the first time, quota sales were established. The new regulations, which came into force only on 7 May 1557, had the aim of resolving the disputes between 'rich and poor tanners', the Gonfaloniere being moved solely by considerations of 'justice, tranquillity and peace'. The members of the guild were divided into three 'classes', amongst which 550 hides were distributed every month. The first class (six tanners, including the head of the guild and the Council officials) had the right to buy 215 hides; the second class

---

[63] *Statuti Pellacani*, pages unnumbered.   [64] Letter to the Vice-Legate.

[65] *Statutorum Artis Pellacanorum*, fos. 1v–4.

[66] Ibid. On 25 March 1551 a new agreement was made between tanners and butchers over the manner of selling the hides, which prohibited not only monopolistic practices but also sale by weight (so correcting the decision of 1541), with the exception of hides from the countryside (ASB, *Statuti Pellacani*, pages unnumbered). It is clear from this agreement that both buyers and sellers of hides, forced to 'spot' buying, also bet on the weight of the hides while they negotiated the price. This practice was severely condemned. The *Statuti Pellacani* contain the official decisions until 1551, the *Statutorum Artis Pellacanorum* the acts and decisions from 1541 to 1643.

(eight members) were allotted 191 hides; and the third class (fourteen tanners, probably including some journeymen) were allowed to buy 149 hides. The number of hides bought by individual tanners within each class could vary. From this point on, quotas were established for periods which varied from one to five years with the exception of 1578 and the long gap between 1637 and 1690 (see tables 4.2 and 4.3).[67]

We can consider these quota assignments as true drawing rights, although they were subjected to numerous conditions. In particular, the complex regulations of 15 April and 8 May 1600 established by the Vice-Legate Orazio Spinola (together with the Senate) laid down that those who were included in the quotas had to give a guarantee of security; that anyone who did not buy the quota assigned to him for two consecutive months would be suspended from the right to buy hides for the whole year; that the hides which were not bought or which were 'free' should be 'distributed amongst those of the same class' until new quotas were drawn up; that when the new quotas were decided upon, two representatives from each of the three 'classes' should be present; and that those who had drawing rights should work with their own hands, the penalty for non-observance being the termination of their privilege. The provisions also forbade, as previous legislation had done, the commercialization of these rights (as happened with the formation of tanners' companies, which freed one or more member from the need to work with his own hands), the penalty being expulsion from the guild. The 'poor tanners of the third class' were forbidden from buying hides in the country, something which was thus implicitly allowed to the other two classes. To prevent the accumulation of drawing rights in the hands of individual families, another regulation excluded from the quota system sons who could not show that they had been independent of their father in terms of 'habitation, food and clothing' for at least five years. When the father died (especially if he had been a member of the guild council),

---

[67] *Statutorum Artis Pellacanorum*, fos. 17v–22v. In 1546, at a time of leather shortage and with the growing danger of monopolistic practices, the authorities had already made a step towards the quota system 'in order that the poor men of the trade of tanners can support themselves and their families by their labour and industry... and also for the public utility of everyone.' According to the new rules, the tanners would have been divided into three groups: that of the 'rich men', that of the 'not so rich men' and that of 'the poorest men'. Every week the category which would have the right (and obligation) to buy all the hides the butchers put on sale would be established by lottery. But this lottery had to serve another purpose as well. It had to be done in such a way that half of the hides would go to the rich tanners, a third to the 'middle' tanners, and the rest to the poorest (about 17 per cent) (order of the Gonfaloniere, 30 September, 1546, in *Notizie attinenti l'Arte dei Pellacani*, vol. I).

Table 4.2 *Distribution of hides among tanners, divided into three classes*

Year		I	II	III	Total	Undivided total
			Class			
1577	T	6	8	14	28	
	H	212	191	149	552[a]	—
	%	38.41	34.60	26.99	100	
1586	T	5	8	15	28	
	H	238	200	172	610[a]	
	%	39.02	32.79	28.20	100.01	
1595	T					12
	H					499
	%					
1600	T	7	6	7	20	
	H	337	100	92	529	
	%	63.77	18.90	17.39	100.06	
1604	T	6	6	8	20	
	H	328	128	114	570	—
	%	57.54	22.46	20.00	100	—
1609	T	—	—	—	—	30
	H	—	—	—	—	620
	%	—	—	—	—	
1612	T					29
	H					585
	%					
1613	T					30
	H					640
	%					
1614	T					32
	H					640
	%					
1619	T					29
	H					632
	%					
1627	T					21
	H					562
	%					
1632	T					23
	H					578
	%					

Notes:
[a] according to the source: 555
T = Tanners; H = Hides

Source: Statutorum Artis Pellacanorum.

Table 4.3 *Field of variability of hides bought within each class*

Class	1577		1586		1600		1604	
	Min.	Max.	Min.	Max.	Min.	Max.	Min.	Max.
I	27	50	39	62	14	82	20	80
II	20	25	20	30	12	23	14	25
III	6	8	4	20	13[a]		17.50[a]	

Notes:

[a] Average number given in the source.

Source: Statutorum Artis Pellacanorum.

the drawing rights would be passed on to the heir following the normal rules of inheritance – first the eldest son, then the other sons and the brothers and finally the other relatives. The condition for this inheritance was that the heir should be male, that he should be over twenty and that he should belong to the guild.[68] Subsequent rules (13 May 1609) laid down by the Cardinal Legate Giustiniani in accordance with the Senate, decreed that those who already had a right to a quota could not inherit that of the father unless their quota had originally been subtracted from that of the father, and as long as no one ended up with a monthly quota of more than fifty hides (excepting rights which had been acquired previously). This clause, disadvantageous to the richer tanners, was to some extent compensated by another which exempted the tanners from manual work as long as they at least bought and sold the skins personally.[69]

This set of regulations, although based upon a hierarchy of privileges (the three classes), seems to be dominated by a concern to safeguard the rights of the weaker social groups. While they permitted the realization of profits, they also tended to favour the survival of independent producers. However, it would be naive to believe that rules established at the end of the sixteenth century continued to operate unchanged for whole decades and indeed centuries. The rich tanners, all council members and officers of the guild, had what may be called an effective political lobby. They exploited their position of power to increase their

[68] *Statutorum Artis Pellacanorum*, fos. 27–32. In principle the countryside hides were not included in the quotas. In 1753, the Tribuni stated that the cattle hides of Poggio Renatico and of Samoggia, the estate belonging to the Lambertini noble family, were excluded from the 'comparto'.

[69] Ibid., fos. 37–37v.

drawing rights, to decrease or at any rate keep within limits the quotas of the 'poor', to capture the quotas which remained 'free', and to gain control over eventual increases in the total number of hides. This lobbying, an activity which was carried out more or less openly, gave rise to protests especially from the 'poor' tanners. They came not only from those who were really in a state of poverty, but also from those who, out of ability or ambition, hoped to climb rapidly up the social scale and whose low quotas operated as a brake.

In fact, the 1609 clause which set a ceiling to the number of hides was aimed at correcting abuses which by this time had become common practice. In 1595, the four most powerful tanners (Antonio Pedrini, Giovanni Andrea Volpara, Battista Gappi and another Giovanni Andrea Volpara) had managed somehow to accumulate an average of eighty hides a head, completely upsetting the quotas fixed in 1586. In 1600, the same tanners, although they had lost some of their power, still bought seventy hides each. Between 1604 and 1612, their quotas decreased slowly, but it was only in 1632 that no tanner – 'not even the richest ones and the oldest members of the guild' – bought more than fifty hides.[70]

Table 4.2 shows that the drawing rights of the rich tanners jumped from the 38–9 per cent of the first two occasions in which the quotas were set (1577–86) to over 50 per cent in the years between 1600 and 1604.

Unfortunately, for 1595 and for the years after 1604 I have not been able to find the division of the quotas into classes but only the quotas assigned to each tanner. This is important quantitative data, but it does not enable to us to reconstitute the classes. In 1600, for example, two tanners were assigned to the first class, even though they were only allowed 14 hides, while others, in the same year, with 20 hides, remained in the second class. Those whose quota increased, then, sometimes rose to the class above and sometimes did not. Without wishing to deny that there were economic differences between the three classes, I would say that they seem to be orders rather than groups based exclusively on wealth.

The tendencies towards accumulation, particularly noticeable around the turn of the century, gave rise to strong protests.[71] Thus on 6 March 1596, the shoemakers' guild accused 'four or five' tanners

[70] Ibid., fos. 25–57v.
[71] The stories which follow come from the dossier *Ricorsi e Proteste*, in *Notizie attinenti l'Arte . . . dei Pellacani*, vol. II.

(arrogant rather than powerful) of undertaking the division 'to the great damage of the tanners' guild and the general public' but also to the shoemakers who were forced to submit to their monopoly and to pay high prices for 'bad quality' leathers. Another protest, the date of which is not certain but it is probably around the same period, accused the same group of 'four or five tanners' of setting quotas in a way which was contrary to the statutes and of gaining control of the hides of dead tanners 'without the authorization of the Senate'. Those who increased the number of their own hides necessarily decreased the number which went to the 'poor'. On 11 April 1615, the five heirs of Daniele Dell'Arosto protested against a quota which gave them only sixteen hides (little more than three per person), when even to newcomers at least 'six per person' were allotted. Given their 'poverty and difficult family situation', they asked for considerable increases and two separate quotas, as only three of them lived together. Even quotas already in force were open to corruption. Thus Paolo Vocieri paid for his admission by renouncing for three years the quota to which he had a right. In 1624, Giovan Battista degli Alemanni, a 'very poor tanner', protested because his quota of 'eight hides every month had not been raised in twelve years', even though he had 'always worked with his own hands'. He asked to be allowed to participate in the division of the forty spare hides in order 'to sustain his family with his own industry' and to pay the rent of his workshop (200 lire a year). On 25 June 1625 Domenico Maria Salomoni, who had been turned down on more than one occasion from the guild council onto which he wanted to be co-opted, accused the members of the council of 'grave malignity' in preferring to give quota rights to 'gentlemen who, neither they themselves nor their predecessors, have ever worked as tanners'. Among the many complaints which I have recorded, I will cite only one other – that of a group of poor tanners who, on 12 February 1627 and in the lead-up to the new quotas, asked the Senate that the 'good rules and healthy regulations' should be enforced as they were by now seriously disregarded 'with damage to the public and to private individuals'. In particular, they invoked 'distributive justice' so that the poor could have what was due to them and so that 'the rich do not rule the guild with arrogance and tyranny'.

Complaints and protests were made to the Senate and the Cardinal Legate, but it was often with these authorities that abuses originated. The quotas the poor considered to be unjust were countersigned by the Cardinal Legate and/or the Gonfaloniere. The Legates were greeted with grumblings and protests each time they used their authority to have civil or military members of their court co-opted onto the guild. Over the years, colonels, captains and artisans of other guilds appointed by the legates appear among the members of the tanners' guild.

The best-documented case is that of the barber Domenico Ruinetti, made a member of the guild 'by the grace of' the Cardinal Legate Matteo Barberini (later Pope Urban VIII), who had served the Cardinal 'with great fidelity in France' at the time when the latter was the Apostolic Nuncio.[72] The Cardinal Legate's heavy-handedness is apparent from the threatening tone of his letter to the head of the tanners' guild, dated 26 August 1614, demanding the immediate co-option, with full quota rights, of Ruinetti to the post left vacant by the death of Cristoforo Salomoni, on pain of depriving him of quota rights and 'corporal punishments'. The council, 'after long discussions' (*post multa colloquia*), approved the co-option unanimously, but recorded in the minutes that the decision had been taken 'to avoid threatened punishment', contesting its legitimacy.

Later, on 9 November, the council met again and, in an attempt to defend the rights of Domenico Maria Salomoni, brother of the dead tanner, confirmed (again emphasizing the illegality of the imposition) the full validity of all the statutory regulations relating to the hereditary transmission of quotas, by which brothers were the legitimate successors in the absence of sons. The guild took Ruinetti to court to exclude him from the quota. After various appeals, the case ended up before the Tribunale della Rota of Rome, which issued an ambiguous judgement. The barber was given guild membership but not quota rights. During the trial, the guild stressed the need to respect the rules regarding hereditary transmission and the professional qualification laid down in their statutes. They feared that co-opted members, unable to work the hides 'with their own hands', would 'enter into trade', selling them to tanners at double the price negotiated with the butchers. This is the first (and up to this point the only) evaluation of the price of drawing rights. The evaluation is perhaps exaggerated, but it does shed light on the aggressive strategies of the butchers during the failed negotiations of 1637. Domenico Ruinetti's lawyers, on the other hand, argued that the membership rules of the guild were not usually respected, as was demonstrated by at least seven irregular applications for membership

---

[72] See the dossier *Domenico Ruinetti Processo*, in *Notizie attinenti l'Arte . . . dei Pellacani*, vol. II.

granted since 1595, and that quota rights could not be passed on 'from one heir to the next . . . but were subject to the decisions of the higher authorities'. They pointed out that the authorities, in fact, were responsible for lowering quota rights which were too high and raising those which were too low, referring clearly to the rules laid down by Cardinal Legate Benedetto Giustiniani in 1609 and to their initial application.

Later, the two parties reached a compromise. When the quotas were renewed in 1619, the Gonfaloniere and the Cardinal Legate Ubaldini allocated ten hides a month to Ruinetti on condition that he learnt the tanners' trade within four months.[73] It was in this year, too, probably for the first time, that seven tanners were expelled from the guild because they had been selling their quotas in a way that 'was contrary to the statutes'.[74] This severe decision, affecting about a quarter of the members, left an extra seventy hides to be divided up amongst the remaining tanners.

The question of the influence of hereditary systems on the distribution of the skins is a fascinating one. But the series of surnames (set down only for the quotas from 1577 to 1627) is not sufficient to allow us to reconstruct horizontal or vertical lines. It is also necessary to bear in mind descent via the female line (above all through widows and daughters). The long-term reconstruction of families and relatives must also be linked to that of property, not just inherited property, but also property which was accumulated, bought or sold. Above all, in the eighteenth century social mobility existed not only downwards, but also upwards, as tanners' sons become lawyers and notaries, while still continuing to demand their quota rights. However, research on these lines, while already under way, cannot be considered part of the present study.

Up to now, although I have discovered traces of the existence of a number of eighteenth-century quotas, I have had little success in

---

[73] *Statutorum Artis Pellacanorum*, fo. 49.

[74] Ibid., fos. 54–5. The authorities made sure that the 'consignments' of hides took place smoothly. In the eighteenth century at least, in cases of disagreement between individual tanners and butchers, it was possible to request an alternative distribution of the assigned quotas. Thus, for example, on 22 April 1768 the butcher Giacomo Bedini informed the Tribuni that 'he no longer wanted to deliver his hides' to the tanner Giuseppe Capurri because of 'difficulties with him regarding weight and money'. He therefore asked 'that the said Signor Capurri be substituted and that the hides be delivered to another tanner'. Twenty years earlier the Assunteria al sollievo delle Arti had already suggested that the butchers be granted the right to request the substitution of tanners who failed to pay for hides delivered to them.

actually finding them.[75] I have, though, found an ideal quota model of about 1730 formulated by the Assunteria Arti.[76] This ideal model, although respecting the established hierarchy, aimed to introduce or reintroduce principles of justice in an area in which abuses had become common. According to this project, ordinary members of the guild would receive an annual quota of 200 hides, while members of the guild council would be given 300. The head of the guild would receive 450 hides, over and above the 300 to which he was entitled as an ordinary member of the guild council, and 150 additional hides would be given to the guild officials. Furthermore, the eight most senior members of the council would receive an extra 1,450 hides to divide among themselves. In short, the quotas were calculated on the basis of two principles: position in the guild hierarchy and seniority in terms of length of guild membership. But the income scale, to which the size of the quotas corresponded, was conceived of according to the principles of distributive justice, so as to ensure to everyone, even those who received the smallest quotas, a 'decent livelihood'. Ordinary guild members, with quotas of 200 hides, would earn 680 lire a year (slightly more than the cost of their labour), which was less, but not much less, than that of those tanners who received larger quotas but who had to hire one, two or more journeymen. According to some calculations (the reliability of which needs to be checked) members of the guild council with quotas of 300 hides would earn 1,020 lire a year, whereas the head of the guild, with 750 hides, would earn 1,635 lire a year (see table 4.4).

This mode of exchange, embedded in the fabric of social relations, offers close analogies with well-known anthropological models concerning primitive societies. But the reciprocal obligations of primitive societies were based on unwritten customs, were non-monetary (with the

---

[75] The system was practised at least until 1793. In Bologna the division by quota applied only, but not always, to intermediate goods. We know, for example, that the corn-reed makers bought ox horns by quota. In any case, this way of buying and selling was part of the urban transactional culture. In 1665 the shoemakers had to buy by quota all the unsold leathers, by order of the authorities. In 1770, the silk merchants were obliged to buy by quota, again by the authorities (in an order which was not formalized as a decree, however) all the unsold raw silk of the cocoon merchants, who did not have the right to organize weaving (a privilege held exclusively by the silk merchants). It could be said, then, that the damaged parties (and the authorities) had recourse to selling by quota each time the bilateral institutional monopolies of the guilds situated in the same productive line got jammed, the alternative being the abolition of the bilateral monopolies and the freedom to expand the size of the firms vertically.

[76] *Seconda parte d'informazione al Legato sopra il regolamento delle tre Arti.* See the recent exploration of 'market principle' and 'market place' in S. Kaplan, *Provisioning Paris. Merchants and Millers in the Grain and Flour Trade during the Eighteenth Century*, Ithaca 1984, pp. 23–40.

Table 4.4 *Skin quotas (comparti) and (attributed) income in relation to internal hierarchy of the tanners' guild*

Position in the hierarchy	No. of skins attributed	Income (in Bolognese lire)
Master	200	680
Council member	300	1020
Senior council member	480	—
Head of the guild	750	1635
Senior head of the guild	930	—

Source: Seconda parte d'informazione al Legato sopra il Regolamento delle tre Arti

exception of the exchange of shells), had no formal punitive enforcement and concerned goods destined for immediate consumption. In contrast, exchange by quota in early modern Bologna was sanctioned by written rules, concerned only intermediate goods, required monetary payments and, in principle at least, sanctioned punishment of violators by the authorities. Moreover, these rules were deeply imbued with principles of moral economy: the just price, the common good, distributive justice, the right to life. These values came from Thomist–scholastic culture but had their deeper roots in the Bible and the Gospels. If we use other conceptual parameters, though, we can 'read' the complex transactions between the tanners and the butchers with the help of the modern notion of the bilateral institutional monopoly, with division by quota and the recovery of the residual increases – an extraordinarily modern structure.

5 ❧ Group strategies and trade strategies: the Turin tailors' guild in the late seventeenth and early eighteenth centuries

Simona Cerutti

Introduction

In this chapter I shall deal with the tailors' guild in Turin at the end of the seventeenth and in the first half of the eighteenth century. The analysis proposed is based on a desire to understand the nature of trade associations and the factors which led individuals and different social groups to come together in such associations, and which contributed to their success or to their decline. The association, rather than the trade itself, is the focal point of this paper.

Studies about guilds, even recent ones, have tended to identify the activities of a trade with the organizations representing it.[1] By failing to separate their analysis into two parts, such studies have implicitly postulated complete identity between guild and trade. In fact they have tended not to separate the two aspects – guilds and trades – and thus have in effect implicitly postulated a complete identity between the two. This is also the case for studies of conflicts between guilds and their base, since these conflicts have been analysed purely in an economic, or in any case a trade context. Once broad chronological periods dictated by political history are identified, the trajectories of individual guilds are analysed principally in terms of the economic context of the trade or productive roles and mercantile politics. (In the case of Piedmont the

[1] W.H. Sewell's controversial book is the clearest example of this tendency: *Work and Revolution in France*, Cambridge 1980; see M. Sonenscher, 'The Sans-culottes of the Year II: Rethinking the Language of Labour in Revolutionary France', *Social History*, 9:3, 1984, pp. 301–28; in French in *Annales ESC*, 5:5, 1985, pp. 1087–108.

[2] All the major, important syntheses from the middle of the last century agree on such a global interpretation of guilds in modern times. See, in particular, E. Levasseur, *Histoire des classes ouvrières en France depuis la conquête de Jules César à la Révolution*, Paris 1859; E. Martin Saint-Léon, *Histoire des corporations de métier*, Geneva 1897; H. Hauser, *Ouvriers du temps passé (XV–XVI siècles)*, Paris 1899; and, more recently, E. Coornaert *Les Corporations en France avant 1789*, Paris 1940.

periodization substantially follows the lines of that widely proposed for France – and hence has centred on progressive phases of subjection of the guilds to royal authority.)[2]

On the other hand, their relations with other urban social groups, with other institutions not connected to the trade, have remained obscure. Factors of a political nature, such as privileges granted to certain organizations or signs of prestige enjoyed by them within the city, have often been superimposed on the analysis of guilds as outside elements (or disturbances) rather than as characteristics which can clarify the nature, the internal composition and the success of the guild throughout its history. In short, the element of *choice* that led individuals and social groups to unite and create a new group has not been seriously looked into. Rather there has been immediate identification with the productive function which the guild formally fulfils.[3]

In this chapter, I intend to demonstrate that factors related to the urban political configuration and the morphology of different social groups are most significant for analysing the history of a trade association. The Turin tailors' guild's varying success during different periods, the peculiar prerogatives it enjoyed and its extremely heterogeneous internal composition, cannot be adequately explained by the characteristics of the trade the guild was supposed to represent. These aspects can, however, be explained in relation to the vicissitudes of other institutions and to the possibilities of economic and political control present in the urban area.

The identification of this 'broad' context within which the life of the tailors' guild could be analysed evolved during the course of my research. It emerged with a series of more general questions concerning the nature of a social organization linked to a trade: its function with regard to the distribution of work; the allegiances required from its

---

[3] On this 'substantialist' interpretation of social groups, see the important observations of L. Boltankski, *Les Cadres. La formation d'un groupe social*, Paris 1982. But important ideas can already be found in K. Polanyi, 'Our Obsolete Market Mentality', *Commentary*, 3, 1947, (reprinted in *Primitive, Archaic and Modern Economies*, edited by G. Dalton, Garden City, NY 1968). On the analysis of the formative processes and institutionalization of social groups, a classical theme of the sociological–anthropological literature of the 1960s and 1970s, the ideas of S.N. Eisenstadt in *Essays on Comparative Institutions*, New York–London–Sydney 1965, first part, seem to me very important. See also the critical survey by D.E. Brown, 'Corporation and Social Classification', *Current Anthropology*, 15:1, 1974, pp. 29–52, with a thorough bibliography on the theme of 'voluntary associations'. For a recent empirical analysis of the creation and transformation of interest groups, see J. Fewsmith, 'From Guild to Interest Group: the Transformation of Public and Private in Late Qing China', *Comparative Studies in Society and History*, 25:4, 1983, pp. 617–40. More generally, the synthesis of ideas about guilds by A. Black (*Guilds and Civil Society*, London 1984) constitutes an important occasion to reconsider the theme.

members in terms of alliances and matrimonial ties, and the expression of a group identity (through common religious and charitable activities, etc.); its relationship to the family strategies of its members (transmission of the trade, professional diversification, etc.). Even more crucial were other questions, specifically connected with the Turin tailors' guild, which was one of the oldest in the city (second only to the shoemakers in drawing up statutes and a definite internal organization at the end of the sixteenth century),[4] and amongst the most important because it had to organize one of the most widely practised trades in Turin over the course of the two centuries we are studying.[5]

1 What factors contributed towards determining the hierarchy between guilds and their greater or lesser prestige in the town? Around the 1680s the tailors' guild had achieved universally recognized success which, for example, assured it a 'ceremonial primacy' with respect to other trade guilds. A period of expansion and growing prestige was followed by a relative decline from the 1730s to the 1740s, although the guild continued to represent one of the most widely diffused trades in the city. What was the context which can help explain the causes of this irregular pattern?

2 What were the prerogatives which allowed individual guilds to claim privileges and immunities with respect to other associations? What is particularly striking in the history of the tailors' guild is the relative judicial autonomy it managed to maintain even during the eighteenth century, when all guilds were deprived of their own special judges and subjected to the government's control through the Commercial Tribunal (Consolato di Commercio). This was an absolutely exceptional prerogative, considered to

---

[4] The guilds of Piedmont, and particularly those of Turin, have an anomalous history with respect to those of the other Italian states. Their importance during the Middle Ages was very limited. The 1582 regulations by which the Duke of Savoy reorganized the guilds can therefore be interpreted as the authentic creation of trade guilds (see C. Duboin, *Raccolta per ordine di materia delle leggi cioè. editti, patenti, manifesti, ecc. emanati – negli Stati di Terraferma dal principio dell'anno 1681 sino agli 8 dicembre 1798*, 23 vols. Turin 1818–68, vol. XV, pp. 73–5). For the implications related to this late birth and to the peculiarities of Turin guilds, and for elements of possible comparison with the case of France, see S. Cerutti, 'Corporazioni di mestiere a Torino in età moderna: una proposta di analisi morfologica', in *Antica università dei minusieri di Torino*, Turin 1986 (Catalogue of an exhibition of the Archivio di Stato di Torino). More generally, see I.M. Sacco, *Professioni, arti e mestieri in Torino dal secolo XIV al XIX*, Turin 1940; and E. De Fort's useful synthesis, 'mastri e lavoranti nell'università di mestiere fra Settecento e Ottocento', in *Storia del movimento operaio, del socialismo e delle lotte sociali in Piemonte* (edited by A. Agosti and G.M. Bravo), Bari 1979, pp. 89–142.

For the statutes of the guild, which date back to 1594, and for successive ones, see Archivio di Stato di Torino (henceforth AST), Sezione I, Commercio, cat. IV, m. 20 *bis*. The present study was unable to use the private archives of the guild (admission books or listings of the entire membership) which have apparently been lost. However the Archivio di Stato di Torino, as will be seen, conserves a relatively rich documentation of the guild's activities.

[5] The trade of tailor was already registered in 1619 as the most important numerically, on the occasion of the first tax on crafts. This was confirmed in the 1625 'cotizzo'. See AST, Sezioni Riunite, art. 177, paragraph 9, and ibid., art. 358.

be of capital importance. What were the sources of the power the guild demonstrated in maintaining such a privilege?

3 Lastly, what causes determined the varying forms of conflict experienced by the guilds? In this case too the tailors' guild offers original characteristics. Its conflicts had little to do with the most obvious divisions within the guild (men's and women's tailors, the presence of men and women workers) or with the more typical 'boundary' problems faced by most trade guilds during the same period (conflicts between producers and repairers, for example). Rather the conflicts were concentrated on the problem of the choice of a symbol to unify the whole group, the cult of a saint to be universally recognized as the protector of the trade. This was a conflict which was atypical in the relations between master tradesmen, and it mirrors the tensions and diverse orientations that divided the guild in this period. What was the nature of these conflicts? What divisions did they reflect?

The research then identified different areas of analysis capable of providing answers to these questions. I thought it necessary to relate the guild to the whole urban population involved in the trade, and thus to analyse the social characteristics of the Turin tailors. Using the 1705 census of Turin, I was able to identify the tailors present in the city and (in at least half the cases) to determine their geographical origin, reconstruct their family groups, their choice of neighbourhood, their strategies of handing down the trade. Fifty of these families have been analysed in depth. An examination of parish registers has enabled me to reconstruct the politics of alliances through the choice of godparents and wedding witnesses and, in at least some cases, the politics of marriage choices.

At the same time I have reconstructed the individual and family biographies of some officers and councillors of the corporation between 1698 and 1711. Parish registers, but above all notarial acts indicating status, choice of alliances, and range of economic activities, provided the sources.

This analysis brought into focus the considerable distance separating the members of the guild from the broader base of the trade – a division measurable in terms not only of wealth and social prestige but also of interests and social and political identity. This led me to study the reasons behind the coming together of very different people and social groups within a single organization during this period. It was necessary, that is, to explain the economic and political motivations which led silk merchants and cloth traders to desert their own organizations and massively join the tailors' guild precisely in this period. What prerogatives was this guild able to offer with respect to other urban social groups? And, vice versa, to what extent did this 'heterogeneous' character contribute towards determining the image of the guild?

I traced back the trajectory of the social groups which I had found to be closely linked to each other in the guild between the 1680s and the 1730s – tailors, silk merchants and cloth traders. I tried to identify the characteristics of their associations and above all to reconstruct the institutional and informal possibilities of economic control and social and political representation existing within the urban area. The investigation was therefore broad, beginning within the corporation and the trade and then extending outwards to a reconstruction of the associations present in the city and of the resources which each of these offered.

This analytical approach, dictated by the composition of the guild, has provided replies to the questions originally raised. In the case of the Turin tailors the vicissitudes of the guild, its special prerogatives, even the form of its conflicts, can be explained only in relation to a broader political process. This process involved a progressive restriction of the possibilities of exercising political control by merchants and traders from the last quarter of the seventeenth century. Control of local powers and of economic and political direction was increasingly asserted by the Ducal court and its bureaucracy. Such a development had been studied in general terms, but had hardly been analysed in terms of its implications for the morphology of urban social groups, and even less so with respect to the trajectories of the trade guilds. Yet this political process can not only explain the composition of the tailors' guild, of its good fortune as well as of its abrupt decline, but can also provide useful elements for an understanding of the exceptionally uniform chronology of 'corporative development' in Turin during the 1730s.[6]

This analysis has revealed that there is no necessarily direct identification between *guild* and *trade* and that these two categories are not synonyms of shared interests or even shared activities. In the case of the Turin tailors the language of work alone was not able to explain the characteristics of their organization. If there was a crucial passage, that is the decision to unite and contribute to the formation of a social group, thus bringing together the two terms – guild and trade – then an analysis of trade guilds must begin with a study of the reasons for this choice. And the analysis of a choice can only be conducted through the reconstruc-

---

[6] For an interpretation of that chronology, see S. Cerutti, *La Ville et les métiers. Naissance d'un langage corporatif (Turin, XVIIᵉ–XVIIIᵉ siècles)*, Paris, 1990.

tion of the broad spectrum of possibilities offered by the urban milieu to different social groups.

The tailor population

The census of the population of Turin I have used was drawn up in August 1705 – just before the French attack on the city – with the basic purpose of registering the number of men fit to bear arms. There are therefore some distortions which need to be taken into account. These include a possible underestimate of the male population and a definite partiality in the registration of the families and individuals employed by the court of the Duke of Savoy, residing in his palaces and therefore privileged.[7] With respect to the tailor population, one can legitimately assume that, besides the five employees of the Ducal house, registered as 'his Highness' tailor', 'tailor of the court' or of the Prince, there were others who were not registered.

The population of Turin in 1705 was 33,773 inhabitants, in 7,759 family groups. In all, 376 persons declared that they practised the art of tailoring. Of these, 288 worked independently (258 men and 30 women), while 88 were apprentices or journeymen (64 men and 24 women).[8] At this date, if we exclude the various food trades and domestic services, tailors were the most numerous group in the city's population.[9] As registration was very incomplete in terms of geographical origin, we only have information about 207 individuals, 170 masters and 37 journeymen and apprentices (55 per cent of the total). The distribution of the two groups was analogous in many respects: more than 48 per cent of the masters were citizens of Turin or its suburbs, as were 40.5 per cent of the 'youths'. A high proportion, 13.5 per cent, came from the provinces of Cuneo and Mondovì, with a strong contingent from the city of Mondovì; 27 per cent of the 'youths' came from these provinces. The number of masters from Savoy (6.4 per cent), Nice (5.2 per cent) and

---

[7] The census can be found in AST, Sezioni Riunite, art. 530. For its characteristics, the way in which it was prepared and an elaboration of the total data, see E. Casanova, 'Censimento di Torino alla vigilia dell'assedio', in *Le Campagne di querra in Piemonte (1703–8)*, Turin 1909. See especially pp. 10ff, for comments on possible distortions. The census has another important limitation – the registration of fifteen of the city's 126 'blocks' has been definitively lost.

[8] My data are slightly different from those registered by Casanova. I believe this is because the latter assimilated servants, workers and apprentices, which does not seem justifiable.

[9] For comparison: shoemakers numbered 331; velvet manufacturers 307; carpenters 174; construction masters 136, etc.

France (4.1 per cent) was lower, notwithstanding the considerable prestige of French fashion at the Court and amongst the Turin nobility. Only two workers were French, while none were from Nice or Savoy.[10]

It was a rather homogenous population, therefore, characterized by two major poles of concentration – first, Turin and the surrounding area; second, the province of Cuneo and the Mondovì area, situated at the border of the state of Genoa. I shall come back to this point later and shall try to provide some interpretations for such a specific distribution of geographical origins.

We shall now look at the composition of the family groups of the Turin tailors (table 5.1).

As shown in the table, most of the families were of restricted size, with a limited number of children. In a significant percentage of cases the families consisted of only one person in the 20 to 39 age range, signifying young people who took up the trade separately from their family of origin. This is confirmed, conversely, by the large number of couples without children in the over-50 age group, and again by the scarcity of multiple family groups in which two generations live in the same home.

The general picture then is one of a prevalence of nuclear families in which adult children, to a considerable extent, did not live with their families. This point needs to be studied closely in order to understand the behaviour of these children, both sons and daughters, towards their families of origin. To verify when and how sons and daughters left their families, I have chosen to organize the data according to three important ages: 10, since apprenticeship could begin at this point,[11] and 15 and 20, marking the probable end of apprenticeship and the possible beginning of an autonomous activity.

The data, when considered in relation to the presence of younger children, did not reveal any significant correlations which could lead to the conclusion that there was an 'expulsion' connected with cyclical family problems, caused by an unfavourable ratio of consumers to producers. The most striking result is the total number of children of both sexes who lived with their parents at the ages of 10, 15 and 20. The

[10] Other data concerning geographical origins: 9 masters and 6 'youths' were from the province of Ivrea and the Canavese area, north of Turin. Otherwise, the dispersion was very wide, with 6 masters from Flanders, 2 from Tuscany and one tailor from Turkey.
[11] The tailors' guild did not have rules as to the age at which apprenticeship could begin. The length of time needed to 'learn the art' during the period considered was five years, although the guild's request (as early as 1612) was to make the comprehensive period eight years.

Table 5.1 Family groups of tailors (calculated as a percentage of the individual age brackets)

| Age | Number of cases | Unmarried | | | | | | Couples without children | | Total unmarried childless | | Widows (widowers) | | | | | | Children | | | | | | | | | | | | | | | | Multiple families |
		M.	%	F.	%	T.	%	T.	%	T.	%	M.	%	F.	%	T.	%	1	%	2	%	3	%	4	%	5	%	6	%	7	%	12	%	
10-19	2	2	100.0	—	—	2	100.0	—	—	2	100.0	—	—	—	—	—	—	—	—	—	—	—	—	—	—	—	—	—	—	—	—	—	—	—	—
20-9	36	7	19.4	—	—	7	19.4	18	50.0	25	69.4	1	2.7	—	—	1	2.7	6	16.6	3	8.3	2	5.5	—	—	—	—	—	—	—	—	—	—	—
30-9	83	10	12.0	5	6.0	15	18.0	12	14.4	27	32.5	2	2.4	5	6.0	7	8.4	22	26.5	12	14.4	12	14.4	4	4.8	5	6.0	1	1.2	—	—	—	—	1
40-9	77	4	5.1	1	1.3	5	6.5	15	19.4	20	25.9	2	2.6	7	9.0	9	11.7	10	12.9	9	11.6	16	21.7	7	9.0	7	9.0	5	6.5	2	2.6	1	1.3	2
50-9	43	1	2.3	2	4.6	3	6.9	6	13.9	9	20.9	1	2.3	6	13.9	7	16.2	10	23.2	6	13.9	8	18.6	4	9.3	3	9.3	2	4.6	1	2.3	—	—	4
60-9	36	2	5.5	1	2.7	3	8.3	10	27.7	13	36.1	5	13.8	5	13.8	10	27.7	12	33.3	4	11.1	3	8.3	2	5.5	2	5.5	—	—	—	—	—	—	4
70-9	4	—	—	—	—	—	—	2	50.0	2	50.0	—	—	—	—	—	—	1	25.0	1	25.0	—	—	—	—	—	—	—	—	—	—	—	—	—
80+	2	—	—	—	—	—	—	1	50.0	1	50.0	—	—	—	—	—	—	1	50.0	—	—	—	—	—	—	—	—	—	—	—	—	—	—	—
%		9.1		3.1		12.3		22.6		34.9		3.8		8.1		12.0		22.0		12.4		14.5		6.0		6.0		2.8		1.0		0.3			1
Total no.	283[a]	26		9		35		64		99		11		23		34		62		35		41		17		17		8		3		1		11

Notes:
[a] In five cases we have no indication of the age of the head of the family (three unmarried and two couples without children).

Table 5.2 *Families including children older than 10, 15 and 20 years of age*

Age of head	Total number of families	Children											
		Between 10 and 14				Between 15 and 19				Over 20			
		M.	F.	M. and F.	Total	M.	F.	M. and F.	Total	M.	F.	M. and F.	Total
10–19	2	—	—	—	—	—	—	—	—	—	—	—	—
20–9	36	1	—	—	1	—	—	—	—	—	—	—	—
30–9	83	6	7	1	14	1	1	—	2	—	1	—	1
40–9	77	17	17	14	48	14	9	4	27	4	2	—	6
50–9	43	3	14	11	28	4	10	6	20	4	7	1	12
60–9	36	5	10	7	22	8	5	4	17	6	2	2	10
70–9	4	—	1	1	2	—	1	1	2	—	1	1	2
80–9	2	—	—	—	—	—	—	—	—	—	—	—	—
Total	283	32	49	34	115	27	26	15	68	14	13	4	31
% of total number of families					40.6				24.0				10.9

figure drops decisively and continuously from 40.6 to 10.9 per cent. However, the table illustrates even more interesting characteristics. In the first place there is a differentiated behaviour pattern for sons and daughters. While almost all sons seem to have moved away from the family of origin when its head was aged 50 to 59, the presence of daughters remained constant for at least another decade. At this point their patterns diverged: with aged parents, the number of sons tended to increase, though to a limited extent, while the presence of daughters became unusual, and the age of marriage seems to have coincided with an abandonment of the family. In fact cohabitation between sons-in-law and parents-in-law was present in only two cases, and in only one was the son-in-law a tailor.[12]

Thus, in the same period that daughters moved away from the family for good, sons tended to return to the family of origin. These cases, however, are limited in number and are primarily significant for the contrast they offer to the daughters' behaviour. In terms of the continuity of the trade, the presence of sons seems to have been more important than that of daughters. In fact, out of 126 cases in which the nuclear family included sons over the age of 10, 13 declared themselves tailors, while in 141 cases in which daughters were present only 2 were considered to be tailors. The persistent presence of daughters during the period of the family cycle when cases of widowhood were most frequent leads to the conclusion that collaboration at work was less important than assistance and support. This is confirmed by the extremely small number of women tailors in the sample.

The information so far presented about the behaviour of the children seems to converge in creating an image of limited continuity in the trade as a consequence of infrequent cohabitation between generations. However this picture is corrected by other indications in the same census. While multiple families were rare, we find twenty-two cases in which members of the husband's family of origin lived with the new family – the elderly mother, a younger brother and particularly younger sisters. This may indicate that the father was replaced by the son as the head of household. In addition, in reconstructing the 'indices of continuity of the trade', we must also note the existence of six *frérèches* in the sample.

But a study of the names in the census reveals a more important fact:

12 The other son-in-law declared himself as a soldier of the Duke.

the same surname is to be found for various family groups, and a study of the parish registers shows that, in at least some cases, their heads of household were brothers. In fourteen cases there was a separation from the family group in the second generation. Brothers chose the same profession, often neighbouring homes, but not cohabitation. The constant aim of keeping down the size of the domestic group is confirmed. Tailors wanted a small, nuclear family, which did not seem to tolerate the presence of too many adults. Succession in the trade therefore had to follow less direct paths, as we shall see, which did not include the presence of adult children. For the moment, to our construction of a hypothetical 'index of transmission practices of the trade', we can add to the preceding data the distinct groups of brothers shown in table 5.3.

Apprentices and journeymen

I believe that the separation of nuclei of siblings is significant in family decision-making in terms of domestic ideals and transmissions of the trade. Certain questions need to be raised, such as when the separation of the siblings took place, and whether the father's death and the systems of transferring the patrimony constituted the bases of family reorganization.

The census gives us the possibility of reconstructing this process in its various phases. Again we must use a procedure of nominal research, linking the surnames of the masters to those of journeymen and apprentices in the various workshops. In fifteen cases the parish registers confirmed that identical surnames identified family relationships: at the time of the census the youngest son of the master tailor was an apprentice or journeyman in the workshop of one of his father's colleagues, while the eldest brother in all cases lived with the father, most probably in order to succeed him in the workshop when he died. There was thus a 'wide' tendency to transmit the trade which involved more than the eldest son, accompanied by a more rigid transmission of the workshop. The separation of brothers therefore had to occur, in a considerable number of cases, before the death of the father, when the second-born was ten years old and could begin an apprenticeship. Thus the family nuclei of tailors split up at a certain point – which needs to be more precisely determined – and lost some of their members. The configurations that resulted can be illustrated by the example of the Stachino family. This family will be studied in more detail later, as one of its members became a

Table 5.3 *Transmission of the trade*

Children – tailors[a]	13
Multiple families	11
Frérèches	6
Presence of mother of head of family	6
Presence of sister of head of family	11
Presence of brother of head of family	5
Nuclei of siblings not living together	14
Total number	66 (= 22.5%)

Notes:
[a] Only those cases in which the profession was explicitly stated
in the census have been counted

Table 5.4 *Age of apprentices and journeymen*

	Total no.	M.	F.	10–14	15–19	20–4	25–30	31 +
Apprentices	24[a]	16	8	7	6	2	—	—
Journeymen	64[a]	49	15	2	18	20	6	9

Notes:
[a] For nine no age is given

guild officer. In the 1705 census, members of the family lived in three domestic nuclei. Francesco, the 61-year-old father, declared himself, his son Pietro and two single daughters, aged 18 and 20, one of whom worked outside the home. In the neighbourhood lived his son Giò Antonio with his wife and six children. Giò Antonio's sister Ludovica Stachino appeared as his journeyman, while his younger brother Giò Batta was at the time journeyman for one of the most prestigious tailors in the city, Carlo Merval, one of the Duke's tailors.

A strategy of dispersion, and thus a limitation of the household size; circulation of masters' children to other workshops: these are some of the elements through which the characteristics of the tailors' domestic groups can be analysed. Let us take a more detailed look at the situation, studying particularly the apprentices and journeymen in order to understand when and in what family situations their presence was most frequent.

We have already considered their geographical origins, which basi-

Table 5.5 *Distribution of apprentices and journeymen by workshop*

Apprentices and/or journeymen	Number of workshops
1	26
2	23
3	4
4	1

Table 5.6 *Age groups of masters with apprentices or journeymen*

Age of masters	Number of masters
20–9	4
30–9	16
40–9	19
50–9	11
60–9	4
70–9	—
80+	—

cally coincided with those of the masters. The apprentices ranged in age from 10 to 22, with the 10 to 16 cohort as the most important. The age range of journeymen was wider, from a minimum of 12 years (one case) to a maximum of 40; the most concentrated group was that of the 15 to 25 cohort. This disparity can be explained by the ambiguity of the category 'journeymen', which may indicate either the phase following apprenticeship or the salaried-employee category which will never lead to 'mastership'.

Let us now turn to the distribution of apprentices and journeymen in the various domestic groups.

Apprentices and journeymen were present in only fifty-four households (table 5.5); in addition, their number was always very limited. This fact confirms the restricted size of domestic groups to which we have already referred. It is interesting to observe the distribution of apprentices and journeymen in the different phases of the family developmental cycle, especially in terms of the differing ratio between producer and consumer members. Apprentices and journeymen were more numerous

Table 5.7 *Distribution of apprentices by age group of master*

Age of masters	1 apprentice	2 apprentices
20–9	1	—
30–9	3	1
40–9	3	4
50–9	3	1
60–9	1	—
70–9	—	—
80+	—	—

Table 5.8 *Distribution of journeymen by age group of master*

Age of masters	1 journeyman	2 journeymen	3 journeymen	4 journeymen
20–9	2	1	1	—
30–9	7	5	—	—
40–9	7	7	1	—
50–9	2	3	1	—
60–9	2	1	—	1
70–9	—	—	—	—
80+	—	—	—	—

in households in which the head was of mature age, but particularly in the 40 to 49 range (tables 5.6, 5.7, 5.8); whereas the phase in the family cycle in which the greatest degree of imbalance between consumers and producers existed was between 30 and 39. In other words, the presence of external help is not adequately explained by the need for additional labour to substitute for children still too young to work. In fact, the 40 to 49 cohort of heads of household corresponded to family groups with a strong presence of sons and daughters over the age of ten. Nor did the presence of apprentices and journeymen reflect the loss of the contribution of relatives: the distribution of relatives is not visibly lower with respect to that of the 30 to 39 cohort. The taking-on of apprentices and journeymen would seem rather to be a prelude to – and in some way a preparation for – the departure of sons from the family of origin. A comparison of tables 5.6 and 5.9 shows that apprentices and journeymen were most frequently taken on when the tailors' families included the greatest number of sons over ten years of age. This number dropped considerably in the next age bracket of heads of household. Journeymen

Table 5.9 *Age of sons of masters with apprentices or journeymen*

Age of masters	Only under 10			Only over 10			Both
	M.	F.	M.&F.	M.	F.	M.&F.	(over and under 10)
20–9	1	—	—	—	—	—	—
30–9	1	4	1	—	—	—	3
40–9	—	1	2	1	1	—	7
50–9	—	—	—	—	2	1	4
60–9	—	—	—	—	—	—	1
70–9	—	—	—	—	—	—	—
80+	—	—	—	—	—	—	—

and apprentices seem to have entered the family just before one or two sons left it, either to follow some other career (we have seen that the continuity of the trade remained limited), or to enter other master-tailors' employment.

This circulation of sons between the various masters (found in fifteen cases or 17 per cent of the total population of apprentices and journeymen) needs to be more closely analysed. In fact, in the guild's statutes there was no regulation, either before or after the 1705 census, which favoured the eldest son relative to the younger ones. Moreover, the fact that masters' sons could remain in the paternal home during the period preceding 'mastership' seems to have been taken for granted.

But let us look at the protagonists of these exchanges. All fifteen cases involved rather prestigious and wealthy families: three of the five tailors of the Duke of Savoy, who both received apprentices and journeymen and sent their children to other masters; four were families from which mayors or guild priors came. The others were masters with high social status, attested for by the titles given them by the census takers (*messere, signore*) and by their flourishing activity, ample evidence of which is found in the notarial acts. The exchanges were therefore amongst equals, and were not attempts to seek protection nor to form relationships of clientage. Rather, this kind of circulation of apprentices and journeymen seems to have been tied to problems of alliances and cohesion involving the upper ranks of the trade. Thus, for this social group entrusting one's own younger sons to other masters had a double, simultaneous purpose. It eased the tensions related to the transmission of the workshop and obtained for the son in question and the family in general more solid alliances.[13]

Such patterns of behaviour, while limited to less than one-fifth of the total population of apprentices and journeymen, allow us to see that workers in a shop were not as uniform as they might seem. They also allow us to assess more carefully cases of apparent social mobility in which journeymen attained mastership or became related to masters through marriage. For the Turin tailors there is evidence which allows us, albeit partially, to verify the possibilities of making a career in the trade, and more generally to measure the stability and transmission of the trade over time. Many years after our census, in 1742, a list of those belonging to the trade was drawn up.[14] It gives no information about geographical origins, age or family situation, but it allows us, at least in general terms, to check the picture that has emerged from the analysis of the census and gives us a better-defined image of the trade over the course of time (see table 5.10).

The entry 'recurring surnames' is of course generic and difficult to evaluate (how many cases of homonyms? How many children or relatives of people not registered in 1705?), and therefore does not allow for real measurements. But even assuming these indices to be purely indicative, they merit some comments. Above all, they seem to confirm the existence of a stable group within the ranks of tailors representing about 25 per cent, a figure analogous to that found in the census.[15] As to the identity of the persons clearly identified in the 1742 document, only eight were registered as apprentices or journeymen in 1705; of these, six were youngest sons of masters and so were among the protagonists of the circulation described above. The 1742 document thus confirms the importance of this movement of apprentices in any close assessment of the real possibilities of career and mobility offered by the trade.

---

[13] Other indications confirm this 'upper' circuit of apprentices, reserved apparently to families who could spend a considerable sum of money to initiate their sons' careers. In fact in two cases that I was able to verify the apprenticeship involved a considerable payment to the master; see AST, Sezioni Riunite, Insinuazione di Torino, 1712, libro 1, c. 3; ibid., 1698, libro 7, c. 559.

[14] AST, Sezioni Riunite, I, archiviazione, Archivi delle Regie Finanze, Commercio e manifatture, m. 1, Register of traders and craftsmen of the city of Turin and its suburbs, 1742.

[15] A similar figure was found for trades in Dijon during the eighteenth century by E.J. Shephard Jr., 'Social and Geographic Mobility of the Eighteenth-Century Guild Artisan; an Analysis of Guild Receptions in Dijon, 1700–90' in S.L. Kaplan and C.J. Koepp (eds.), *Work in France. Representations, Meaning, Organization and Practice*, Ithaca 1986.

Table 5.10 *Turin traders, from 1742 register of traders and craftsmen*

Persons still alive (since the 1705 census)	15
Children (of persons listed in the 1705 census)	15
Recurring surnames	32
Apprentices and journeymen from 1705	8
% of the 1742 total	24.8

Choice of neighbourhood and alliances

The data analysed so far indicate an internal stratification of the trade which contradicts the uniformity of the census. There seem to have been two distinct behavioural patterns. By far the most common experience was where the tailor's trade does not seem to have been linked to family traditions and continuity. The modest investment required probably made the craft an occupation which could be temporarily taken up by a varied population.[16] Alongside this category, another much smaller but more cohesive group was made up of individuals whose choice of trade was connected with family strategies for handing down the trade.

Let us continue with the analysis of the workers in the workshop. Besides the first set, whose identity we have been able to ascertain, there is another equally important group, posing different problems of interpretation. In eleven cases the journeymen and apprentices in the tailors' workshops were not masters' sons. They appear to have been recruited following specific criteria, which we can see in the census. They were sons of silk merchants or cloth traders, whose families lived in the same neighbourhood, or street, as that of the family to which they moved. So in these cases the choice of apprentices or journeymen would seem to have been based on criteria connected with the type of trade, but also with questions involving neighbourhood relations. This last point brings us to a theme we have not yet considered: which neighbourhood the tailors chose.

[16] Tailoring is not a craft requiring costly instruments. Even in the most well-to-do workshops the instruments strictly related to the trade were the least expensive among those inventoried. A 'wooden tailor's table with three legs' cost only 5 lire, while '2 women's dummies, headless, with wooden feet' cost 4 lire. Cf. the inventory in AST, Sezioni Riunite, Insinuazione, 1711, libro 9, vol. 2, c. 611, and 1713, libro 1, c. 751.

The city of Turin did not present rigid trade subdivisions, in the sense of entire blocks dominated by a trade specialization. The considerable mobility of the population obviously influenced the shape of the urban social fabric, organized around small groups based on region of origin and only occasionally characterized by trade preferences.[17] The 1705 census reveals only two significant trade groups which can be identified with specific zones. One was that of the services at the court, concentrated around the Ducal palace. The other consisted of the velvet weavers or manufacturers and craftsmen of precious cloths who lived in the southern parts of Turin.[18] However the rest of the city was not just a professionally undifferentiated space. By looking at the neighbourhood choices of tailors, we can recognize areas larger than the administrative and fiscal quarters, with patterns in the forms of settlement.

Although tailoring was one of the most practised trades, it was neither uniformly distributed across the city, nor concentrated around the Ducal centre, where not only the court, but also the great number of officials and ambassadors could furnish a substantial and secure clientele. Of the 111 squares of houses in this planned rectangular city, in 48 there were no tailors; in 44, from 1 to 5 families of tailors; in 19, tailors' families were more concentrated (from 6 to 18 families). In some squares more than 30 per cent of the population consisted of members of the trade and their families; 161 families (56 per cent of the whole trade) were grouped together in 15 of the 111 squares in Turin. These were the squares situated in the heart of the city, those neighbouring on the town hall and the two most prestigious urban institutions – the congregation of San Paolo (a lay institution which promoted financial and charitable activities) and the chapel of the merchants and traders. These last two categories were obviously also concentrated in the same zones, but above all so was 60 per cent of the entire urban population of silk merchants and cloth traders.[19] A high percentage of tailors and merchants lived in

---

[17] See Casanova's observations in 'Censimento'. On the mobility of the population and its influence on the urban settlement of social groups, G. Levi, *Centro e periferia di uno stato assoluto*, Turin 1985, pp. 50ff. For seventeenth-century examples of ethnic groups' residence and an analysis of their behaviour, see S. Cerutti, 'Matrimoni del tempo di peste. Torino nel 1630', *Quaderni Storici*, 55, 1984, pp. 65–106.

[18] In particular the parishes of S. Sebastiano, S. Giulio, S. Cristoforo, S. Antonio Abate, S. Maurizio, S. Bonifacio.

[19] Once I had identified this regularity in neighbourhoods and (as will be better seen further on) among relations, I catalogued all the families of merchants (merchants of silk, canvas, cloth, traders, drapers, etc.) registered in the entire urban area. This facilitated the identification of many of the relationships of tailors not included in the single squares.

the same squares and their combined presence sometimes represented as much as 50 per cent of their inhabitants.[20]

The choice of neighbourhood seems, at least for the tailors, to have been dictated by the needs of the trade and by the possibility of facilitating production. But we have to note that this topographical convergence between suppliers and distributors of raw material (merchants and traders) and their processors (tailors) is not found in any other case in the 1705 census. No other craft ever followed so regular a pattern of settlement directly related to the productive process.[21] Moreover, although we have no documents analogous to the 1705 census, other historically earlier evidence leads us to believe that such choices of neighbourhood began to be made at some definite point in the history of the city. The artisans' census of 1625, though incomplete,[22] reveals, in a much more limited urban area than that of 1705,[23] a wide distribution of the city's population of tailors, and gives no indication of such a deliberate effort to be close to the cloth merchants.

Hence we must look for more precise explanations of these behavioural patterns, and above all try to understand their implications. Economic productivity, as a motivation which could underlie the tailors' choice of neighbourhood, cannot really explain the merchants' choices. It cannot explain what led at least some of them to entrust their sons to craftsmen during the precious years of apprenticeship. Such close neighbourhood relations must have created forms of relations and alliances which need to be carefully studied. In order to deal with this level of analysis and to collect important elements not contained in the census – the marriage and alliance choices of the tailors – I limited the analysis to fifty families whose trajectories could be reconstructed through parish registers. The choice of the sample, not an ideal one, was in fact dictated by the possibility of finding the documentation.[24] I had to choose the parish of

[20] For example, S. Rocco where tailors, silk merchants, and traders accounted for 47.7 per cent of the total population.

[21] I checked the following professions: leather merchants and shoemakers and cobblers; wood merchants and carpenters, coopers, etc.; iron merchants and locksmiths, sword-makers, etc. In no case were there significant correlations.

[22] I was able to find the documents which prepared the *cotizzo* of 1625, and thus the census of merchants and craftsmen. However the source is incomplete because it does not include all the trade, but only the better-off members. Cf. AST, Sezioni Riunite, art. 449, m. 2. For undated passages referring to the same census, cf. ibid., art. 449, m. 3 not inventoried.

[23] After its 1619 enlargement, Turin experienced another important expansion from 1673.

[24] Unfortunately S. Rocco, the parish under whose jurisdiction the largest number of squares inhabited by tailors was to be found, was suppressed and so no longer possesses its own registers, which seem to have been irremediably lost.

San Tommaso, under whose jurisdiction only five of the fifteen squares most densely inhabited by tailors were to be found. The data provided by the registers are distributed unevenly and reflect the incompleteness of the registers themselves. The birth register is uninterrupted and allowed me to register 105 baptisms, and thus obtain fruitful information about godparents and alliance relationships. On the other hand, I was only able to find twenty-five marriages involving my families, and all were concentrated between 1680 and 1720. This could be indicative of exogamy in the neighbourhood – particularly on the part of the men – but certainly also reflects less careful recording (which is evidence from the condition of the registers).[25]

I shall begin with an analysis of the data referring to alliances created through godparents or marriage witnesses. We have 264 names, actually corresponding to about 200 families, given the recurrence of some of the same persons at weddings and baptisms. Of the 140 persons I could identify with certainty, tailors and silk or cloth merchants were called upon with equal frequency, in about 60 per cent of the cases, to participate in baptisms or weddings. The remaining 40 per cent consisted of either titled persons, lawyers or Ducal officials; or individuals of unknown profession, but definitely neither tailors nor merchants: they seem to have been chosen because of common geographical origin.[26] This high proportion already denotes the importance attributed to relations between tailors and merchants and hence the attempts to create alliances. On the other hand the data are difficult to interpret as they may have tautological explanations: since merchants were among the wealthiest and most prestigious personalities of the neighbourhood, they were certainly sought after as godparents and marriage witnesses. Less obvious is the inverse process, the effort made by merchants to maintain close relations with tailors. I did not analyse the godparents in the merchants' families in such detail, yet a sample of twenty-four families shows the reciprocity of these relationships. Nine of these family groups repeatedly called upon neighbourhood tailors to be godparents or witnesses.

Marriages need to be considered next. Of the twenty-five marriage ties involving tailors or their descendants, four concerned people I could

---

[25] The numerous pages loose or bound in much later volumes attest to irregular recording.

[26] This was certainly the case of the Lintroppo, Guinivel and Span families, for example, who regularly chose their witnesses or godparents amongst the Spaniards and Flemish residing in Turin.

not identify.[27] Six were marriages contracted with people I was able to identify by means of the census. Their professions or those of their parents were rather varied: there were a Ducal usher, two soldiers, a leather craftsman, a button-maker, a hairdresser. Nine were inter-trade marriages and six were marriages contracted with members of silk-merchants' or cloth-traders' families.

The neighbourhood relations between tailors and merchants also implied stronger and more important ties. This is confirmed by data based on parish registers. In five cases I was able to discover that they came from the same families as tailors and merchants living in the same parish, whereas I had thought they were simply homonyms. They are in fact examples of trade diversification within a single family whose head – a silk merchant or cloth trader – sent his own children into different trades. One son followed in his footsteps while the second enrolled in the craft of tailoring. This is another indication of the development of relationships and exchanges between these professional categories. But, at least apparently, it also seems disproportionate in terms of trans-mission of the trade, considering that the art of tailoring had less prestigious connotations than that of the merchants.

We should now try to understand the sense of these linkages and exchanges between tailors (or at least the upper stratum of the trade) and merchants; in particular we should explore the reasons for the attraction exerted by the members of a numerous but dispersed craft, little noted for professional qualifications or for the stability of their trade, on the much more prestigious group of silk merchants and cloth traders. As already mentioned, in the early eighteenth century the tailors' guild was experiencing ever-increasing good fortune. To what extent was this reflected in or determined by these exchanges? What reasons had merchants to apprentice their own sons to tailors or to create a spectrum of trades within their own families? Choices of neighbour-hood and godparents are evidence of a widespread search for relation-ships between these two categories. Exchange of apprentices, marriage alliances and the examples of trade diversification obviously involved the 'upper' group of the tailor population – the group of more stable families within the trade, who were more attuned to problems of transmission and continuity. This was a group which publicly identified

---

[27] These were marriages contracted by daughters who then left the parish.

with the trade of tailoring in that it was called to represent it through the guild. As the analysis of the census has revealed, around it revolved a population much less certain about its allegiance to the trade.

We shall now analyse this elite group within the trade. A reconstruction of its identity and behavioural patterns – the individual and family choices – allows us to measure the weight and significance of the alliances with other trade groups, the characteristics of the tailors' guild during this part of the eighteenth century, the sources of cohesion and conflict, the relationship between the guild and the trade, and, finally, the reasons for the considerable good fortune the guild enjoyed during this period.

The guild elite

The fifteen individuals whose life stories we shall analyse all took an active part in various ways in the life of the guild between 1698 and 1711. They all participated in the guild council and some played a very important role, such as syndic – both for men's and women's clothes – and prior of the guild.[28] The geographical origins of this group basically reflected that of the members of the trade (Turin and suburbs; Mondovì and its province), with a barely greater presence of Savoyards and French. It is interesting to note that the age of the syndics and priors ranged quite widely, from 35 to 63. This means that access to such responsibilities was not always tied to seniority in the trade. Those who found themselves side by side in assuming the most prestigious positions in the guild did not belong to the same generation and of course were at different stages of their life and career.

Let us look at their family situation (table 5.11), insofar as I have been able to reconstruct it through parish registers and notarial acts.[29]

---

[28] The summit of the guild was composed of two syndics representing men's tailors, two for women's tailors, and one prior, the highest office. The succession of 'statutes' of the tailors from 1594 to 1737 illustrates the attempt to formalize and restrict access to official posts and to the guild council. While the 1594 regulations ensured an annual rotation of the offices, as early as 1633 there was a ruling that the office of prior was to be occupied by one of the syndics, lest 'once the syndics and priors are removed and others take over their posts, the latter be not informed of their negotiations'. In the 1737 regulations the prerogative of electing their own representatives was restricted in practice to a small part of the guild, on the pretext of the difficulty in summoning them. The legal number was not more than thirty individuals.

[29] The biographical reconstruction was facilitated, in the case of Piedmont, by the existence of the 'Insinuazione', or centralised registration of all notarial acts, from 1611 onwards. I examined the registers of the Turin Insinuazione systematically for the years 1680 to 1720 in terms of the biographies of guild officers. For the tailors' guild I examined the registers from 1610 to about 1780.

Table 5.11 *Guild officers and councillors*

Origins	Father's profession	Position in the family	Profession of brothers	Profession of wife's father	Wife's origins
Anatolia	?	Only child	—	(1682) Tailor	Turin
Savoy	?	Third-born	(1) Hairdresser (2) ?	(1695) Cloth-trader	Turin
Turin[a]	Tailor	First-born	Tailors' journeyman	(1685) Silk merchant	Turin
Turin	Silk merchant	Second-born	Silk merchant	—	—
Turin	Silk merchant	Second-born	(1) Silk merchant (1) Tailor	(1693) Silk merchant	Turin
Turin	Silk merchant	Third-born	(1) Silk merchant (1) Tailor	(1698) Tailor	Moncalieri (TO)
France	Tailor	Only son	—	(1685) Cloth trader	Oneglia (GE)
Savoy	?	First-born	Tailor	(1680) Cloth trader	Turin
Savoy	?	Second-born	Tailor	(1686) ?	Turin
Mondovi	Tailor ?	First-born	Tailor	(1687) Cloth trader	Mondovi
Mondovi	Tailor ?	Second-born	Tailor	(1702) ?	?
Mondovi	Tailor ?	Third-born	Tailor	(1706) ?	?
Cocconato (AT)	?	First-born	Tailor	(1686) Tailor	Turin
Cocconato (AT)	?	Second-born	Tailor	(1701) Silk merchant	Turin
Rivoli (TO)	Tailor	First-born	(1) Soldier (1) Upholsterer	(1687) Cloth trader	Mondovi

Notes:

[a] The bracket indicates groups of relatives, not living together: in the first case they are two brothers-in-law; in all the others they are brothers.

AT: Asti; GE: Genoa; TO: Turin

In such a limited sample what is striking is the very high proportion of nuclei consisting of non co-resident brothers (in the 1705 census their importance was limited with respect to the totals). Analogously, we find three cases of merchants' sons (never the eldest) sent to become tailors, whose marriage choices (in at least one case) attested to the close relationship maintained with their original milieu. But, more generally, the marriages contracted by these small groups were formed, in a high percentage of cases, with the families of silk merchants or cloth traders. This is of interest for two reasons. First, it indicates that such alliances were given priority over craft and especially over guild endogamy, which is what one might have expected to encounter, particularly within the elite group. Second, it is striking that this leading group moved towards both silk merchants who possessed looms – therefore merchant– manufacturers – and simple shopkeepers, two categories whose antago- nism, considered traditional, was to explode violently (as we shall see) from the 1730s onwards. We shall return to this point and to the significance of this joint presence.

Thus the leading group of the tailors' guild was not characterized by marriage exchanges within its own ranks. It was marked by the presence of groupings of relatives, but these were siblings. In only one case did the presence of brothers-in-law attest to an internally created alliance. This absence of crossed linkages was what struck me most in the biographies of guild members.

The choice of godparents was also relatively indifferent to group allegiance,[30] even during the years in which an important post was held within the guild. Marc'Antonio Bruno and Giovanni Chiesa, Gaspar Ton and Giò Antonio Colombato, syndics respectively of men's and women's tailors between 1708 and 1710, did not choose each other as godfathers for their children born during these years. In only four of the cases did they choose tailors (all from the same neighbourhood). Their choice once again involved merchants, sometimes very wealthy ones such as the Triuls, Presenda or Tempia, silk merchants with many looms,[31] or important cloth traders like Carlo Michele Villanis or Giuseppe Lanzon of Mondovì. At the same time the witnesses to the notarial acts and particularly to wills drawn up by some syndics and

[30] Five of the fifteen individuals were identified through parish registers as well and I was thus able to follow their choices of godparents and marriage witnesses.
[31] For a list of Turin silk merchants with working looms in 1702, see AST, Sezione I, Commercio, cat. IV, m. 7.

councillors when they assumed office – a sign that this was considered an important moment in a person's life – were not guild members and only rarely tailors.[32] The wills furnish interesting evidence for reconstructing indices of the cohesion of the trade and of the existence of a sense of identity linked to guild membership. None of the burial instructions contained in the wills refer to the parish with the altar of Saint Francis of Assisi's tailor, patron saint of the guild. What is more, devotion to Saint Albert, Saint Bonaventura's successor as patron of the art (guild syndics and priors were elected on Saint Albert's day), was indirectly attested to in only one case. In the inventory drawn up by Pietro Francesco Gianaletto, a councillor, who had asked to be buried in the church of the brotherhood of the Holy Spirit, amongst the many paintings invoking religious subjects we find a representation of Saint Albert 'with varnished frame', of very modest worth.[33] Thus we do not find any forms of sociability, common symbols or alliances linking these personages.

Did these individuals share the same social position in terms of material wealth and status? We know that only one of the officers was attached to the Ducal court. This was Gerolamo Motta, from Turkey, Prince Eugenio's tailor and treasurer of the Princess of Savoy. During the thirteen years we have studied he was the only court tailor who held office in the guild. This is again not what we would expect, considering that this group must have represented the most prestigious members of the trade. But, as we shall see, other characteristics seem to have been common to the guild officers.

A first index of wealth, the dowries paid and received, reveals a relative uniformity within the group. Dowries regularly amounted to between 500 and 700 lire, with only one high point of 1,100 lire in the event of daughters being born to Amedeo Re.[34] However, dowries, in any case, may not be fully reliable; for they were not paid only to daughters nor received from wives, but were also given to sisters and in three cases to nieces or other relatives. Hence they are a very heterogeneous category. To determine both the wealth and the social status of

[32] See the wills of Carlo Giovanni Aymetto (in AST, Sezioni Riunite, Insinuazione Torino, 1709, libro 11, c. 249); Claudio Chiarmet (ibid., 1709, l. 3, c. 495); Giovanni Chiesa (ibid., 1709, libro 12, c. 151); Bartolomeo Chiesa (ibid., 1711, libro 4, vol. II, c. 663); Pietro Francesco Gianaletto (ibid., 1712, libro 2, c. 169); Gerolamo Motta (ibid., 1703, libro 9, c. 539); Carlo Re (ibid., 1706, libro 6, c. 505); Amedeo Re (ibid., 1710, libro 8, vol. I, c. 295).
[33] Ibid., 1713, libro 1, c. 751.
[34] But the absolute originality of the will of Amedeo Re illustrates that it was a liquidation of the inheritance meant to free the sole heir (in this instance, most unusually, the wife) from any obligations. See the will cited above, n. 32.

these individuals, it is better to look more closely at their activities during these years. This can enable us to define their identity and explain why they grouped together within the guild.

Economic activity and social identity

Two of the fifteen personages stand out in terms of their presence in the notarial acts and their high status; they are Claudio Chiarmet and Marc'Antonio Bruno. The first, from Savoy, had lived in Turin for some years, as had many members of his family, including a hairdresser brother and a relative in a much more prestigious position, Nicola Chiarmet, customs director of Turin.[35] Marc'Antonio Bruno, from Mondovì, belonged to a numerous kin group (two brothers also held office in the guild), divided between Turin and their province of origin, where they maintained important interests. Their biographies, like those of the other officers, merit lengthy description because of the significant information they contain. I shall limit myself to a very brief outline only of the main characteristics essential for an understanding of their social identity. The numerous notarial acts in which they figure demonstrate that tailoring was not the principal activity of either of them. Chiarmet and Bruno were important merchants and genuine court financiers, who lent money at high rates of interest 'to deal with traders' money as the trader deals in many things'.[36] From the beginning of the century, besides his personal earnings, Chiarmet was responsible for the property of his orphaned nephews and nieces. He administered their fortunes carefully, by continually lending money at high interest rates to cloth merchants and court circles.[37] His tailoring activities are never mentioned, not even in the arrangements concerning his estate. Childless, he established a considerable fund for relatives in financial difficulties, in both Piedmont and Savoy. He made his nephews his sole heirs, without indicating the profession they were to practise.

[35] While Chiarmet's other relatives lived in the same square, Nicola lived with his own family in the S. Spirito neighbourhood; see the census cited.

[36] Insinuazione, 1701, l. 12, c. 1325.

[37] For the principal notarial acts regarding Chiarmet see Insinuazione, 1701, l. 4, c. 845; 1701, l. 5, c. 707; 1701, l. 8, vol. II, c. 812; 1702, l. 2, c. 269; 1703, l. 3, c. 401; 1703, l. 4, c. 816; 1704, l. 12, c. 720; 1705, l. 4, c. 775; 1706, l. 4, c. 717; 1709, l. 3, c. 495; 1709, l. 2, c. 501; 1709, l. 9, c. 311; 1709, l. 10, c. 484; 1710, l. 10, c. 663; 1711, l. 4, vol. I, c. 331; 1713, l. 2, c. 614 v.; 1713, l. 5, c. 145; 1715, l. 6, vol. III, c. 1450 v.; 1717, l. 11, c. 575; 1718, l. 3, c. 894; 1718, l. 5, c. 1409; 1719, l. 7, c. 611; 1721, l. 9, c. 205; 1721, l. 12, c. 691; 1722, l. 5, c. 287; 1722, l. 6, c. 991; 1723, l. 8, c. 633.

Bruno's career was analogous but much more intense.[38] A 'merchant and banker', as he was defined in the notarial acts, he was involved in an extraordinary number of business and monetary affairs. He purchased estates at Mondovì and property in Turin, but above all engaged in investments and companies with traders and big silk manufacturers, such as Travo, Olivero and Mangardi.[39] He gave his daughter in marriage to Mangardi, with whom he developed particularly intensive relations of cooperation in the purchase of properties and lending activities.

Bruno's relations were also concentrated in a specific circle which only marginally included tailors. However his circle was wider than Chiarmet's, since his relations with traders included (and perhaps gave priority to) those of his province of origin, and were based on continuous business deals with Turin. For example, together with Giuseppe Lanzon, cloth merchant, fellow townsman and godfather of one of his daughters, he made loans on security (*censi*) and purchased property in the city, bought with credit from earlier loans at Mondovì.

As in the case of Chiarmet, Bruno's tailoring activities were never mentioned. The inventory drawn up when he died – at an unhappy point in his career – makes one wonder whether this activity ever existed since it does not mention any tools relating to the trade. When he dictated his will, in the presence of three silk merchants, he gave no burial instructions which might indicate loyalty toward the guild of which he had been a member and even syndic.

Chiarmet and Bruno were thus important merchants and financiers. Their presence in the tailors' guild could be interpreted as the desire of its members to increase the prestige of the guild with the leadership of wealthy men. But their identity, while particular, does not differ basically from that of the other officers and councillors whose careers I have analysed. In fact all were more or less publicly known as merchants before they were tailors. On a lower level than Chiarmet and Bruno, they dedicated themselves to huge investments – *censi* in Turin or their community of origin, purchase of lands and high interest loans.[40] Their

[38] For the principal notarial acts concerning Bruno see: Insinuazione 1705, l. 5, vol. II, c. 943; 1711, l. 3, c. 162; 1711, 1.3, vol. II, c. 491 v., 1711, 1.3, c. 591; 1712, l. 5, vol. IV, c. 1925; 1712, l. 8, c. 349 and 350 v.; 1715, l. 11, c. 197; 1717, l. 1, c. 341; 1717, l. 12, c. 1009; 1720, l. 3, c. 376; 1720, l. 4, c. 1617; 1721, l. 6, c. 663; 1723, l. 1, c. 881; 1723, l. 6, c. 73; 1724, l. 10, c. 627; 1725, vol. II, c. 3; 1725, l. 3, c. 735.

[39] See the list of silk merchants cited in n. 31.

[40] See, as examples, the purchase of ashes by the community of Cocconato for the Chiesa brothers: Insinuazione, 1707, l. 3, c. 563, and some of the numerous purchases by the Brunos in Mondovì,

status as traders was often explicitly written in the notarial acts[41] and implicitly recognized by the city authorities. For example, two of them were appointed by the civil court as administrators of considerable sums inherited by unrelated minors. They were to invest these sums until the heirs came of age, a responsibility which would hardly be assigned to craftsmen, however wealthy.[42] Their very homes, in the few cases in which I found inventories or less complete descriptions of their contents, reflected a life style and possessions (such as a great quantity of arms) not to be found amongst even the richest artisan families.[43]

In the light of their economic activities and biographies, their marriage relations and their continual alliances with merchants (who in these cases were also witnesses to wills and notarial acts and neighbours) take on a different meaning. They were choices made within the same social circle rather than attempts at professional differentiation or expressions of social mobility. In reality, we are not dealing here with craftsmen who personally dealt in the small quantities of cloth required for their own products; they were, in a way, members of the upper class of a trade who could appropriate merchants' prerogatives for themselves. Indeed, the distance which separated them from the 'base' cannot be measured exclusively in terms of wealth; rather, it expressed a different social and professional identity.[44] The elite of the guild in these years consisted of big cloth dealers. They were individuals who – as we have seen in the case of godparents and even more in that of the exchange of apprentices – were sought after as important allies by the city's traders and silk manufacturers.

Yet stronger proof of their importance is that the relationship which

their town of origin: 1711, l. 3, c. 162; 1711, l. 3, vol. II, c. 491 v.; 1711, l. 3, vol. II, c. 591. The reconstruction of the biographies of this group (excluding Bruno and Chiarmet) involved the examination of 309 notarial acts. For obvious limits of length I shall only cite the most significant and pertinent to the subject.

[41] For all: 1705, l. 5, vol. II, c. 943; 1711, l. 4, vol. II, c. 663.

[42] The traders were Francesco Bonaveri and Amedeo Re. See 1702, l. 1, c. 317; 1706, l. 1, c. 75; 1707, l. 2, c. 583; 1707, l. 10, c. 273; 1708, l. 5, c. 453; 1709, l. 1, c. 295; 1711, l. 9, c. 373; 1712, l. 1, c. 3; 1712, l. 4, c. 1,227; 1712, l. 6, vol. I, c. 95v.; 1712, l. 6, vol. II, c. 6; 1713, l. 1, c. 163; 1713, l. 3, vol. I, c. 363; 1713, l. 4, vol. II, c. 551; 1714, l. 11, c. 761; 1715, l. 6, c. 1,279.

[43] See the inventories cited in nn. 37 and 38. On the presence of arms in merchants' houses and the total absence thereof in those of artisans, even in a different geographical context, see I. Palumbo Fossati, 'L'interno della casa dell'artigiano e dell'artista nella Venezia del Cinquecento', *Studi Veneziani*, N.S. 8, 1984, p. 42.

[44] In fact, the range of their economic possibilities was much wider than that which generally seems to have separated the upper class from the base in trade guilds. For an analysis of economic cleavages in the case of Lyons, see M. Garden, 'Ouvriers et artisans au XVIII siècle. L'exemple Lyonnais et les problèmes de classification', *Revue d'Histoire Economique et Sociale*, 1, 1970, pp. 28–54.

should have existed between tailors and cloth suppliers was curiously reversed. The suppliers were in fact often indebted to the so-called craftsmen. Thus the guild of those who processed the raw materials seemed to supply the same raw materials to those who were supposed to be its suppliers.[45]

Tailors, merchants and dealers

At this point we must ask ourselves what led cloth merchants to desert their own trade guilds and join that of the tailors, becoming proper members and officers of this guild; to ally themselves by marriage to this professional category; to apprentice their sons to them; and to seek godparent linkages? More generally, what determined the good fortune of this trade guild during the years under study? We know that the possible presence of merchants within the guild was only referred to, and then rather vaguely, in the guild's first constitution of 1594, which foresaw the possibility that merchants who employed journeymen tailors could enter the guild. This clause was never mentioned again. In fact, the privileges later enjoyed by the guild – effective jurisdictional autonomy – were explicitly based on the declared, total separation of the craft from any form of trading.

Perhaps this last point offers an explanation of the guild's composition. The tailors' guild, unlike that of the merchants and, after 1723, unlike any other trade guild, managed to maintain a substantial autonomy from central bureaucratic control and above all from the Commercial Tribunal. In 1687 the Tribunal, the principal organ of economic control, composed of 'doctors', jurists and not merchants, saw its sphere of competence notably extended. Silk merchants and cloth traders were placed firmly under its jurisdiction with respect to commercial cases, control over the election of officers and even internal conflicts; whereas the tailors' guild (like, generally, all 'processing' crafts) maintained its own judge and was free from any central control. Moreover, the tailors' guild managed, against the tide, to maintain a condition of relative autonomy– unique amongst Turin craft guilds – even when special guild magistrates were completely abolished by a new regulation

---

[45] See in particular the inventory of Bartolomeo Chiesa; in addition, the activity of Francesco Antonio Gianotto and his credits with Jewish merchants: 1710, l. 3, vol. III, c. 1139; 1711, l. 2, c. 871, and some acts concerning the Bruno brothers and C. Chiarmet: 1708, l. 9, c. 179, and 1712, l. 8, c. 349; 1713, l. 2, c. 614 r.

of the Tribunal in 1723. It achieved this by pleading that it did not engage in commerce, and remained responsible only to the judge of the city of Turin. This was an extremely privileged condition, allowing the guild to look after all the affairs of the craft from within its ranks, from the election of syndics to internal disputes, and to avoid such external Tribunal intervention as visitations of workshops in order to check the quantity and quality of the merchandise.

The significance of this autonomy and its implications were brought out extremely clearly and violently by the Tribunal officials themselves in 1731 during a serious quarrel with the tailors' guild. According to the declarations of the guild syndics to the Duke, the quarrel was the result of the Tribunal's undue interference in tailors' affairs:

despite the fact that the exercise of their stated craft of clothes-making *has no relation to commerce nor to the manufacturing trades subject to the jurisdiction of the Tribunal . . . since such a craft does not involve any purchase or sale*, but only the fashioning of garments for private individuals, the Tribunal of this city has claimed the right to examine the accounts of some administrators of this guild.

What was worse, against all usage the Tribunal had demanded that the election of syndics and the council take place in its headquarters, under the control of its officials. The Tribunal's version was of course very different and, in the light of our evidence, closer to the truth. It maintained that it was defending a large part of the guild which had complained about the bad conduct of the syndics and the councillors.[46] The Tribunal requested that the tailors' guild be declared subject to its jurisdiction because there were significant irregularities in the election of the council, and above all because

this art involves considerable commerce in that many are those who trust their tailors to purchase and provide garments without their personal intervention . . . *but even more so . . . due to the ties with the silk and brocade merchant–manufacturers, through which they can easily obtain prohibited foreign merchandise* . . . That they are involved in purchasing and selling is verified by the books of Christian and Jewish merchants, indicating that most of these merchants have open accounts with them [the tailors].[47]

---

[46] According to the Commercial Tribunal, the syndics, when called upon to present the admission books to the guild, altered their own registers and seriously underestimated the real membership in order to avoid accounting for sums received. The court's intervention was thus caused by the remonstrances made by the many 'excluded' masters, who denounced the dishonesty of the officers.

[47] All the numerous documents relating to the lawsuit, the statements and appeals are in AST, Sezione I, Commercio, cat. I, m. 1 (my italics).

We shall return later to the reasons that led the Tribunal to take a stand against the tailors' guild at that particular moment. For the present, the Tribunal's declarations are useful above all because they confirm the non-homogeneous composition of the tailors' guild during this period, and substantiate the numerous pieces of evidence that came out in the comparison between trade and guild. The considerable fortune enjoyed by the guild from the 1680s is obviously tied to its composition or at least to that of its elite. Cloth traders and silk merchants joined the guild or allied themselves to its members when the guild could provide a wide range of opportunities and privileges. The guild's composition was therefore strictly linked to problems of control over economic and (as we shall see) political areas. As the analysis of the census of its executive group has brought out, its configuration was more that of an internally diversified social group than a homogeneous body linked to the common practice of the trade. The guild's internal hierarchies reflected not only different levels of wealth but also different motivations at the root of the very choice of association.

But what were these motivations? The Tribunal's declarations tended to underline one in particular, economic advantages, presenting tailors as smugglers, importers of 'forbidden' cloths, yet covered by legal immunity. These illicit activities do not leave much documentary evidence. However many elements confirm such underground activities. We have already noted that the tailors were creditors with respect to merchants and traders, reversing the traditional relationship between processors and distributors of raw materials. But an analysis of the inventories of two council members, Bartolomeo Chiesa and Pietro Francesco Gianaletto, explicitly confirms the existence of a trade in valuable cloths, the import of which was prohibited at the time. In the Chiesa workshop, for example, besides large quantities of more common materials, there were 'satins with gold and silver', 'taffeta from China', 'the finest broderie anglaise'. The import of all such materials was still strictly prohibited in the 1730s, as they were not produced by Piedmontese looms.[48] Illegal imports, therefore, were undoubtedly facilitated by the superficial controls imposed upon the art of tailoring; and that activity was easily accessible to other guild councillors. The brothers Bartolomeo and Marc'Antonio Bruno, for example, although they

---

[48] See the inventories cited in nn. 37 and 38. For a list of the materials whose import was forbidden, see *Nota dei lavori che vengono forestieri*, compiled by a master velvet manufacturer during the 1730s in AST, Sezione I, Commercio, cat. IV, m. 8.

resided at Turin, maintained extremely intensive buying–selling relations with their town of origin, Mondovì, near the Genoese border. At the time the Mondovì area was a genuine thorn in the side of the Turin government because it was notoriously the site of illegal and clandestine traffic of various goods: salt and tobacco, and especially valuable cloth, Genoese silks and velvets.[49] The characteristics of this area, so strongly marked by smuggling, must have had something to do with the numbers of Mondovì 'tailors' in our sample; although of course a more detailed analysis of all of their biographies would be necessary to determine the extent and the nature of their relations with their town of origin, which are striking in the case of the Bruno brothers.

Underlying the merchants' choice to join the tailors' guild or to ally themselves with its members were, obviously, the economic advantages clearly revealed by the Tribunal's denunciation. But these were not the only elements, and perhaps not even the most important ones, in explaining the social configurations we have found in this particular period – the association of tailors, merchant–manufacturers and cloth traders, the latter two traditionally antagonistic categories and in later years divided by strong contrasts. Besides economic resources, the tailors' guild, as the Tribunal's complaint revealed, could offer these groups more ample opportunities, related to its relative self-government and political autonomy from central control. This political aspect was particularly precious at this time, because the institutions which traditionally guaranteed merchant–citizen political representation were increasingly threatened by the interference of the central authority, the Duke and his officials. In fact the vicissitudes of the Turin merchants and the history of their relations with the tailors must be considered within a far broader process of progressive limitation of political resources. This process deserves to be treated in some detail; but here I shall only outline its more general aspects.

Spheres of economic and political government within the city

We have mentioned the new constitution of the Commercial Tribunal of 1687 and the control the Tribunal wanted to establish, not only over the silk merchants' and traders' economic decisions but over the relations

<hr/>

[49] On contraband in the Monregalese area, see S. Lombardini, 'Appunti per un'ecologia politica dell'area monregalese in età moderna', in *Valli monregalesi: arte, società, devozioni*, Mondovì 1985, pp. 189–212, and especially in 'Appendice', doc. 1 which refers specifically to cloth smuggling.

within their organizations. What were the implications of this? The New Tribunal was founded barely a year after the creation of the Turin silk guild, which united masters, journeymen and merchant–manufacturers.[50] These were the years of the first real boom of an industry which was to be the major source of revenue to the state in Piedmont.[51] In reality, the 'New Tribunal for commerce, cognizance and expedition of legal affairs regarding traders, merchants and others' dealt mainly with the control and organization of 'merchants and operators of silk and other works'. It was a body with both economic and judicial powers, composed of three lawyers who could consult with bankers and merchants. The presence of 'gown' members and the relegation of merchants to a purely consultative role clearly reflected the government's new interest in, and determination to control the guild. It was a moment of important change, because the New Tribunal replaced, for all purposes, the Tribunal created by the merchants and traders of Turin themselves in 1676 to replace their special judge. In the old Tribunal merchants and traders were pre-eminent. At its head were two bankers, a cloth merchant, a silk merchant, a chemist and only one Ducal representative.[52]

The new organization of the major economic body signified important consequences. It placed merchants and their organizations under centralized control and threatened their autonomy to govern their own guilds. The sharpest conflicts derived in particular from this latest point. The irregularity of the registration of assemblies of silk and cloth merchants – the meetings in which syndics were supposed to be elected in the presence of Ducal officials – during the first few years of the Tribunal's life, and the conflicts characterizing these assemblies, illustrate the level of resistance to the central authority's exercise of control over the selection of the guild's executive groups. Syndics often remained in office for more than their one-year appointment because the guild refused to meet. Assemblies did not take place for years because Ducal

---

[50] For the act setting up the New Commercial Tribunal, see Duboin, *Raccolta*, vol. IV, p. 794.

[51] Some data on the volume of production in G. Arese, *L'Industria serica piemontese*, Turin 1922, and in L. Bulferetti, *Agricoltura, industria e commercio in Piemonte nel secolo XIII*, Turin 1963; for data concerning export in the later eighteenth century see G. Levi, 'La Seta e l'Economia Piemontese nel Settecento', *Rivista Storica Italiana*, 79: 3, 1967. Silk spinning in Piedmont has been extensively studied by C. Poni, 'All 'origine del sistema di fabbrica: tecnologia e organizzazione produttiva dei mulini da seta nell'Italia settentrionale (secc. XVII–XVIII)', *Rivista Storica Italiana*, 88, 3, 1976.   [52] See Duboin, *Raccolta*, vol. III.

representatives demanded to be present,[53] along with the outgoing officers who were to elect the new officers through an open vote. While the resistance to such control over the organization often met with success, the New Tribunal certainly managed to limit the merchants' sphere of political autonomy, to permit the first divisions within the guild[54] and, above all, to deprive the merchants of a fundamental judicial weapon. Without their own magistracy the merchants were under the jurisdiction of a tribunal in which they were not represented for all legal affairs concerning commerce and labour relations. The situation was to change again in 1723 with the third restructuring of the Commercial Tribunal, but by then the merchants had definitely lost authority and real political control in this area.

The consequences of the creation of the new Commercial Tribunal, controlled by Ducal officials, affected other important mercantile institutions. By assuming the right to adjudicate cases concerning trade guilds in general, the Tribunal diminished the power of other institutional figures traditionally tied to or elected by merchants: the senior urban magistrate (*vicario*), the weights and measures officers and the 'politicians' responsible for the government of the city – the major city officers. In the same year 1687, the Town Council itself was to be the object of a serious attempt to downgrade its social identity. This institution, most representative of the merchants, was the victim of a regulation approved by the Duke aimed at reorganizing its internal hierarchies and closely controlling its revenues.[55] The attempt to counter this move led to a severe weakening of the Town Council and its officers. During the following months and years they were obliged to accept many state officials in their ranks (until then formally excluded from the City Council) and give up the right to election to many posts, thus losing control over them.[56] Merchants' participation in the life of the Town Council became progressively weaker. Under tight financial control and largely populated by Ducal officials with their own loyalties and

[53] See AST, Sezioni Riunite, Consolato di commercio, vol. 32 *bis*, in particular cc. 6, 31 and 43. The volume cited includes the assemblies held between 1687 and 1701. The documentation recommences only in 1740 because of a fire which destroyed the other volumes.

[54] Evidence in the documents cited reflects not only a common tension towards court officials, but friction between the summit and the base of the guild.

[55] See Archivio del Comune di Torino (henceforth ACT), Statuti n. 416, 19 December 1687, *Regolamento per la città di Torino*.

[56] See in particular, for the immediately following period, ACT, Ordinati, 1687, cc. 340 v. ff.

clienteles, the Town Council lost its special prerogatives and was deserted by the merchants and traders.[57]

The central authority's aggressive acts of interference in institutions traditionally governed by these social groups were not isolated episodes in this period. They were part of a broader strategy of control of local authorities involving the whole of Piedmont. It was a political strategy which should not be interpreted as purely repressive. It expressed the emergence and strength of a new social elite whose careers consisted of the offices held in the State bureaucracy and which claimed its own spheres of control and political power. But the 1680s in Turin and the two instances we have briefly outlined – the attempt to deprive of authority the two most important and prestigious bodies in which the merchants were significantly represented – mark a fundamental point in this process which was to have major consequences on the group choices made by Turin's merchants over the following years. The general outlines of this process are well known,[58] but the important consequences it was to have on the morphology of urban social groups, which were profoundly altered, have been little analysed.

With the taking over of the merchants' magistracy and the narrowing of their authority in the Town Council, the importance of formally marginal or highly specialised institutions increased. They now became central and clearly representative of group identity. The most important example perhaps is the Brotherhood of merchants and traders.[59] Founded in 1663, based on the symbol 'the most Holy Madonna of the Faith', the Brotherhood was a strictly devotional association whose activities (which seem very irregular during the first twenty years of its life) were concentrated around the preparation of the annual procession, the distribution of torches and the purchase of ashes. From 1683 the minutes of the meetings became more regular, attesting to charitable

---

[57] The reconstruction of this process – of extreme interest in the study of relations between the central authority and local governments – required a systematic examination of the municipal *Ordinati* from the end of the seventeenth century to the 1740s. For a more detailed analysis, see Cerutti, *La Ville et les metiers*, cited in n. 6.

[58] This theme has dominated Piedmontese historiography. See also G. Symcox, *Victor Amadeus II. Absolutism in the Savoyard State, 1675–1730*, London 1983, which offers a useful synopsis and a rich bibliography.

[59] For the reconstruction of the activity of this institution see Archivio Storico della Cappella; I have consulted: F11 (Accounts of treasurers and Ordinati 1663–1741); G1 (Ordinati 1740–1784; H1 (Inventory furnishings 1663–1748); E (Documents relative to the foundation); F1 (Accounts of treasurers 1662–1777); I3 (List of members). I was able to study this archive thanks to the help of Dr Lanza.

activities – visits to the patients of the Charity Hospital – and attempts were made to play a role in the sphere of urban ceremonies. But around 1690 the Brotherhood assumed a more clearly defined physiognomy and began to engage in acquisitions which were to make its chapel one of the most prestigious monuments of the city. Between 1692 and 1702 pews, altars and stained-glass windows were purchased. By 1697 the chapel possessed seven precious paintings donated by its members, amongst whom were many silk merchant–manufacturers and traders who were united in this institution despite important differences in income and status.[60] From the beginning of the eighteenth century, the Brotherhood became an increasingly cohesive group and a source of strong identity for its members. They were buried in the Brotherhood church, and enjoyed the exceptional privilege of participating in the spiritual exercises of the Jesuit fathers, and had priority here even over the Companies of San Paolo and Annunziata, the most prestigious in the city. The numerous legacies of its members provided for conspicuous and efficient systems of charity. During these years the Brotherhood became a centre of strong social identity and of charitable aid and distribution of resources. So it became a kind of reconstruction of the community of Turin merchants and traders, which in some way replaced the institutions – particularly the Town Council – which no longer provided such attractive openings. The symbolic and also political value implicit in the proposal it made in 1705 to elect itself repository of the cults of Saints Solutore, Avventore and Ottaviano (the city's oldest cult), which had long since been neglected by the Town Council, seems to me extraordinarily significant.[61]

The growth of institutions which previously had been marginal in the life of the town should be considered within this context of attempts to find spheres of economic control, political representation and also social identity. The success of the tailors' guild from the 1680s, its heterogeneous composition and its special traits also need to be seen in this context. What the guild could offer to merchants and traders, and what cemented their unity, despite hierarchies and internal differences was, as we have seen, an arena relatively independent of the interference and control of central authorities. It offered the possibility of organizing their

---

[60] We know that merchant–manufacturers were much wealthier than traders, whose ranks were highly stratified. See the considerations and the analyses of income and status in this group in the documents cited in n. 81. .   [61] Archivio Storico della Cappella, F11 Ordinati 1705, c. 142.

own hierarchies without being subject to the Tribunal's approval; of exercising economic controls and avoiding those imposed by the central authorities; and lastly, of maintaining a special magistracy and thus of resolving within the guild itself cases involving commerce, labour relations and even personal and family quarrels.[62]

Merchants and traders, in an at least temporary alliance, came together in this organization, both taking advantage of and determining its own particular characteristics, those very characteristics that are so striking when one studies the guild without finding an explanation in the context of the trade. This explains the considerable strength obtained between the 1680s and 1730s by a guild representing a trade which was not very closely knit, since it was composed of members who, to a large extent, did not have to consider the activity of clothes-making as a stable choice. The craft regulations, while tending to upgrade membership by, for example, putting a high price on the granting of 'mastership', were oddly indifferent to trade standards and very vague about the master-piece.[63] The very kind of conflicts that divided the guild during this period of its life were different, for these conflicts did not express the more traditional problems of restrictive practices – the major source of identity of an art, one might say – but rather reflected the tensions created by an extremely diversified social composition. As we have said, the tailors' guild was to have a difficult time agreeing upon a common symbol with

---

[62] This last point is of capital importance. The enormous value attributed to particular magistracies by the single crafts is due to the fact that they offered the possibility of completely avoiding the jurisdiction of ordinary courts. I have tried elsewhere ('Corporazioni') to demonstrate how this element was the central point of the very birth of guilds in Piedmont at the end of the sixteenth century.

[63] Arguing that 'taste' was dominant in clothes-making, and that therefore it was impossible to impose a precise standard of production, the guild's statutes refer vaguely to an examination to which the workers were to be subjected. In this sense the Turin guild differed from the Paris one, for example, which provided for the confection of the masterpiece in the presence of guild officers. There were in fact many differences between the two guilds. One striking difference indicates the importance of the political configuration in determining the trajectory of the guild. While in Piedmont, as we have seen, the guild was accused of trading cloth, in Paris the conflicts characterizing the guild were strangely inverted; above all, they concerned the competition of the *merciers*, who in reality had clothes made, while they should only have sold them. See S. Kaplan, *The Luxury Guilds in Paris in the Eighteenth Century*, contribution to the conference 'Möbelkunst und Luxusmarkt im 18. Jahrhundert', Nürnberg, 23–25 April 1981; see P. Vidal, *Histoire de la corporation des tailleurs d'habits, pourpointiers, chaussuriers de la ville de Paris*, Paris 1926. The Turin guild presented original traits even compared to tailoring guilds in other Italian states (see, for example, though with respect to an earlier period, C. Violante, 'L'Arte dei sarti nello svolgimento del sistema corporativo (secoli XIII–XV)', in *Economia, società, istituzioni a Pisa nel Medioevo*, Bari 1980, pp. 253–97); or to the tailors' guild of York analysed by D.M. Pallister, 'The Trade Guilds of Tudor York', in P. Clark and P. Slack (eds.), *Crisis and Order in English Towns, 1500–1700*, London 1972.

which all its members could identify. It was the only group in Turin successively represented by three saints: Bonaventura, Alberto and Omobono. The choice of the last saint – traditional protector of tailors in Italy – made only around the 1730s,[64] marked, as we shall see, a change in the guild, its 'normalization' with respect to the more complex vicissitudes it had experienced.

An analysis of the *real* composition of the guild therefore explains its peculiar traits. During the period we have analysed, the tailors' guild, rather than a trade organization, was a composite social group, governed by an elite whose group choices were related to problems of economic control and judicial and political autonomy. Total identity did not exist between the practising of the craft and the guild that represented the trade. Between the two aspects there was an essential passage, i.e. the decision to unite to form a social corpus, which could involve a great variety of contents and aims. The 'language of the trade', in short, is insufficient for the study of its organizations. The characteristics of the guild and its position compared to other urban trade guilds are incomprehensible if detached from the social and political context that led different social groups to choose alliances and share common roles. Alongside economic contingencies, we need to analyse the opportunities present in the urban area if we want to explain the fortunes and sudden transformation of the guilds.

Attacks on the guild and its transformation

While the period considered is the richest in which to analyse the vicissitudes of the tailors' guild in Turin, the guild's trajectory needs to be followed, albeit briefly, over the course of a few more decades. We have already outlined the guild's success, but have not explained its unpredictable decline after the 1730s. The guild in fact lost its preeminence and, though tailoring remained one of the numerically most important arts of the town, the guild's prestige diminished relative to that of other guilds. The starting point must be the 1730s and the tensions the guild was experiencing. At this moment the gap between elite and base was at its most clear, a gap which allowed for and encouraged the intervention of the Commercial Tribunal.

---

[64] I was not able to determine the precise year in which the cult of St Omobono was confirmed, but a 1731 document refers to this as a very recent event. See the *Stato della controversia di giudizio tra il Consolato e il giudice della città di Torino*, in AST, Sezione I, Commercio, cat. I, m. 1.

The reporting of the embezzlements perpetrated by the tailors' guild and of the illicit commercial activities the guild acted as a cover for, certainly expressed the tensions that such an unbalanced group must have felt. It was indicative of that divergence between elite and base already revealed by the comparison between our analysis of the census and the biographies of syndics and officers. But above all it was a symptom of a profound division which was to deepen within the social group of merchants and traders from the 1730s, a process of fragmentation which, because of its consequences, was to affect the lives of all trade guilds, creating a kind of shared chronology of internal strife and tensions which continued through the second half of the eighteenth century.[65] In this chapter I can only outline the stages of this chronology, emphasizing above all those elements useful in understanding the later trajectory of the tailors' guild.

There is an apparent paradox in the 1731 denunciation which we should try to understand. The Tribunal accusing the guild was at that date made up of the same social figures and professional categories as was its target. In 1723, in fact, the regulations of the Tribunal were rewritten for the third time, and for the next ten years it was to be headed again by bankers, merchants and traders. We therefore need to ask, what was the meaning of this new composition? And what scission within the same social group was strong enough to cause an acute period of strife? Why had merchants and traders, a social group which we have seen acting together, become so divided?

The third Commercial Tribunal was created in the framework of the Royal Constitutions, the principal administrative and judicial reorganization formulated by Victor Amadeus II.[66] Its main intent was to centralize authority. The trade guilds' special magistracies were suppressed and control over all crafts involved in business was concentrated in this tribunal. Considering the importance attributed by these groups to judicial self-sufficiency, this was a drastic measure. The 1723 Tribunal and the merchants and traders at its head were faced with a very difficult task. The Tribunal had to assert itself as the only judicial body able to resolve litigation concerning crafts. But it was hindered in reaching this goal by a judicial definition which was much more fragile than appeared

---

[65] Cerutti, La Ville et les métiers.
[66] On the Royal Constitutions and the innovations they contained, see M. Viora, Le Costituzioni piemontesi, Turin 1928.

at first glance. In fact its powers of intervention only included lawsuits between traders and not the much more frequent ones originating from the sale of products to individuals, for which the ordinary local judge was responsible.

This crucial clause[67] severely restricted the Tribunal's authority. Its own members could not resolve all their disputes through the Tribunal, but were called to appear in other tribunals (most of their complaints were based on this point).[68] At the same time it was difficult to avoid the Tribunal's jurisdiction by claiming that the case was private. The weakness of the judicial definition created serious problems of authority which characterized the tormented life of the Commercial Tribunal during these ten years. As its judges were 'civilians' without legal title, their authority was disavowed by the Ducal officials, by lawyers and judges, according to whom their sentences 'besides derision, provoke appeals and complaints',[69] and by the Duke, who received and supported protests and remonstrances.[70] Lastly, they were disavowed by the merchants and traders themselves, who on many occasions demonstrated, sometimes violently,[71] their intolerance for a magistracy which attempted to regain force and authority by simply confirming a hierarchy.

The conflicts the Commercial Tribunal underwent (which deserve further attention) are important signs of the splits and divisions which were created and revived within the group of merchants and traders, a

---

[67] As we have seen, the immunity of the tailors and their election of the judge of Turin as arbitrator of their litigation was lost because of the ambiguity of this formulation. It was the subject of much discussion, of which we still find traces in 1771: see 'Rimostranza del Consolato di Torino al Gran Cancelliere per averne la sua decisione sopra la competenza del Magistrato o del giudice di Torino nella lite tra artigiani per le società di negozio', in Duboin, *Raccolta*, vol. XV, p. 47, footnote. Besides the 'immunity' of the tailors, this document deals with an analogous condition shared by carpenters and cobblers. In the case of the former, at least, an examination of the guild's private archives (recently and accidentally discovered) demonstrated how the attempt to avoid Commercial Tribunal control failed in the 1720s. The case of the cobblers requires further research, but various indices lead me to believe that their story was analogous.

[68] In particular *Rappresentanza del Consolato di Torino a Sua Maestà perché le cause di vendita di merci a particolari si trattino avanti esso Tribunale*, 1724, in AST, Sezione I, Commercio, cat. I, m. 1.

[69] See *Supplica a S.A. dei mercanti del Consolato*, 1731, and in general the entire set of documents entitled 'Scritture riguardanti il Magistrato del Consolato'.

[70] Ibid.: numerous examples of appeals presented and accepted.

[71] Ibid., *Relazione del Consolato circa la parlata men rispettosa fatta dal mercante Ughes cui fece seguito un provvedimento per consentire al Consolato di punire quanti gli mancano di rispetto*, 1726. For the provisions referred to, ibid., m. 1 da ordinare, *Copia di lettera con la quale il Guardasigilli per ordine di S.M. fa noto al Consolato che nel caso venga ad esso mancato di rispetto, rimane autorizzato a punire i contravventori con l'arresto personale*, 1726. And see throughout this documentation the numerous examples of disputes between the Commercial Tribunal and lawyers, etc.

composite and hierarchical group which until then had managed to stay together because it shared a common opponent and a common pursuit of spheres of autonomy.

The 1730s and the production crisis which struck silk manufacturing in particular were years in which these conflicts accelerated sharply. They appeared on many fronts contemporaneously – the merchants' and master cloth manufacturers' guild, the Brotherhood of merchants and traders, within the Commercial Tribunal and in the Tribunal's relations with other guilds, above all that of the tailors. Let us look at some of the consequences of this strife.

The stagnation of production in Piedmont between 1729 and 1730 was the first serious crisis the silk industry experienced.[72] It left about half the industry's workers jobless, causing the city and government authorities serious problems of provision of charity and control of a population reduced to poverty.[73] The impoverishment of so many masters could not but rigidify the hierarchical structure of an extraordinarily stratified guild which included both workers and the richest merchants of the city, those who provided jobs. Through petitions to the Duke and the Commercial Tribunal in 1730, the master workers requested customary measures to assure themselves control over the distribution of work and oppose the absolute power of the silk merchants. The most important rule was that of 'the four looms', destined to provoke protests and appeals from the merchants, and source of such extreme clashes that it could only be irregularly applied during the following years.[74] The most open signs of a fracture between merchants and masters within the guild date from the same year. The masters considered themselves 'persecuted by some of the officers'. They complained about the monopoly of work established by the merchants. They denounced the supporters of the Commercial Tribunal, claiming that they tried to prevent application of the four looms rule and showed partiality in favour of the merchants.

To sum up, the crisis caused strife between masters and merchants

[72] Arese, *L'Industria serica*, pp. 109ff.

[73] For a description of the dramatic effects of the crisis on the urban population: ACT, Ordinati, 1730, particularly the months of September and October. The Council of Commerce, composed of high magistrates, seconded the Commercial Tribunal as early as 1723, but the election of its first members and the effective start of its activities occurred a few years later (1729): Duboin, *Raccolta*, vol. XV, p. 16. This Council controlled the Tribunal and its existence demonstrates the limited power of the latter.

[74] On the four-loom regulation (which was meant to limit the number of looms that each manufacturer could manage), and on the disputes caused by it, see Arese, *L'Industria serica*, pp. 110ff., and particularly AST, Sezione I, Commercio, cat. IV, m. 7, containing petitions, appeals, etc.; ibid., *Supplica di Giacomo Giuseppe Casale e Gio Antonio Beltramo mastri, a nome anche delli 200 e più mastri della loro università*, February 1730.

which was never resolved. Within a few years, this led to a total separation between the two categories, which could never again belong to the same guild. This meant a significant impoverishment of the masters but, for the first time, it also seriously threatened the position of the silk merchants. The merchants were able to appreciate the inefficiency of their institutional instruments. The members of the Commercial Tribunal were broken by the continuous interference in their affairs by State officials who claimed rights and authority over a Ducal magistracy and by the continuous disavowals of their authority by merchants or traders who threatened their status and even their reputation;[75] finally, in 1731, they drew up a petition in which they asked to be assigned a lawyer as leading member. In fact, a lawyer was to replace them definitively in 1733, when they gave up the direction of the Commercial Tribunal.[76]

The fear of being overwhelmed by the crisis, but also the genuine absence of any efficient institutional instrument through which to claim their economic pre-eminence and their status, led the silk merchants violently to reclaim their leading role and openly to attempt to assert sole rights and monopolies. These two factors led, perhaps for the first time, to genuine corporative claims and marked divisions within the social group. The divisions were not only between masters and silk merchants but also between the latter and other categories closer to them in terms of status and hitherto allies. These were the cloth traders, who traded but had no working looms and constituted dangerous competitors in textile sales and imports. The silk merchants were to attack them violently during the 1730s, the worst of the crisis years. They attempted to block their activity at any price and claimed monopoly rights for themselves, as the mainstay of the state's principal industry.

It is in the context of this new conflict that we must interpret the divisions and contrasts of which we find signs within the merchants' and traders' Brotherhood during these years,[77] as well as the Commercial

---

[75] In 1730 a very serious case occurred: two consuls were dismissed from their offices, accused of having directed in their own favour a case against other traders, and 'with great prejudice to their reputation and trade'. A few months after this episode the merchants requested that they be supported (in practice, substituted) by lawyer members. See AST, Sezione I, Commercio, cat. IV, m. 1.

[76] For the creation of the new Commercial Tribunal: Duboin, *Raccolta*, vol. III, p. 781; and again in AST, Sezione I, Commercio, cat. IV, m. 1, the documents entitled 'Diversi pareri per la formazione di un nuovo regolamento per li consolati'.

[77] Archivio storico della Compagnia, F11, cc. 234ff., year 1732: for the first time, the Brotherhood manifested problems of 'internal democracy', leading some of its members to demand a stronger presence in the council and assemblies.

Tribunal's denunciation of the tailors' guild. Through this attack and the unmasking of the ties that some of its members had with the cloth trade, the silk merchants intended to claim their right to a monopoly of the trade (so much more essential at such a critical time), and the legitimacy of controls over the economic life of the town. To reveal the 'ties' of the tailors to the traders meant denouncing the existence of uncontrolled import channels. This was dangerous for those who wanted to obtain a monopoly. It also meant eliminating a 'free' zone, the economic and political importance of which was well appreciated by the merchants, since they themselves had created and shared it, but which at that moment went against their interests. The 1731 episode is an example of the new fractures and divisions which the crisis, together with the peculiar political configuration described above, created in the group of merchants and traders.

The division deepened over the following years and was definitively ratified in 1738. In that year a guild of 'Merchants keeping workshops and shops open and manufacturing silk stuffs',[78] distinct from that of the masters and any other category of traders, was officially created. The petition presented was basically a summary of all the problems we have seen presented by the silk merchants during the first half of the 1730s. By creating a distinct organization they claimed to limit the sale of all materials to those matriculated in the guild, with the aim of preventing masters from having their own sales assistants. At the same time they claimed the monopoly of textile imports, maintaining that foreign cloths could only be imported by those with working looms producing the same type of cloth. The traders would thus have either to give up their trade or install at least five looms in their shops, which involved considerable investment.[79]

The two targets of the petition were very clear and were the protagonists of the strife that began in the 1730s. They were the master workers on the one hand and the cloth traders on the other. The implications of this petition in terms of monopolies and privileges could not escape the notice of the Ducal counsellors to whom it was submitted: their recorded opinions were very blunt in unmasking the merchants' desire to gain complete control over the sector, hidden behind paradoxes

[78] The guild, as we have seen, elected its own syndics as early as 1687, and was in fact an independent body. However, before this time it had never given itself autonomous regulations. See Duboin, *Raccolta*, vol. XVI, p. 312. But see also the interesting differences between the version of the Memorial approved and the first version in AST, Sezione I, Commercio, cat. IV, m. 8.

[79] The original request included the installation of twelve looms, a number later reduced due to the opposition of the Commercial Tribunal.

and falsehoods.[80] The first clause concerning the sale of textiles too visibly threatened the survival of masters during a crisis period and so was not accepted in its restrictive form. But the second clause regarding the import monopoly was accepted in the end, despite adverse opinions, numerous appeals made by traders and the obvious impossibility for most of them to afford the installation of looms.[81] The silk merchant–manufacturers became, at least officially, the only legal importers of cloth and therefore the only distributors of textiles in the city.

I believe two factors favoured the success of such exorbitant claims, for which the merchants had fought with less success in earlier years. The first was a new production crisis, even more serious than the former one, which induced many masters to emigrate and hastened the adoption of the first authentic plans of state subvention of workers.[82] Merchants could threaten to close and bankrupt the shops in the event of refusal. The second was their renunciation of the Commercial Tribunal (from 1733 their role was again purely consultative). They thus eliminated the ambiguity of their presence in the magistracy which the government authorities had felt to be competitive, and so deserved a reward in terms of pre-eminence in production. Once again, two inseparable factors, economic and political, explain the success of the merchants and, more generally, 'corporative development' in Turin during these years.

The economic implications of such a throttle-hold on production and import channels needs to be analysed in relation to the Turin textile manufacturers' failure to 'take off' despite their rosy beginnings. The political process of 'corporatization' of social groups can provide more precise and useful answers than those to be found in the burden of import duties or the short-sightedness of investments.

But this story, besides its particular interest, is useful in allowing us to return to the vicissitudes of the tailors' guild and analyse the conse-

---

[80] See in particular the opinion of one of the members of the Commercial Tribunal (signed Beraudo di Pralormo) who wrote of the 'almost real monopoly' the merchants were aiming at. The same aim had also been hidden behind the request to impose a period of apprenticeship as a condition for admission to the guild, an apprenticeship not justified by the characteristics of the craft: AST, Sezione I, Commercio, cat. IV, m. 8.

[81] Ibid. See particularly the appeals of the 'Merchants of fashion, cloth and embroideries', which provides an attentive and interesting analysis of the stratification of this category, and in which each point of the merchants' petition is accurately interpreted as a wilful attack against them.

[82] On the 1738 crisis, Arese, L'Industria serica, pp. 111ff., and in particular AST, Sezione I, Commercio, mm. 8 and 22, in which is to be found the project, compiled by Conte di Salmour, trade councillor, to create a company, with capital provided by royal finances, which would offer work to textile workers during crisis years.

quences which the next order was to have on its history and composition.

I have already noted that the guild, after its moment of glory from the 1680s, suffered a relative decline, at least in terms of its prestige, around the second half of the eighteenth century. In the 1742 'list of professions' (already discussed) tailoring still figured as one of the most numerically important crafts of the town. But in 1750 different data, referring less to the consistence of the trades and more to the relative importance of the guilds in the urban area, demonstrated that the tailors' guild occupied a lower position than formerly. On the occasion of the reception of Duke Vittorio Amedeo and the Infanta of Spain in 1750, when all trade groups were called upon to attend the solemn entrance, the tailors' guild had lost the 'ceremonial supremacy' to which it had been entitled in the 1730s. This decline became more marked with time, as was evident on a much later occasion, the arrival of the Prince of Piedmont and his consort in 1775.[83] The guild occupied only fourth position in terms of the number of members called upon to represent it.

These indices of a loss of prestige were however accompanied by a more intense internal life, which produced richer documentation between the 1730s and 1770s. A memorial dated 1737 redefined the formalities required to join the guild, the length of apprenticeship and the duties tied to office-holding. For the first time considerable attention was given to the defence of the guild's boundaries, perhaps the most typical problems of the Turin trade guilds from the beginning of the century. Jews were expressly prohibited from producing clothing 'under pretext of their dealings'.[84] During the 1740s a series of notarial acts and guild ordinances were to follow which attested to a more regular functioning. The payment of apprenticeship and that for the attainment of 'mastership'[85] were among these. The cult of Saint Omobono, which had itself emerged during the 1730s, was continuously raised. An ordinance of the 1760 council informs us that the cult was officially accepted by the entire guild. The saint's altar was to bear a sign, never to be removed, 'that says he is of the tailors' guild'.[86] These signs of a 'normalization' of the guild, which had lost its elusive characteristics and was more marked by the trade and more cohesive, can be at least partially confirmed indirectly by an analysis of the 1742 state of traders.

---

[83] See ACT, loose papers, nn. 1101 (1705); 1111 (1775); see also the entrance of Carlo Emanuele and the Princess of Lorraine, in 1737 (no. 1095).

[84] AST, Sezione I, cat. IV, m. 20 bis da ordinare; see in addition the opinion on the petition of the Substitute Attorney Gentile Botto, ibid., m. 6.

[85] In particular, AST, Sezioni Riunite, Insinuazione Torino, 1740, l. 2, c. 737; 1740, l. 10, c. 436; 1740, l. 10, c. 501.   [86] AST, Sezione I, cat. IV, m. 6.

We have already used this document to verify indices of continuity of the trade amongst the tailors found in the 1705 census. It provides other interesting information which emerges from the lists of silk merchants and cloth traders. Ten sons of tailors found in the 1705 census were registered under these two categories (four merchants and six traders) in 1742.[87] They were the sons of the guild's most prestigious members (four belonged to families of guild officers). For them, as we have seen, the trade of tailoring was either marginal or non-existent, while their commercial activities were rich and intensive. The change of profession cannot therefore be interpreted as a sign of social mobility, or at least not exclusively. Such a change seems to have been closely linked to the vicissitudes of the guild and its new life.

The events of the 1730s and the fragmentation of the merchants' guild profoundly transformed the significance of formerly shared spheres. The denunciation of the peculiar composition of the tailors' guild and the conflicts expressed by this denunciation, which divided groups previously responsible for forging the corporation's character, took away from the guild the economic and political possibilities which had determined its good fortune. The guild was given back to the trade.

Only a detailed analysis of guild members in the second part of the century could reveal to what extent and in what way the social composition of the guild actually changed, whether the choice of 'deserting' the tailors' corporation made by the ten sons we have registered was really the sign of a transformation of the guild and of its abandonment by merchants and traders. Its lesser fortune, the rebirth of its internal life, the recomposition of its symbolical unity, the new nature of the conflicts – all lead us to hypothesize that, from a composite social group, the tailors' guild, at least with regard to a part of its life, once again represented the trade.

This part of the research needs to be followed up and amplified. But even at this still partially documented stage it shows how the life of a trade guild could vary and profoundly change during the course of its history. A guild could aggregate different social groups and thus change its own distinctive characteristics. The choice of the historical moment in which to study a guild cannot neglect the reconstruction of other associative forms present in the city or other possible alliances available to individuals and social groups.

---

[87] This check also showed that none of the sons of merchants and traders to be found working as apprentices for master tailors in 1705 later practised the trade.

6 ❧ Conceptions of poverty and poor-relief in Turin in the second half of the eighteenth century

Sandra Cavallo

Introduction

The idea that poverty is a relative rather than an absolute concept appears to be widely accepted. Historians recognize that different societies define need and the necessity of relief in different ways. It has even been proposed that the term 'poverty' be replaced by 'deprivation', in that this automatically suggests greater flexibility and points to the dependency of the threshold of need on culturally determined variables.[1]

The relative nature of the concept of 'poverty' is usually attributed to two considerations. First, to a series of conventions about what is regarded as a necessity which define acceptable standards of living. Then, there are boundaries, which are also liable to change, that distinguish between the deserving and the undeserving poor, according to various sets of values and ideological frameworks.[2]

Even though they underline the importance of a relativist approach, historians, it seems, hold on to an element of objectivity in the shape of a hierarchy of need, albeit based on the notion of convention. This is seen as the key criterion through which different social and cultural milieux were accustomed to identify and measure poverty and to model their systems of welfare. Such assumptions, in my view, have deeply influenced studies in the field, imposing two major methodological orientations. On the one hand, such studies have considered that the population in receipt of welfare could be taken as revealing the structure if not the dimensions of poverty. Thus, lists of recipients have been used

Translated from Italian by Robert Lumley.

[1] W. Blockmans, 'Circumscribing the Concept of Poverty', in T. Rijs (ed.), *Aspects of Poverty in Early Modern Europe*, Stuttgart–Brussels–Florence 1981.

[2] The different definitions of poverty adopted by historians are discussed in P. Slack, *Poverty and Policy in Tudor and Stuart England*, London–New York 1988; see also W. Beckerman, 'The Measurement of Poverty', in Rijs, *Aspects*, and A. Sen, *Poverty and Famines, An Essay on Entitlement and Deprivation*, Oxford 1981.

as sources for discovering the age, gender, and situation of those most hard hit by poverty. On the other hand, many studies have tried instead to measure the effectiveness of the systems of poor relief, comparing those receiving relief with the profile and estimates of the scale of poverty as shown by other sources. In both instances, an assumption is made of a continuity or an equation between the poor population as a whole and the poor in receipt of relief. Such an approach underestimates the complexity of the dynamics behind the selection process and reflects the premise that evaluation of need was the principal criterion on which that selection was based.

My research on Turin has aimed at tackling this very question of the criteria underpinning differences in access to poor-relief by analysing the logics of discrimination that were in operation. In order to do this, I was able to take advantage of the rich documentation concerning the activities of the major institution in Turin providing poor-relief, namely the Ospedale di Carità. Its records, kept from 1743 onwards, have enabled me to analyse the criteria of selection adopted in the hospital and to compare the composition of those selected with that of the poor requesting relief. In addition, I have been able to trace the different developments in the models of relief and conceptions of poverty over a forty-year period.

The research reveals how the provision of relief was only in part based on the 'structure of poverty'. It was influenced to a greater extent by the relationships between rich and poor and by the consequent favour shown to certain sections of the poor rather than to others. The connections running through the social hierarchy created differentiations of status and concomitant privileges among the poor which flowed much more from bonds of protection than from criteria based on necessity or morality. Far from covering all the different factors involved in selection, this chapter points to the importance of exploring the categories of status that divided the society of the poor into a hierarchy and created differentials in access to relief. It suggests that the definition of new attitudes and policies towards the poor must be linked to the emergence of new models of vertical relations in society. Consequently, the shift in the boundaries defining deserving poverty, which is usually explained as an outcome of reflection 'on the poor' seen as alien beings,[3] is understood here as emanating from the ties of interdependence and

---

[3] This is the main approach found in G. Himmelfarb, *The Idea of Poverty*, New York 1984.

reciprocity that connected the poor to those who controlled charitable resources.

Criteria of status appear to be essential in defining the poor worthy of receiving relief. The very deafness shown for so long by the institution in question towards factors of economic inequality and social difficulty (in contrast to those due to natural causes) evidently constituted an ideological defence mechanism concerning the untouchability of status as the principle regulating the provision of poor-relief. It is clear that these criteria were open to manipulation by the poor and so it was not always the case that many of the needy were excluded. Yet it is important to note the existence of a link between the categories of those deserving relief and the ideology of that specific structure of power, even when it only meant that the poor, in order to be heard, were obliged to recite words using a language that insisted on the rhetoric of natural disasters to which they had fallen victim.

Sometimes the qualifications for receiving poor-relief explicitly referred to categories of status. This was the case with the requirement of citizenship, which remained an indispensable condition for a long period. On the one hand, the primacy attached to citizenship reflected the importance of being a party to the local dynamics of patronage and protection. On the other, it appears to be closely related to the dynamics of ongoing conflicts of power. In the Turin political situation of the time, the exaltation of the status of citizen worked to reinforce the identity and force behind municipal power in the conflict with Ducal authority. Not by chance it clashed with the Duke's promise to protect all his subjects without exception.

However, criteria concerning social worth usually operated in a less explicit manner. For example, it is possible to observe how the centralization and expansion of state bureaucracy in the second half of the eighteenth century brought with it an enhancement of the status of state employee, greatly benefiting workers in state-controlled industries when it came to seeking poor relief. Again, such a shift did not coincide with a new structure of poverty, but it did strongly articulate the ideological discourse that accompanied the new forms of state control. An examination of the changing configurations of power and the sets of vertical relations that they entailed thus becomes essential if we are to explain the emergence of different images of the deserving poor and changes in the allocation of privilege among categories of the poor.

The Turin Ospedale di Carità and the suppression of begging

During the eighteenth century the Ospedale constituted the institution responsible for providing for the needy sections of the population. Established in 1649 as a result of the joint efforts of different bodies representing the city elites (the Senate, the Camera dei Conti, the Court, the Municipality, the craft organizations and the largest lay confraternity),[4] it had progressively absorbed most of the charitable work which had been monopolized for about a hundred years by the municipal authorities and which had been mainly based on outdoor relief. After an initial period of friction and economic difficulties, the Ospedale had begun to win the support and financial backing of the citizens. Consequently, it was in a position in 1683 to start work on a new and bigger building which it would then occupy until the late nineteenth century.[5] The monumental building was situated in the heart of the city not far from the royal palace and the other major centres of power and court life. It housed a considerable number of the poor, oscillating between about 500 and over 2,200 in the course of the century (figure 6.1).

These included mainly old people, children and adolescents, and adults unable to work. In addition, the hospital assisted recipients of outdoor relief – babies whom the hospital maintained through wet-nurses, and poor families to whom bread was distributed each week.[6]

Meanwhile, medical treatment for the sick was entrusted to the long-established hospitals of San Maurizio e Lazzaro and Santissimo Sudario, and, more importantly, to the more spacious Ospedale San Giovanni,

[4] The hospital founded in 1649 should not be confused, as often happens, with the hospital for beggars set up in 1626 as a result of a special initiative by the Duke. The latter had a troubled and fairly brief existence and closed down definitively at the end of the 1630s. Even its incomes did not go to the Ospedale di Carità, which replaced it, but were incorporated into the incomes of the hospital for the infirm of San Maurizio e Lazzaro, which was also the product of Ducal patronage. G.B. Borelli, *Editti antichi e nuovi di Sovrani Prencipi della Real Casa di Savoia*, Turin 1681, p. 232, *Eretione di un hospedale per i mendicanti.*

[5] Although the inmates had been transferred as early as 1685, the building went ahead in stages with long gaps in between. The cruciform building envisaged by the project, in line with the hospital architecture of the time, was actually only finished in 1715. Subsequent extensions and extra storeys were built in the 1730s and 1760s.

[6] From 1733, however, the hospital extended its functions, establishing a new ward for contagious diseases (especially venereal), which was built with the legacy of the banker Bogetti, as stipulated in his will. The activity of the *Opera Bogetti* (or *Opera Nuova*), which was separately administered, is not considered in the present study.

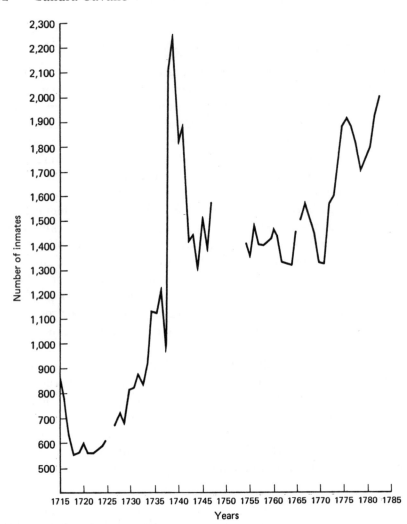

Figure 6.1 Numbers of inmates at the Ospedale di Carità, 1715–85. Turin population (with suburbs): 1715: 54,964; 1723: 62,258; 1733: 67,734; 71,128; 1763: 76,504; 1773: 83,175; 1783: 86,510. Source: Archivio Storico del Comune di Torino, Collezione XII, *Statistica della popolazione 1714–1832*. The series is incomplete, but I was able to supplement data (drawn from various records of the *Archivio dell'Ospedale di Carità*) for 1765, 1768, 1776, 1779. However, the years 1748–50 and 1752–3 are not covered.

the second major city charity. Traditionally, the latter also cared for the children found abandoned in the city. It had, moreover, a section for incurables which in practice, thanks to the patronage of one or other of the families or institutions responsible for assigning beds, housed old people guaranteed a refuge and a kind of life-pension, rather than the chronically ill and infirm.[7]

Lastly, the Albergo di Virtù was one of the institutions meant to provide for the very poor. About 100 boys were admitted when aged from 12 to 15, and they stayed there for at least six years, during which time they learned a trade under the instruction of one of the masters resident in the Albergo. Established in 1580, the institution was almost immediately placed under the control of the Duke of Savoy. Its foundation has usually been seen as designed to promote the spread of manufacturing, notably the silk industry, which was still little developed in Piedmont. However, apart from its declared intentions, the institution also constituted a means for the reinforcement of Ducal power at a time when it was still weak and threatened by rival centres of power, such as the Municipality. By granting generous concessions to both the pupils and their masters, the institution became an important sphere of protection and hence of support for the Duke.[8] From that time onward, it remained a terrain for royal patronage and was the only one of the city charities to be directly administered by appointees of the sovereign, in contrast to those representing various laymen's corps and organizations.

Many city charities, however, were characterized by the relief they gave to the 'privileged poor' – those affected by a temporary or permanent loss of status rather than the really indigent. In the eighteenth century, four institutions (three going back to the previous century, one founded around 1720) provided a respectable refuge for a few years for girls coming from the so-called 'educated classes' (popolo

---

[7] For the city's medical charities, and the hospital of San Giovanni in particular, see my 'Charity, Power and Patronage in Eighteenth Century Italian Hospitals: the Case of Turin', in L. Granshaw and R. Porter (eds.), *The Hospital in History*, London–New York 1989.

[8] As far as the masters were concerned, privileges ranged from the exclusive right to manufacture certain products to exemption from payment of duties. Furthermore, the institution did not have to pay tolls for supplies and raw materials for its manufactures. All the residents were placed under the jurisdiction of the governors who ran the Albergo. With the establishment of craft guilds, the apprentices were assured favoured treatment on completion of the mastership, while the masters obtained additional privileges. Many of the provisions favouring the Albergo are detailed in the informative book by G. Ponzo, *Stato e pauperismo in Italia: l'Albergo di Virtù di Torino (1580–1836)*, Rome 1976, pp. 99, 120. See also Duboin, *Raccolta*, vol. XIII, p. 203, *Lettere Patenti*, 15 September 1587; Archivio di Stato di Torino (henceforth AST), Sezione (henceforth Sez.) I, Luoghi Pii di quà dei Monti, m. 16 d'addizione, Albergo di Virtù, fasc. 3.

civile) – daughters of aristocratic families, or, more commonly, those of notables and state officials who had fallen on hard times, or in decline due to deaths or ill-fortune – and then a dowry adequate for a marriage in keeping with their class of origin. These were small institutions (they accepted a total of some 300 inmates), but this type of charity endured: even in the last decades of the century, two large new institutions were built for women of such social origin, indicative of the importance in the charitable system of the logic of privilege and assertion of status, as opposed to economic definitions of poverty.[9] Nor, as will be seen, was the distribution of charity to the poorest sections of the population an exception to this rule.

The Turin Ospedale di Carità, according to most accounts, was set up as a result of the measures adopted to get rid of begging and to enclose the poor – measures, it is maintained, that were put into practice in Italy since the seventeenth century in the wake of developments in France, such as the establishment of the *hôpitaux généraux* and the *bureaux de charité*. In the Italian case reference is usually made to an extended period, given the difficulties of fitting it into Gutton's model developed for France,[10] due to the range of moves to institutionalize the poor and the gaps in time between them. With these qualifications regarding dates, the analysis first developed by Foucault – according to which the seventeenth-century initiatives, characterized by an ideology and practice of repression, marked a turning point in policies towards poverty – has been widely applied to Italy. Moreover, the new institutions are normally seen as emanating from central directives and expressing a new sense of responsibility for dealing with questions of poverty and relief on the part of the state.[11]

The body of measures called '*sbandimento della mendicità*' (the suppression of begging), adopted in Piedmont in 1716–17, is often regarded as a special example of these developments, and as one of the most interesting cases of action taken by an Italian government in relation to the poor.

---

[9] On these institutions and on other forms of provision for the privileged poor, see Cavallo, 'Charity', pp. 99–101.

[10] J.P. Gutton, *La Société et les pauvres; l'exemple de la généralité de Lyon, 1534–1789*, Paris 1971; M. Rosa, 'Chiesa, idee sui poveri e assistenza in Italia dal Cinque al Settecento', *Società e Storia*, 10, 1980; G. Assereto, 'Pauperismo e assistenza. Messa a punto di studi recenti', *Archivio Storico Italiano*, 141, 1983; A. Pastore, 'Strutture assistenziali fra chiesa e stati nell'Italia della Controriforma', in *Storia d'Italia. Annali 9*, Turin 1986.

[11] For a recent overview in this regard, see B. Pullan, 'Support and Redeem: Charity and Poor Relief in Italian Cities from the Fourteenth to the Seventeenth century', *Continuity and Change*, 3:2, 1988.

The first edict, in August 1716, outlawed begging and giving alms in the capital and the surrounding area, and ordered all beggars to present themselves within three days at the Ospedale di Carità. Here they were to be examined and given relief if thought deserving of it. However, the poor who were outsiders had to leave and return to their places of origin. Anyone caught begging after the edict became law was liable to arrest by the hospital guards and to due punishment. A few months later, in May 1717, a new edict made the measures applicable to the whole of the kingdom, and ordered the building of a network of Ospedali di Carità, or, in less important centres, of Congregazioni di Carità, which would play the same role in providing for repression and relief as that of the Turin hospital in relation to the poor of the capital.[12]

The Piedmontese case became famous not least because of the comprehensive nature of the measures proposed in the 1717 edict. It is possibly the only Italian plan for dealing with poverty that can be compared in ambitiousness and range to that initiated by Louis XIV in 1662. However, its fame also owed much to the influence exercised by the pamphlet *La Mendicità Sbandita*, written by the Jesuit, Father André Guevarre, to coincide with the issuing of the edict.[13] In fact, later historians totally swallowed the interpretation and rhetoric of Guevarre, in terms of both the assessment of the novelty of the measures and the attribution to the king, Victor Amadeus II, of the role of organizer of a centralized system of poor relief that took control away from church and private hands.[14]

While it is true that the territorial scope of the plans deserves serious attention, the novelty of the functions assigned to the Ospedale di Carità and the originality of the forms of intervention proposed in the edicts have certainly been overemphasized.

[12] Duboin, *Raccolta*, vol. XII, p. 280: *Regio editto col quale si proibisce di mendicare nella città e nel territorio di Torino*, 6 August 1716; p. 34: *Regio Editto per lo stabilimento di ospedali generali o di congregazioni di carità in tutti i Comuni dello Stato*, 19 May 1717.

[13] A. Guevarre, *La Mendicità sbandita col sovvenimento dei poveri*, Turin 1717. This work belongs to a very large number of pamphlets printed in various Italian and French cities to mark the inauguration of similar projects in relation to the poor, beginning with the publication of *La Mendicité abolie par un bureau de charité à Toulouse*, Toulouse 1692. An English edition, entitled *Ways and Means for Suppressing Beggary and Relieving the Poor by Erecting General Hospitals, and Charitable Corporations* was also published in 1726.

[14] Such an interpretation is already proposed by the biographer of Victor Amadeus, A. Carutti, in his *Storia del regno di Vittorio Amedeo II*, Turin 1897, p. 460. It is taken up by G. Prato, *La Vita economica in Piemonte a mezzo del secolo XVIII*, Turin 1908, p. 332; G. Quazza, *Le Riforme in Piemonte nella prima metà del Settecento*, Modena 1957, p. 313 ff.; more recently by G. Symcox, *Victor Amadeus II. Absolutism in the Savoyard state, 1675–1730*, London 1983, pp. 199–200.

Table 6.1 *Inmates of the Ospedale di Carità by sex and occupation, 1713*

	M.	%	F.	%	Total M.&F.	%
Infirmary	35	10.0	58	11.2	93	10.7
Under sevens	27	7.7	72	13.9	99	11.4
Old and disabled	14	4.0	99	19.1	113	13.0
Pensioners	—	—	5	1.0	5	0.6
Various crafts	50	14.3	78	15.2	128	14.8
Woollen mill	112	32.1	58	11.2	170	19.6
Silk manufacture	2	0.6	84	16.2	86	9.9
Weaving	3	0.9	—	—	3	0.3
Farms	5	1.4	2	0.4	7	0.8
Royal silk mill	11	3.2	—	—	11	1.3
Services	85	24.4	49	9.5	134	15.5
Nurses	5	1.4	12	2.3	17	2.1
Total	349	100.0	517	100.0	866	100.0
Total at work	183	52.4	222	42.9	405	46.8
Total at work (including services)	273	78.2	283	54.7	556	64.2

Source: AST, sez. I, Luoghi Pii di quà dai Monti, m. 18, fasc. 5, *Tabella dei poveri esistenti all'Hospedale della Carità . . .*, 2 April 1713.

Let us take the case of Turin for the moment. The 1716–1717 measures did not bring 'reform' nor a 're-opening' of the Ospedale di Carità whose new headquarters, begun in 1683, were just being completed at that time. The volume of relief provided by the hospital and the state of its internal organization before the supposed reforms can be seen from a register of inmates compiled in 1713 (table 6.1). This shows that the institution housed over 800 inmates, all of whom were employed in the manufactures set up by the hospital, with the exception of the sick and disabled.[15] Figure 6.1 also indicates that the new edicts did not lead to a rise in numbers; if anything, there is a fall-off.

In practice, Victor Amadeus' orders only reinforced the mixed functions of relief and repression that the hospital already undertook in relation to the poor. A comparison between the Regulations of the hospital contained in the edicts of 1717 and a description of its activities

[15] Nor was this a highpoint. A few years earlier, in 1709, when the state had not yet recovered from the French invasion and the exhausting siege of the capital, the number of inmates had reached 1350 (AST, Sez. Riun., la archiv., Confraternite e Congregazioni, m. 1, fasc. 2, *Congregazioni per provvedere all'emergenza dello Spedale di Carità di Torino*, 1709).

drawn up in 1700 confirms the total continuity in the measures adopted towards the poor: that is, the combination of shelter for children, the old and the disabled and the weekly distribution of bread to families, with the expulsion and punishment of able-bodied persons caught begging.[16] The Minute Books, for their part, enable us to establish that these were practices undertaken by the hospital since its foundation in 1649.[17] Even before then, measures directed at the poor undertaken from the mid sixteenth century by the hospital of San Giovanni (and subsequently taken over by the municipal authorities) followed the same criteria. According to the first major plan for city poor-relief drawn up in 1541, the hospital of San Giovanni had the job of admitting 'orphans, the sick and the weak', while other categories of poor seen as deserving but able to survive on their own would receive a fixed quantity of bread and money each Sunday. Furthermore, begging was prohibited on penalty of 'being irremissibly whipped'.[18] From 1568 the provisions stipulated the expulsion from the city of beggars regarded as undeserving – a measure which, even if new to the city, brought to mind the orders expelling foreign beggars from the state already adopted in the fifteenth century.[19]

From then on numerous orders reaffirm the prohibition of begging and establish the arrest and examination of all beggars found in the city. There were a further four issued in the second half of the sixteenth century and at least another nineteen between 1601 and 1700.[20] They all

[16] See in particular clauses 1 and 2 of the *Deliberazione della congregazione dell'ospedale della carità di Torino*, 1 June 1700 in Duboin, *Raccolta*, vol. XII, p. 272; and p. 286 *passim* and the regulation included with the *Regio editto col quale Sua Maestà conferma l'erezione e le prerogative dell'ospedale della carità di Torino*, 17 April 1717.

[17] Archivio Ospedale di Carità (henceforth AOC), Cat. III, *Ordinati* 1664–1945.

[18] Archivio Storico del Comune di Torino (henceforth ACT), C.S. 657, *Regolamento del modo e governo della Congregazione dei Poveri nell'Ospedale di S. Giovanni di Torino*, 1 May 1541.

[19] See, for instance, *De mendicantibus validis et aliis otiosis et vagabundis*, 17 June 1430 in Borelli, *Editti*, p. 711; *Lettere di Sua Altezza colle quali nomina un cavaliere di virtù e di polizia per la città di Torino, con autorità di scacciare gli oziosi mendicanti*, 5 April 1568, in Duboin, *Raccolta*, vol. XII, p. 248.

[20] See the document dated 11 February 1571, in which the Duke accepted the supplications of the governors of the hospital of San Giovanni to create a post specifically for the expulsion of beggars (ACT, C.S, 3234). This was followed by a series of provisions undertaken by the city itself: ACT, *Ordinati*, 10 September 1586; Ibid., C.S. 4701, 1 August 1587; Borelli, *Editti*, pp. 228–9, 29 May 1592; ACT, *Ordinati* 13 December 1601, 29 June 1603, 1 November 1611, 9 August 1623; Duboin, *Raccolta*, vol. XII, p. 249: *Ordine di Sua Altezza*, 10 March 1627; Ibid., p. 254 for the plague, *Ordine del Magistrato di Sanità*, 27 November 1629 and *Ordine di Vittorio Amadeo I*, 15 June 1631. During the period of plague, civil war and its aftermath, there do not appear to have been further banning orders until the edict of 9 May 1650 (Borelli, *Editti*, p. 236). There followed the provisions of 11 January 1651, 20 August 1654, 20 March 1657, 30 March 1661, 1 April 1664, 24 September 1666, 8 January 1670, 31 March 1672, 4 February 1676 (ibid., p. 237ff.); ACT, *Ordinati* 29 November 1679, and *Ordine di Sua Altezza*, 5 July 1700 in Duboin, *Raccolta*, vol. XII, p. 277.

resemble one another, though they emanate from different authorities
(the governors of the hospital of San Giovanni, the Municipality, the
rectors of the new Ospedale di Carità, or the Duke himself). The only
points of difference relate to the penalties for recidivist beggars, for those
giving them lodgings and alms, and for gatekeepers at the city gates
responsible for allowing them entry.[21] Over the period, there is also some
oscillation in the relative importance attached to citizenship between the
poor deserving of relief and those to be expelled. Sometimes the banning
orders seem to be designed specifically for 'the poor from outside, of
which the city is full, so that the poor of Turin, already great in numbers,
shall not suffer!' On other occasions they seem to be more generally
directed against beggars who 'appear able to work and earn their
living'.[22] The differences in emphasis are probably connected to the
conflicts between the different authorities over the control of action
concerning the poor. It is clear, for example, that the longstanding
antagonism between the Duke and the Municipality comes out in the
conflict between the idea of charity open to all subjects and that of
charity reserved only for citizens. The 1716 edict, by establishing that
the poor were only to be given relief in the place where they had stable
residence (or what in the English system would have been called
'settlement'), restored full legitimacy to the requirement of citizenship as
the indispensable condition for receiving relief.

Seen in terms of continuity, the changes introduced by the new
provisions of 1716–17 seem marginal. They amounted to instructions to
exclude from poor relief children under seven ('so that the hospital does
not fill up with useless persons') and those with contagious diseases. In
addition, they laid down that the number of governors of the Ospedale di
Carità should be increased from thirty-one to thirty-five, but this
amendment did not alter the balance between the different centres of
power in the city which the Board of Governors reflected.[23] On the
administrative level too, far from marking a shift to state control of relief,
the edict confirmed the existing situation whereby the hospital was
dependent on the bodies that had founded it in 1649, leaving a mixed

[21] The penalties for recidivist beggars generally consisted of whipping, but sometimes prescribed
the shaving of their heads, a beating or imprisonment. Anyone giving lodgings or alms to beggars
was liable to various fines, and officers responsible for their repression who failed to carry out
orders were liable to loss of pay or removal from their post.
[22] ACT, *Ordinati* 11 November 1601 and *Lettere di Sua Altezza*, 5 April 1568.
[23] In reality, the distribution of the governors elected by the different bodies (eleven in all)
remained unchanged. These, in turn, had to nominate another twenty-four (previously twenty)
governors.

and uncentralized form of management typical of the running of city government. Not until the 1730s, with the introduction of a royal officer (the *Regio Protettore*) into the administration of the various institutions, did the central authority begin to lay claim to the control of poor relief. Nevertheless, the acknowledgement of the role of the state in the administration of poor relief would meet with a hostile response and would not take root until the second half of the century.[24]

The 1716–17 edicts are therefore in line with previous attitudes and measures related to the poor. Although these were seen as an expression of a new policy (largely repressive in nature) towards the poor, previous legislation and practices contained all the elements subsequently proposed in Victor Amadeus II's edicts. Rather, what was new was that for the first time a project was designed to cover the whole kingdom with a network of hospitals and Congregazioni di carità in every parish, and subordinated, since 1719, to a pyramidic structure of control emanating from the capital.[25] However, the centralization contained in this project should be looked at anew. Its formal unity does not correspond to a uniformity of criteria for provision, nor to a direct administration of the charities by the state. On the one hand the edict left ample space for local ideas and variations over time in the treatment of poverty. It only supplied very general guidance on the age-groups and categories to be given relief, acknowledging that the administrators of each institution had to adapt such criteria 'according to the needs of the poor and to the customs of the locality and its forms of government'. The latter included the age at which children were sent to work, the area's trades, and the income levels and forms of household and social organization which prevailed locally.[26] Even over the formation of the administrative bodies of the hospitals and congregations due to be set up, the new provisions

[24] For a reconstruction of the ongoing conflict that accompanied the centralizing process, see Cavallo, 'Charity'.

[25] Although a hierarchical structure had been spoken of from the outset, its features remained very vague in the earlier provisions. Not until 1719 did a Royal Edict establish the foundation of *congregazioni generali* in every province and what was called the *primaria generalissima* in the capital. According to the Regulations enclosed in the edict, the *congregazioni generali* had to obtain a statement of accounts every six months from each of the provincial congregations, which took the form of a specific questionnaire, and had to carry out an annual visit. The *congregazione generalissima*, apart from having responsibility for the province of Turin, had to intervene, on request, in aid of other congregations, though its supervisory duties remained completely undefined: *Editto Regio per lo stabilimento di una congregazione primaria e generalissima sopra gli ospizi e congregazioni di carità*, 20 July 1719, in Duboin, *Raccolta*, t. XII, p. 92.

[26] See in particular *Istruzioni degli Ospizi Generali dei Poveri. Parte Prima. Capo* III, clause 9 and *Capo* IV, clause 3.

showed the same respect for the different local structures of power, in that they established that their composition and scope should depend on 'the custom of the locality'. They also allowed that the guidelines on administrative procedures could be altered 'according to the necessities of time and place'.[27]

Victor Amadeus' edict, by recognizing the local bodies' direct administration of charity – that is, their selection of the poor deserving relief – and by making relief dependent on birth or long residence in an area, thus reaffirmed the traditional territorial unit – the Municipality – as the basis for poor relief. It should be noted that the local basis of charity – a key feature of its pre-industrial forms, in both Catholic and Protestant countries – was never called into question by the various laws reforming poor-relief. In fact, the local aspect was closely bound up with the possibility it offered of controlling and selecting the poor deserving of relief not just on the basis of an 'economic' idea of need, but also on less 'objective' criteria. It was this very power to select and, therefore, to carry through a policy of protection and patronage that was at the heart of the social significance attached to charity in *ancien régime* society. The giving and receiving of charity was not a bureaucratic action: it was a matter of benevolence, not a right but a favour, and it strengthened the ties of interdependence and obligation between individuals and often, indirectly, between social groups.

To accept this perspective on the crucial notion of local control in the workings of charity makes it possible to undertake a less literal-minded assessment of the significance of the measures outlawing begging, which recur throughout the history of European poor-relief. Although much emphasis has been placed on the role played by hospitals for the poor in the segregation and violent repression of begging, in Turin the detention of beggars seems to have remained marginal to the hospital's activities, growing in importance only during moments of crisis when the city was invaded by an influx of outsiders. The fact that the banning orders were re-issued in the city's most difficult moments is an initial sign that the repressive policies were occasional, and all but fell into disuse after their implementation during crises. The bans should be read not as permanent policy measures, but largely as warning signals aimed at the immigrant poor.

An analysis of the *Libri dei poveri presi a mendicare* (Registers of the poor

---

[27] Ibid., *Capo* I, clause 3, and *Capo* III, clauses 3 and 6.

Table 6.2 *Origin of beggars*

	Male	%	Female	%	Total	%
Beggars from Turin	117	9.2	102	15.9	219	11.5
Beggars from other places	1,154	90.8	538	84.1	1,692	88.5
Total	1,271	100.0	640	100.0	1,911	100.0

Source: G. Levi, *Centro e periferia di uno stato assoluto*, Turin 1985, p. 64.

Table 6.3 *Age of beggars arrested in Turin in 1740*

	Male	%	Female	%	Total	%
0–9	110	8.2	96	14.4	206	10.3
10–19	654	48.8	162	24.4	816	40.7
20–9	166	12.4	87	13.1	253	12.6
30–9	75	5.6	98	14.8	173	8.6
40–9	78	5.8	68	10.2	146	7.3
50–9	100	7.4	62	9.3	162	8.1
60–9	80	6.0	55	8.3	135	6.7
70–9	56	4.2	28	4.2	84	4.2
80+	22	1.6	9	1.3	31	1.5
Total	1,341	100.0	665	100.0	2,006	100.0

Source: G. Levi, *Centro e periferia di uno stato assoluto*, Turin 1985, p. 63.

detained begging) carried out for the year 1740, throws light on how those detained were largely from outside Turin, where almost all of them had only arrived a few days before; furthermore, they were mostly males, aged 10 to 29 (see tables 6.2, 6.3).[28]

They were the very opposite of the classes looked upon with favour by the hospital. The annual report on the inmates voluntarily admitted in the period 1750–7 shows a considerable number of children and old people as opposed to other age groups and a marked prevalence of women (considering that at the time men outnumbered women by 5–9 per cent: table 6.4).

Moreover, the treatment of these two categories of poor differed markedly. Those arrested were only kept for a brief period in the hospital, and were discriminated against in comparison with other inmates; for example, they did not have the right to eat in the same

[28] G. Levi, *Centro e periferia di uno stato assoluto*, Turin 1985, p. 64.

Table 6.4 *Records of all inmates admitted to the Ospedale di Carità (1750–7)*

	1750	1751	1752	1753	1754	1755	1756	1757	Total	
									Number	%
Male										
0–6	1	1	3	2	—	—	4	—	11	1.1
7–12	62	59	77	32	26	41	47	34	378	37.6
13–15	21	12	21	20	4	12	13	14	117	11.7
16–60	40	25	35	11	20	11	15	15	172	17.1
60–90	58	45	54	33	27	23	42	38	320	31.8
Foundlings	—	—	2	—	—	2	2	1	7	0.7
Total inmates	182	142	192	98	77	89	123	102	1,005	100.0
At wet-nurse	28	16	14	12	11	13	31	19	144	—
Total on relief	210	158	206	110	88	102	154	121	1,149	—
Female										
0–6	1	5	2	1	—	—	2	—	11	1.0
7–12	54	44	49	32	35	31	44	43	332	29.6
13–15	16	14	15	13	5	8	19	9	99	8.8
16–60	39	37	29	27	28	35	46	21	262	23.3
60–90	71	48	66	58	36	40	45	34	398	35.4
Foundlings	4	1	6	4	—	—	2	4	21	1.9
Total inmates	185	149	167	135	104	114	158	111	1,123	100.0
At wet-nurse	18	12	11	13	12	10	19	26	121	—
Total on relief	203	161	178	148	116	124	177	137	1,244	—

Source: AST. sez. I, Luoghi Pii di quà dai Monti, m. 19, fasc. 24 (NB: in the document some age groups overlap).

refectory. They were then released, after signing a statement in which they undertook to return to their places of origin and desist from begging. Heavier penalties were provided for recidivists.

The detention of the poor, therefore, did not strike indiscriminately at all begging, which was an activity large sections of the population resorted to in moments of crisis. Rather, it seems to be a measure taken in certain periods to protect the local poor from unfair competition from outsiders who tended to reduce the available total of the city's charity. In the final analysis, it was a measure to protect the power of the authorities to control the process of assigning poor relief in their locality. The dividing-line between the 'deserving' and 'undeserving' poor was not so much decided on the basis of whether or not people begged. Rather it depended on whether they belonged to the local network of protection that dispensed charity to its own poor – since this allowed a control over distribution and over the social consequences (rewards) flowing from it.

It remains to explain the fate of the edicts of 1716–17 at the hands of historians. As I have indicated already, it seems largely to reflect the rhetoric which accompanied the issuing of the edicts that presented them as a radical work of reform conceived and executed by Victor Amadeus II. In fact, the publication of Guevarre's apologetic was just the last act of a huge publicity campaign surrounding the event. A panoply of celebrations accompanied the promulgation of the renewed provisions outlawing begging; we can only guess as to whether they influenced contemporaries in the way they did historical memory of the event. The Jesuits mobilized attention with a campaign of sermons in the city churches, and alms for the hospital were repeatedly collected from houses. The highpoint of the celebrations was the dramatic ceremony that took place in the spring of 1717. At midday on Wednesday 7 April the poor who were inmates of the hospital, all dressed in a new habit of blue cloth (bought with the proceeds of the third collection of alms) assembled at the cathedral, where they found all the confraternities of the city, each one represented by a flock of boys 'dressed in the guise of angels' and of 'girls adorned as virgins with crowns of flowers on their heads'. The poor processed in single file, each woman having at her side 'one of those virgins crowned with flowers', and each man 'an angel'. The women led the procession, followed by the men. The invalid poor unable to walk were carried on carts and were also accompanied by their angels. There followed six boy choristers dressed in red tunics, and behind them the priests and governors of the hospital, followed by 'a huge troop of the city poor who received bread from the hospital every Sunday'. The remainder of the procession was made up of the confraternities, religious communities and the canons of the Chapter. The procession made its way solemnly between spectators lining the streets to the city centre, terminating at the doors of the hospital where, from the pulpit next to the altar erected for the occasion, Father Guevarre delivered a sermon in which he exhorted the people to give thanks to God, the King and the charity of the clergy, the magistrates and the nobility for their support for the holy work.

The second part of the ceremony then took place. The poor left the hospital in the same order and reached nearby Piazza Castello, at the centre of which were laid six long lines of tables, three for the men and, at some distance, three for the women. All the tables faced the windows of the palace from which the royal family would have been able to watch the spectacle. Here, to the sound of trumpets, the poor were served a meal by the pages of the court and the maids of honour, under the direction of gentlemen and ladies. A line of 200 soldiers enclosed the 'theatre' or piazza, holding back the crowd. At the end of the meal, it was time for the ritual thanksgiving with the poor singing in chorus orations they had learned in the hospital to the good health of the King.[29]

Although executed with greater pomp, the ceremony of April 1717, with its procession and involvement of the clergy and authorities, recalls the earlier ones which had accompanied the opening of the first and second Ospedale di Carità in 1627 and 1649. Yet that of 1717 marked no new foundation. Even the first part, the solemn gathering of all the poor in a place in the city noted for its symbolic or sacred character (the cathedral, the hospital of San Giovanni, or the town hall square) was no innovation. The same rite, aimed at celebrating the solicitude of the city institutions towards their poor and at symbolizing their ability completely to overcome the problem of poverty, had been re-enacted on other occasions to mark the issuing of orders banning begging.[30] However, a new location, Piazza Castello in front of the royal palace, now acquired a crucial importance in the proceedings, and the monarch became the focal point of the celebration. While on previous occasions the sovereign and members of the royal family took part in similar ceremonies simply occupying the place of honour in the procession in front of the clergy, they now occupied a space that was distant and on a higher plane, that was exclusive to them. More than that, the ceremony gave the appearance of being arranged in homage to the royal family.

The reason for attaching so much importance to the edicts of 1717 banning begging, which were really revised versions of old measures, must therefore be found in the desire to construct an event celebrating the monarchy and its reforms. It is necessary to bear in mind that these years marked a turning point in the history of the Savoy dynasty. Following the happy outcome of the negotiations of the Peace of Utrecht in 1713, the house of Savoy had come out stronger in terms not only of territory and power but of status.[31] It represented the only Italian state acknowledged as an interlocutor and courted as an ally by the great

---

[29] The outline of the ceremony and the quotations come from Guevarre, *La Mendicità sbandita*.

[30] The first of the general provisions dealing with the poor of the city in 1541 was already marked by a solemn ceremony in which all the poor were assembled at the cathedral; see ACT, *Regolamento del modo e governo*.

[31] For a recent treatment of these events, see G. Symcox, *Victor Amadeus II*.

powers. The attribution of the title of king, granted for the first time to a sovereign of the house of Savoy, amounted to recognition of the new respect in which the state was held on the international scene.[32] Thus, during the years in which the measures towards the poor were taken, Victor Amadeus was going through a crucial period for the construction of his own prestige as sovereign and for the projection of an image of stability based on his own power and on the organization of the state. The way in which such initiatives were presented undoubtedly contributed to underlining the crucial importance of the monarchy and its ability to shape the future. The work of Guevarre betrays such a purpose by its constant apologetics for the 'Supreme Monarch', Victor Amadeus, and his reforms, as does the language of the edicts which lays great stress on the rhetoric of renewal.

However, as we have seen, these affirmations have a propagandistic ring to them. The year 1717 may be considered a key date that marks the beginning in various parts of the state administration of the major work of reform and centralization through which Victor Amadeus would turn the state of Savoy into one of the most efficient absolute monarchies in Europe.[33] Nonetheless, analysis of the 'new' measures taken in relation to the poor invites us to reflect on the broad ideological function that the launching of reform plans could hold at this time.

Even the part of the reforms that seems most original, namely the measures to establish a unitary system of poor relief for the state as a whole, is in need of further analysis in the light of the political events of the period and the aspiration of the sovereign to put himself on the same plane as the leading European monarchs. Everyone agrees that Victor Amadeus' ambitious scheme of unifying the relief system was a failure. In 1723, six years after its inauguration, the Congregazioni established were few in number and anyway existed only on paper, since they were in no state to operate effectively.[34] However, I would maintain that the failure

---

[32] The two treaties had secured for Victor Amadeus the restoration of the territories of Nice and Savoy that had been occupied by the French, the recognition of his rule over the Monferrato area which had been contested for some time, and the acquisition of territory in Lombardy and of the kingdom of Sicily.

[33] See in particular Quazza, *Le Riforme*, vol. I, p. 55. Nevertheless, analyses which attribute to Victor Amadeus II success in being the first to start reorganizing the state have been queried by the work of L. Bulferetti; see, for example, his 'Assolutismo e mercantilismo nel Piemonte di Carlo Emanuele II', in *Memorie dell'Accademia delle Scienze di Torino*, series 3, vol. II, 1953, and E. Stumpo, *Finanza e stato moderno nel Piemonte del Seicento*, Rome 1979.

[34] Prato, *La Vita economica*, p. 334.

cannot be imputed merely to the inertia or resistance by the local authorities in the face of central directives. It also derived from weaknesses inherent in the measures. The vagueness of instructions made them difficult to carry out. In fact, if looked at carefully, the May 1717 edict which established the Congregazioni can be shown to be an exercise in propaganda, a manifesto of the absolute monarch proclaiming his centralizing aspirations, rather than a piece of legislation designed to be acted on. In the first place, the definition of the territorial unity in which the new structures would arise seems quite unclear. There are generalizations such as 'all the lands and places' of the state, but sometimes 'communities' are mentioned and at other times 'parishes'. Only later would it become apparent that the parish was the basic territorial unit. There are also contradictions in the definition of the centres in which the higher *Congregazioni generali* were to be set up. In 1717 the diocesan seat was referred to, whereas in 1719 it was the provincial capital. It is unclear, moreover, exactly who was responsible for acting on the sovereign's orders and overseeing their implementation. Doubt hangs over the financing of the new institutions. They were due to take over the funds for poor relief belonging to the local *opere pie* (hospitals, confraternities and other bodies) and to administer them according to the new directives. Such an operation, of course, could not be as painless and easy as the edict would have it, given that it meant abolishing many local centres of influence and prestige.

The edict was limited, therefore, to projecting an image or utopian prospect. The fact that it was issued undoubtedly created a climate favourable to a series of local initiatives, but these were often of a different order from those vaguely sketched in the reforms.[35] Not until the second half of the eighteenth century, when the management of poor relief fell more or less under the direct control of state officers, did the centralizing pressures gain the upper hand. From the 1760s onwards, the reinforcement of the relief organizations based on the territorial principles of the state gathered momentum, though without achieving the systematic changes envisaged by the 1717 legislation.[36]

---

[35] A. Torre, 'Il Consumo di devozioni: rituali e potere nelle campagne piemontesi nella prima metà del Settecento', *Quaderni Storici*, 58, 1985, pp. 207–11.

[36] Such developments consisted above all in the erection of new *Ospedali di Carità* in towns of the provinces; see P. Chierici and L. Palmucci, 'Gli Ospizi di Carità in Piemonte. Appunti per la lettura del fenomeno insediativo', in E. Sori (ed.), *Città e controllo sociale*, Milan 1982.

Patterns of poverty and patterns of relief

From the requests for relief made by the poor and the help they subsequently received or were denied, it is possible broadly to reconstruct the criteria informing choices and, thereby, to identify the notions of poverty applied to the population of those thought worthy of charity. The Registers (*Libri delle informazioni*), surviving from 1742 onwards, record the following: descriptions of the families or single poor persons who had resort to the hospital; the type of relief provided, or the reasons for withholding it; all the variations in the amount and forms of aid accorded following the changing situation of a family (births, deaths and departures of its members), in those cases where the receipt of charity was more than fleeting; the various terminations and renewals of contact with the institution. In other words, this source is no ordinary one, and affords the possibility, on occasions, of following the history of certain families and their relationships to public charity over a period of years. The requests presented to the Ospedale di Carità have been analysed for the years 1743, 1753, 1763, 1773 and 1783, making it possible to follow the changes in the composition of the applicants and in the forms of relief over a period of forty years.[37] It has to be borne in mind that the data that will be examined do not refer to all the poor assisted by the Ospedale, but only to new suppliants, whose connection with the hospital began in that year. The way in which the Registers were compiled makes it impossible to arrive at a 'horizontal' overview of the hospital's activities, as the measures to assist individual families were always registered in the book in which the family is described in the year when it made its first application to the hospital. The total number of poor who received assistance was considerably larger than the numbers in our tables, and the difference between the numbers of 'new' and 'old' poor became particularly marked in the last decades.

The requests for charity sometimes mention a particular form of provision – admission to the hospital, wet-nursing for the new-born, the weekly distribution of bread. However, they are more often generic – 'they ask for some aid' – entrusting themselves to the judgement of the Board of Governors. It is worth noting, moreover, that the granting of

[37] AOC, cat. IV, *Libri delle Informazioni*, 1742–1865. An interesting comparison can be made with the work of S.J. Woolf on Florence in the nineteenth century, which uses a similar source: S.J. Woolf, *The Poor in Western Europe in the Eighteenth and Nineteenth Centuries*, London–New York 1986.

charity was partly decided on the outcome of bargaining between the parties. The petitioners had, in fact, to go in person to the hospital, bringing with them the family in its entirety before a select committee of governors. This body then ascertained the gravity of their situation, on the basis, obviously, of the emotional impressions engendered by the suppliants, not to mention the verification of the testimonials presented. Such was the context – a far cry from a neutral encounter of suppliants and charity administrators – in which were compiled the family records, which provided the basis for decisions taken by the Board of Governors in its twice-weekly full sittings.

The records, compiled according to fixed conventions, contain the information thought necessary for assessing the need for relief. Apart from the name, this includes the marital status, age, trade and place of birth of every member of the family or single person (and, in the case of those born elsewhere, the length of residence in Turin); then, the type of infirmity given as reason for temporary inability to work, or the motive for the absence of the head of the family, and hence for a crucial missing source of income. Furthermore, the records provide details of residence (parish, neighbourhood and house) that allowed checks to be made through the parish priest or neighbour, should there be grounds for suspicion. Lastly, they invariably record the declaration to the effect that the person is without means ('without goods or chattels'). This information, recorded in each case according to a conventional formula, is all there is on the economic conditions of the group resulting from the enquiries into a family's situation. The governors did not, in fact, seem to worry about ascertaining the differences in income, depending on a person's trade, that existed between the people asking for charity. Nor did they enquire about the modest property which the suppliants sometimes held in their villages of origin (evidence of which occasionally appears in the inmates' requests for temporary permission to go and sort out their affairs). While close scrutiny was kept of claims concerning place of birth and residence and the number of children – all of which had to be documented with certificates and testimonials (from the parish priest, doctor or surgeon and sworn witnesses) – no questions or enquiries went into a suppliant's income, economic situation or estate.

To begin with, consideration of appeals for relief at the Ospedale di Carità depended on whether the suppliant was a domiciled resident. Lack of the requisite qualifications was the first reason for being denied any poor relief. It is true that the institution's system for processing claims was not waterproof. The suppliant had to show his *fede di battesimo* (certificate of baptism) as evidence of being born in Turin; in the case of a family, it was sufficient for a man or his wife or their children over the age of three to be born in Turin (since this was the minimum period entitling a person to a residence qualification). Obviously, to be born in the city could be a matter of chance rather than evidence of having settled there. However, an analysis of the places of origin of the families in receipt of relief shows that these groups were either from the city or long-established inhabitants. Of the latter, about half of the children born in Turin had at least one parent born in the city. Furthermore, even among the immigrant couples, the majority of children, not only the youngest, were born in Turin, testifying to the duration (usually more than ten years) and continuity of residence in the city of those asking for poor relief.

The Ospedale di Carità thus proves to be an inward-looking institution, concerned more with protecting those settled in the city than with attracting outsiders. Although the existence of charitable institutions has often been identified as one of the factors which explain the influx of people into urban centres in periods of crisis, the Turin case indicates that little help was actually given to such immigrants. Analysis of the distribution of appeals for charity relief does not reveal significant upswings for the months when seasonal migration to the city was at its height.[38]

Naturally, there was frequent abuse of the regulations governing the distribution of relief, and hence the validity of statements (and even documents) about a suppliant's origins should not automatically be taken at face value. However, the instances of fraud most often denounced mainly concern family size. The numbers were often doctored by omitting to mention the death of a child or a husband's return, whereas the falsification of *fedi di domicilio* (testimonial of residence) provided by the parish priest, an altogether more difficult and costly operation, was a relatively rare occurrence.[39]

---

[38] Immigration brought on by hardship, originating above all in the Alpine valleys of the dioceses of Saluzzo, Mondovì and Alba, peaked in November and March (i.e. the beginning and end of winter). The lowpoints were in July and August. This immigration should be distinguished from that providing the capital with manpower always on a seasonal basis; see n. 40 and also Levi, *Centro e periferia*, pp. 58–67.

[39] In the five annual samples examined, I only found one case in which falsification of the testimonial from the parish was uncovered. Instead, checks among neighbours carried out during the annual inspection of households in June often revealed that recipients of relief presented other people's children in place of their own who had died.

The very committing of abuses is, it should be added, tied to a knowledge of and skill in dealing with the urban environment which could only spring from genuine city roots. That is to say, the very lack of qualifications for relief increased the importance of having dependable relationships and sources of support in the city which could provide the cover and back-up needed to tap the charities. Thus the person who was 'deserving of charity' was someone who had roots and was protected; he was not someone marginal to urban society and ignorant of its ways. The crucial factor dividing the favoured from the excluded was their integration into the urban protective network, rather than regular residence in the city – this is the real significance of the principle of citizenship in terms of social relations. Thus it is possible to see the recipients of poor-relief as potentially including not only those entitled to it by the charity statutes, but those 'impermanent' immigrants for whom the relationship to the city had a crucial role in their strategy for survival. The latter constituted a population that gravitated around Turin on a regular basis, while retaining their residence and interests in their village of origin; they could, in consequence, rely both on ties with a parish neighbourhood, and on channels of support within the city.[40]

More generally speaking, the fact that the rights to relief of the poor were ascertained via a strict adherence to information and testimonies gathered in their social environment underlines the value attached in the definition of poverty to belonging to a body, or simply to a social network. This principle of selection, much more than economic or moral considerations, informed the initial process whereby the deserving poor were identified. Moreover, it took place largely outside the hospital and beyond the sphere of intervention of the Board of Governors.

Within the framework of classification of the poor based on citizenship, the institution operated a further set of distinctions. A key consideration for assessing the degree of poverty was the proportion of producers to consumers in a family unit, or, for the single person, whether he or she was fit enough to work for a living. This calculation of need also gives us a definition of what was considered a 'family': that is, the extent of the rights and duties that bound relatives together, the role

---

[40] Giovanni Levi has shown how certain Piedmontese and Lombard villages would be emptied of adult males for several months every year when they moved to the capital to work. These men were concentrated in certain occupations, such as builders, carpenters and wine-carriers, fulfilling the role of a kind of 'appendix to the urban population': Levi, *Centro e periferia*, pp. 50–7.

and economic value of each member, and the age- and sex-thresholds marking the 'strong' or 'weak' producer and consumer.

It is immediately apparent from the information requested that reciprocity of responsibilities within a family unit was not extended beyond the nucleus composed of parents and children 'in their charge'. The head-count does not include adolescents already engaged in some activity (usually apprenticeship in a trade typically commencing when a child was between nine and twelve years old), nor those over the age of fourteen without an occupation. Unless families could point to serious ill-health or disability, fourteen was the age threshold that the institution regarded as marking the children's independence from the family, though they were not in turn made responsible for its maintenance. In fact, the young apprentice was never, in the eyes of the hospital, a potential source of succour for his parents and brothers and sisters.[41]

The same principle of being able to provide for themselves through work was also applied to old people. Normally adult children, especially when married, did not take on the burden of responsibility for aged parents, and the latter were systematically registered as single, or as a couple, once the children had set up a family of their own. Moreover, although the old people who asked for admittance to the hospital were frequently not without close relations, and often had married children in the city, the institution did not apply pressure for them to be maintained, nor make enquiries about the children's situation. Even in the rare cases where they lived in the same household, adolescents and old people were considered as economically independent of the family unit's subsistence requirements.

This image of the family embodied in the institution's assessments corresponds closely to the household structures typical of families who turned to charity. In fact, the requests for relief regularly present units made up exclusively of parents and (mainly infant) children. There were few children of working age living with their families (even if fathers of mature age were well represented) and rarer still was the presence of old people of the generation prior to that of the head of the family. Furthermore, there is a complete absence of multiple family households.

---

[41] Such attitudes reflect, in addition, the nature of the apprenticeship contracts. In Turin, the apprentice did not receive payments in cash (except sometimes the odd sum towards the end), but the master was obliged to provide board and lodging. In some instances, it appears that families had to pay the master to accept an apprentice. In any case, a tax of about two lire was paid to the guild of the craft.

The family as an economic unit seems to have had a very short life-span. Characterized by the early departure of the children and the autonomy of the newly established family unit, it gave no protection for a long period of a person's life-cycle when the individual had to provide for himself.

I am suggesting here that the characteristics of the population seeking relief reflect to a large extent those generally affecting the structure of the family common to the Turin working classes. Obviously this statement needs to be substantiated by further investigation based on different sources. However, it must be pointed out that there are no clues suggesting that, instead of mirroring the patterns of survival of poor people in the city, the composition of people seeking relief was influenced by the institution's own preferences. This view is also supported by the fact that we are dealing here with all the poor applying for relief (many of whom would be rejected), and not only with those already selected and granted relief by the hospital. If this hypothesis is correct, the high number of requests for poor relief presented by single individuals – a large and often greater percentage of the total than that of families (tables 6.5 and 6.6) – would reflect a social phenomenon, not just a concentration of extreme cases. As testified by the number of authorizations of absence granted by the institution (usually for a period of a few months), those admitted on an individual basis – widows, old people, young unmarried – often had roots in the city and strong family ties.[42] It was not lack of ties or social support but the very cycle of subsistence of the poor urban family that swelled the ranks of 'single people' asking for relief. The institution's different kinds of provision did not, therefore, appear to have been addressed to marginal groups and exceptional cases only. Instead, they tended to correct imbalances produced by the household and subsistence arrangements normal to extensive sections of the urban population.

---

[42] Some examples of authorizations; 'Angela Catarina Prina, aged 70, absence of 15 days to assist her daughter', 'Pietro Bernardi, aged 70, 2 months to visit his daughter at Borgo di Po [a *quartiere* of the city]'; or 'Margarita Derocha, aged 16, 25 days for holidays (*per andare a vacanza*)'.

The authorizations are sometimes recorded in the *Libri delle Informazioni* at the foot of the description of the person or family assisted and of the type of relief. They were also recorded separately in the *Libri delle licenze temporanee* (Books of temporary permissions), only existing for the period 1768–93. This latter source (which I suspect is not complete) shows the dimensions of the phenomenon: for example, 390 permissions were listed in 1769, 381 in 1770, 369 in 1779, 459 in 1780, 359 in 1789, 254 in 1790 (in the same years the overall number of inmates in the hospital grew from about 1700 to 1900). The permissions are for a maximum of one to two months (80 per cent of the total) and show a marked seasonality, coinciding with the summer months.

Table 6.5 *Requests for relief according to type of suppliant*

Type of suppliant	1743	1753	1763	1773	1783
Family with children: family-head under 50	72	62	90	218	216
Family with children: family-head over 50	37	15	24	80	61
Couples without children: family-head under 50	4	1	1	8	7
Couples without children: family-head over 50	9	10	21	43	41
Single old persons	65	86	70	166	154
Orphans and foundlings	85	48	29	61	32
Disabled adults	32	24	20	36	45
Total	304	246	255	612	556

Table 6.6 *Requests for relief by families and single individuals*

	Families						Singles		Overall total	
	With children		Without children		Total					
	Number	%	Number	%	Number	%	Number	%	Number	%
1743	109	35.8	13	4.3	122	40.1	182	59.9	304	100.0
1753	77	31.3	11	4.5	88	35.8	158	64.2	246	100.0
1763	114	44.7	22	8.6	136	53.3	119	46.7	255	100.0
1773	298	48.7	51	8.3	349	57.0	263	43.0	612	100.0
1783	277	49.8	48	8.6	325	58.4	231	41.6	556	100.0

Let us now look in detail at the considerations underlying the granting of poor-relief to families, before looking at provision for single individuals. A family deserved poor-relief when two conditions coexisted: on the one hand, the sickness, death or absence of the head of household (due to imprisonment, flight from debt, temporary migration, or, for soldiers, departure for war) that prevented work and hence contributions to the family budget; on the other hand, the responsibility of the parents for several very young children. However, a distinction over responsibility for subsistence was made between the man and the woman. When the head of household was a woman, the existence of more than one 'young charge' was already held to be serious and deserving of charity, whereas the widower only benefited from charity where the family was numerous. Women's ability to maintain the family was always regarded as weaker than the men's, even if in most instances the women stated that they had an occupation.

Once an imbalance between breadwinners and the mouths to be fed had been established, the hospital intervened, granting different kinds of relief according to the age of the children: wet-nursing for the new-born and the weakly and sick among the already weaned;[43] removal of one or more children, if aged between seven and fourteen, from those still at home; provision of bread when children of large families were not old enough to leave home. The relief provided was often a combination of different types (for example, wet-nursing for one child, and the removal of another), and changed, above all, with the family cycle. The forms of provision became more complex in the later eighteenth century: the higher proportion of combinations of forms of relief points to the longer-term commitment of the hospital to the family. Moreover, the practice of distributing bread seems to vary over time, becoming more regular and continuous in the last decades of the century. In the previous period, bread was rarely given, and then only as a temporary measure covering children under seven (the minimum age of admittance). In the first two samples analysed (1743 and 1753), bread remained a grant for young children only, who were recipients of three to four libbre of bread per week.[44]

The admittance of children to the hospital was one of the most usual kinds of provision and, in the first decades under consideration, involved 70 to 75 per cent of families receiving relief. Apart from the much publicized situation of foundling children, who were abandoned anonymously and in most instances definitively (a phenomenon mainly involving outsiders and irregular unions), for whom responsibility was assumed by the Ospedale San Giovanni, this practice of entrusting legitimate children to the Ospedale di Carità for a limited period involved numbers almost equal to those of the foundlings.[45]

[43] The babies were sent to the Canavese, a semi-mountainous area about 50 to 70 kilometres from Turin. They were kept for up to two years, while the older children remained for a few years, until the healthy air of the area strengthened them.

[44] One libbra was the equivalent of 0.369 grammes. It is interesting to note that, from the 1760s, the amount of bread assigned was no longer calculated in libbre but in 'portions' (one 'portion' equalled two libbre, or 0.738 grammes), a measurement more convenient after the extension of bread provision to the older children which took place in this period.

[45] On the relief of foundlings in Turin, see F. Doriguzzi, 'I messaggi dell'abbandono: bambini esposti a Torino nel 700', and S. Cavallo, 'Strategie politiche e familiari intorno al baliatico. Il monopolio dei bambini abbandonati nel Canavese tra Sei e Settecento', both in *Quaderni Storici*, 53, 1983.

The fact that children were not admitted to the hospital until the age of seven provides a clue as to what must have been done with them. If fourteen was the age-ceiling on family dependence, seven seems to be the age at which children were thought capable of working and going into service. As the regulations themselves state, the hospital accepted them when they could already be of use, and employed them for the most basic tasks in its manufactories. According to a document of 1758 on the occupations of inmates, 170 children aged seven to twelve (out of a total work-force of 921) took part in the hospital's work.[46] The majority were spinners and worked in the woollen ateliers, others worked in the hospital as cleaners, while girls also made stockings by hand and sewed cloth. The jobs are similar to those that children were able to help with at home, often working with the mother who was herself a seamstress or spinner, or with parents who were artisans. In fact, in the few instances in which the family rejected the admittance to the hospital of children, stress was placed on their usefulness as helpers to their mother ('the daughter is of a certain assistance to her mother, a seamstress'; 'the small daughter tends the little ones'; and so on). The unit of the poor urban family fits into an economic structure in which the children, prior to being sent to learn a trade, often played an allotted role.

The hospital offered households temporary respite by admitting children aged between seven and fourteen. In many cases, when the crisis was a passing one, they were taken back by the parents after a year or two. More frequently, however, the family left the hospital with the burden of maintaining them until they were able to earn their own living. Finally, the very weak and sick were sometimes kept in the institution after the age of fourteen, as were some of the girls not placed in service or found a partner in marriage, benefiting from one of the seven dowries at the hospital's disposition every year.[47] Some of the children entrusted to the hospital remained all their lives in the charge of the institution. However, admittance did not usually preclude continual contacts between children and their families. As the authorizations of absence show, they carried on playing a part in the household: 'authorization for Rosalia aged nine [an inmate for the past two years] to go for three months to her mother at Villafranca'; 'to go to her mother for a year to learn tailoring [aged eleven, an inmate already for four years]';

[46] AST, Sez. I, Luoghi Pii di quà dai Monti, m. 19, fasc. 24, *Stato generale* 1758.
[47] See S. Cavallo, 'Assistenza femminile e tutela dell'onore nella Torino del XVIII secolo', *Annali della Fondazione Einaudi*, 14, 1980, pp. 127–55.

'Giuseppe Ludovico [aged eleven, an inmate already for three years] to go to his father, a pedlar'.

Only some, therefore, of the considerable number of inmates aged from seven to fourteen were orphans. Crucial to the hospital's activities was its support for family strategies. This can be seen once more in the support given to women who remarried: infants from the first marriage were taken 'in deposit' once the second marriage was concluded. This was normal practice, which allowed young widows, whose extremely weak economic position and inability to maintain their own children was acknowledged, to set up new livelihoods.

If we look instead at the cases of single individuals requesting poor-relief, we can see that for orphans and children without a father, fourteen remained the age marking the threshold of independence and hence the age limit on admittance to the hospital. Above that age, admittance was only granted if they could show evidence of a serious and incurable infirmity that disqualified them from working (physical disability, blindness, insanity). So the category of the 'disabled adult' includes only those aged fourteen to forty-nine who asked for admittance to the hospital. The majority were unmarried persons, cut off from their family, who had to provide for their own subsistence. Their not inconsiderable number (see table 6.6) is likely to reflect the importance in the city's population structure of unmarried individuals of working age who lived on their own resources – a phenomenon also produced by the life-cycle of the urban family and the early age at which children had to fend for themselves.

The charitable activities of the hospital seem, therefore, to interact closely with the forms of subsistence of wide sections of the city poor, meeting the needs of those groups left unprotected. Again, this can be seen in the high proportion of old people admitted, especially women. Their status as solitary individuals, which has already been noted, is confirmed by their almost total absence from the family records. Old people are here understood as those over fifty, because this was the youngest age mentioned as a reason for not being able to maintain oneself ('infirmity of age'). However, few people in their fifties requested admittance. The age group best represented in all the periods under consideration was the over-70s (table 6.7). Furthermore, age itself was no guarantee for receiving relief: the old person normally had to show himself incapable of work due to some other infirmity. Only on rare occasions did old age give rise to such marked feebleness as to be

Table 6.7 *Requests for relief by single old people, and refusals, according to age and sex*

Age	Sex	1743		1753		1763		1773		1783	
		Req.	Ref.	Req.	Ref.	Req.	Ref.	Req.	Ref.	Req.	Ref.
50–4	M	3	—	—	—	2	—	8	3	4	2
	F	1	—	3	1	7	5	3	1	12	4
	Total	4	—	3	1	9	5	11	4	16	6
55–9	M	4	—	—	—	4	—	9	3	10	5
	F	5	—	8	1	5	1	17	5	18	4
	Total	9	—	8	1	9	1	26	8	28	9
60–4	M	4	—	9	1	3	—	12	—	8	4
	F	5	1	11	1	9	1	31	10	21	5
	Total	9	1	20	2	12	1	43	10	29	9
65–9	M	1	—	6	—	9	—	10	1	14	2
	F	7	1	10	1	4	1	27	3	19	—
	Total	8	1	16	1	13	1	37	4	33	2
70+	M	16	—	11	1	13	2	15	2	13	2
	F	20	—	28	1	14	1	34	5	35	2
	Total	36	—	39	2	27	3	49	7	48	4
All ages	M	28	—	26	2	31	2	54	9	49	15
	F	38	2	60	5	39	9	112	24	105	15
	Total	66	2	86	7	70	11	166	33	154	30

Notes:
Req. = Requests
Ref. = Refusals

accepted as sufficient reason in itself. Thus, the person's trade was often given ('formerly a cobbler'; 'formerly a coachman'), and sometimes two consecutive occupations were mentioned; the latter was usually less skilled and demanding than the former, suggesting a shift to a simpler and less well-paid job, requiring less physical strength. Nonetheless, it assured self-sufficiency, at least up to a certain point ('formerly a stocking weaver, now sells used goods'; 'he worked in the country and then was a servant to various people, now infirm').[48] The loss of skill

---

[48] For similar suggestions for early modern England, about the independence of the elderly and their continued relationship to work while still capable of it, see M. Pelling, 'Old people and Poverty in Early Modern England', *Society for the Social History of Medicine*, bulletin no. 34, 1984.

perhaps partly explains the lack of consideration shown old persons in terms of the urban family's subsistence. The stereotype that portrays old age as a condition of dependence on public charity or the modern welfare state peculiar to contemporary society needs to be corrected, at least in relation to pre-industrial urban society.[49]

The fate of old people differed, however, according to whether they were male or female. The man had greater opportunities for maintaining his independence through remarriage to a woman younger than himself. The high number of married couples in which the age difference in the man's favour often exceeded twenty years (table 6.8) shows how frequent must have been men's repeated recourse to marriage as a means of establishing an equilibrium in their mode of subsistence, even if the motive which pushed the second young wife to this sort of marriage requires further investigation. The obligations created by the marriage bond were much stronger than those acknowledged between adult children and parents. This is evident from the hospital's refusal to admit the elderly and infirm when there was a younger wife still able to work and without infant children.

On the other hand, the situation of women made them more likely to be recipients of charity relief. The number of women requesting admittance was much greater than that of men, as was the number that usually obtained it (table 6.7). Old age for women was distinctly more solitary, even if there was a slight tendency for children of working age to continue living with their mother in family units where the head of household was a widow.[50]

This analysis of the requests for poor-relief and the hospital's charitable activities throws light on the demographic, economic and living arrangements through which, at different stages of their lives, the poor faced the problem of subsistence. The interventions of the institution seem to have taken into account a number of situations. These include:

---

[49] See R.M. Smith, 'The Structured Dependency of the Elderly as a Recent Development: Some Sceptical Historical Thoughts', *Ageing and Society*, 4:4, 1984, pp. 409–28; D. Thomson, 'Welfare and the Historians', in L. Bonfield, R.M. Smith and K. Wrightson (eds.), *The World We Have Gained*, Oxford 1986; K.D. Snell and J. Millar, 'Lone-Parent Families and the Welfare State: Past and Present', *Continuity and Change*, 2:3, 1987, pp. 387–422.

[50] The lack of studies of the sex and age structure of the city population prevents us from ascertaining whether the phenomenon of the solitary older woman was due to the greater number of women than men of this age as opposed to variations in their opportunities to remarry. For the position of solitary women in pre-industrial society see the article contained in section C ('La femme seule') of *Annales de Démographie Historique*, 1981; O. Hufton, 'Women without Men: Widows and Spinsters in Britain and France in the Eighteenth Century', *Journal of Family History*, 9:4, 1984, pp. 355–76.

Table 6.8 *Age differences in couples with a partner over 50 years*

		Years							Total	More than	More than
Year	Sex[a]	0–5	6–10	11–15	16–20	21–5	26–30	30–40+	No.	10 years	20 years
1743	M.	4	2	3	8	4	7	6	34	28	17
	F.	—	—	—	—	—	—	—	—	—	—
1753	M.	4	4	3	2	4	—	2	19	11	6
	F.	1	2	1	—	—	—	—	4	1	—
1763	M.	17	8	8	6	5	2	1	47	22	8
	F.	3	2	1	—	—	—	—	6	1	—
1773	M.	18	15	20	12	12	2	4	83	50	18
	F.	6	3	1	—	—	—	—	10	1	—
1783	M.	10	22	10	15	2	5	4	68	36	11
	F.	6	4	4	—	1	—	—	15	5	1

Note:
[a] Sex of older partner

the family unit, based on the wages of two adults, plus the small children's contributions to their work; the independence of the young servant or apprentice; the remarriage of the man; the concomitant abandonment of the children by the woman on her remarriage; and, finally, the relatively early solitude of the widow. Charitable intervention did not, therefore, appear to be limited to extreme cases of isolation or marginalisation, but interacted with the different stages of the urban family's cycle.[51] As a consequence, the main form of relief provided – admission to the hospital – does not seem to have had negative connotations for the poor. Admission, contrary to what is often maintained, was neither forced nor entailed segregation. Regular exchanges and contacts were maintained between inmates and their milieu. The inmate was not lost to the family group. Moreover, admission to the hospital was not a measure extraneous to the practices adopted by the

---

[51] For similar considerations of the English case, see T. Wales, 'Poverty, Poor Relief and the Life-Cycle: Some Evidence from Seventeenth-Century Norfolk', in R.M. Smith (ed.), *Land, Kinship and Life-Cycle*, Cambridge 1984; R.M. Smith, 'Transfer Incomes, Risk and Security: The Roles of the Family and the Collectivity in Recent Theories of Fertility Change', in D. Coleman and R. Schofield (eds.), *The State of Population Theory, Forward from Malthus*, London 1986. Similar remarks about Florence in the nineteenth century, in Woolf, *The Poor in Western Europe*, chapters 7 and 8.

urban family in its search for an equilibrium. As we have seen, the family life of the poor was marked by continuous ruptures: the early departure of the children, the abandonment of the newly remarried mother, the independence of old people and the frequent long absences of the head of the family on account of work.[52] All these factors meant that the family identity was only slightly defined by the criterion of residence.

It is possible that forms of solidarity, contacts and shared strategies held together members of the same family who lived separately and who provided for themselves. However, it is certainly the case that representation of the family as the primary unit of subsistence and point of reference does not seem to hold for Turin.[53] On the contrary, my research indicates that the character of the life of the urban working classes was hardly family centred, but that forms of individual self-sufficiency were of an important and structural nature in pre-industrial societies.

Differences in status and in access to poor-relief

The criteria used by the institutions for deciding whom among the poor should receive relief seem, therefore, to be: membership of the city community, and the existence of exceptional circumstances (like physical weakness, or the death of a member of the family) that lessened the capacities of the individual or group, thereby worsening the living conditions of the family concerned. It is clear that the institution tended to conceive of poverty as a state of need brought about by accidental or 'natural' causes (widowhood, orphanage, illness, ageing) rather than by socially determined factors (like low salary or unemployment). Hence considerations of income and earning remained extraneous to the way in which the hospital examined the poor.

[52] The mobility of the workforce in Turin was not just an 'import' from outside but also affected the resident population. In particular, the migration of the artisans and servants on a seasonal basis or in moments of crisis represented a massive phenomenon. Silk workers, for instance, maintained a stable relationship with manufacturers in Lyons, to whom they turned for work when it was in short supply in Turin.

[53] The image of the family as the focal point of reciprocal obligations that has dominated social historical work for the last twenty years has been dented by recent studies, especially as regards the situation of old people. See Smith, 'The Structural Dependency'; Thomson, 'Welfare'. My study of Turin suggests that responsibilities were limited even in relation to children. For an approach that stresses the weakness of bonds between parents and children see also A. Macfarlane, *Marriage and Love in England. Modes of Reproduction, 1300–1840*, Oxford 1986. However, Macfarlane's claim about the uniqueness of the English case is often questionable.

The intervention of charity thus aimed to restore whatever was regarded as the standard of living in 'normal' times rather than in redistributing income. In fact, overlooking differences in earnings and in ownership of property, and assessing need solely on the grounds of declarations concerning sickness, deaths or births, meant that charity left the inequalities among the poor unaltered.

The adherence to a definition of poverty based on natural, not social causes of distress had a clear ideological significance. It reaffirmed the neutrality of the hospital's activities and underlined respect for a rigid idea of the social order in which everyone had an ascribed place and which could not be changed through welfare measures or by social policy. Charity was closely bound up with the hierarchies which divided the poor. We can see this in the difference in status accorded to various categories of the poor. The treatment reserved for poor 'citizens' (which have already been discussed) and the occupational identity of recipients of relief provide ample evidence. Specific occupations and sectors constantly recur, not, as we shall see, because they were the poorest, but because such groups enjoyed relatively dignified positions and protection.

If we look at the declared occupations of the heads of families who put forward requests for relief we find men of defined and respected trades, not the unskilled or those without a craft (table 6.9).[54] 'Artisans' (including masters in difficulty as well as journeymen) remain consistently the best represented, despite the variations across the period. In the category 'services' have been included a range of workers engaged in transport ('porters', 'carters', etc.), pedlars, ('vendors of fruit', 'vendors of *polenta*', 'of knick-knacks', etc.), not to mention female types of employment, such as 'seamstresses', or 'washerwomen'. It is a rather extended category, due also to the high proportion of women heads of family (between 40 and 50 per cent over the different periods), who figure more prominently in 'services' than in any other occupational group. The relative weight of the male share of service occupations ends up rather diminished, if we bear in mind that many 'seamstresses' or 'vendors' were actually the widows of artisans. We can conclude, therefore, that the families of artisans constituted the chief beneficiaries

---

[54] Table 6.9 provides the figures on occupations declared by male and female heads of families with children. Single people or couples without children are excluded because, in the presence of serious infirmity or inability to provide for themselves, consideration of their membership of particular occupational groups might have been less relevant.

Table 6.9 *Occupations of heads of families*

	1743		1753		1763		1773		1783	
	Number	%	Number	%	Number	%	Number	%	Number	%
Artisans	33	30.3	24	31.2	42	36.9	149	50.0	131	47.3
Services	26	23.9	24	31.2	28	24.6	54	18.1	51	18.4
Servants	11	10.1	11	14.2	20	17.5	33	11.1	43	15.5
Peasants	10	9.2	4	5.2	10	8.8	33	11.1	21	7.6
Soldiers	14	12.8	3	3.9	2	1.7	9	3.0	6	2.2
Traders	4	3.7	1	1.3	4	3.5	5	1.7	3	1.1
Professions	1	0.9	3	3.9	5	4.4	6	2.0	5	1.8
Beggars	1	0.9	1	1.3	1	0.9	—	—	2	0.7
Prisoners	—	—	1	1.3	—	—	1	0.3	—	—
Without occupation	1	0.9	1	1.3	—	—	5	1.7	—	—
Undeclared	8	7.3	4	5.2	2	1.7	3	1.0	15	5.4
Total	109	100.0	77	100.0	114	100.0	298	100.0	277	100.0

of the Ospedale di Carità to a greater extent than the occupational distribution suggests.

The distinction between productive activities and services may seem anachronistic, but it is used here by way of emphasizing the social recognition accorded to such occupations. The distinction, indeed, appears in the records of families in receipt of relief. They describe the transition from a craft to a service occupation as a decline in status associated with old age, invalidity, and, on rarer occasions, unemployment. Usually these occupations are not interconnected, whereas it is easier to find movement between trades. Above all, in the last decades of the eighteenth century, which was a period of serious crisis for the city's industries, the practice of the trades of velvet weaver, tailor, stocking weaver and upholsterer often proved to be interchangeable.

Another group that appeared to have strong links with the hospital is 'servants'. I have included under this rubric the servants of private households, with different positions in the hierarchy (cooks, coachmen, valets, etc.).[55] They merit separate treatment because they seem effectively to constitute a social group in their own right in terms of status and possibilities. Their identity was closely related with the prestige of the family on whom they depended – it is not by chance that their requests

[55] It should be borne in mind that the representativeness of this category is underestimated, since many simply declared themselves to be 'sedan-bearers' or 'coachmen'. In consequence, they were included under 'Services', though they probably carried on these activities in the employ of a gentleman.

for poor-relief often refer to having been in the service of a particular gentleman ('servant of the Count Nomis di Cossilla', 'serves the Canon Vivaldo'). Most of the persons referred to were aristocrats, or at least people of social standing, which doubtless entered into the calculations of the Board of Governors. Similar preferential treatment seems sometimes to have been accorded to 'peasants' (*lavoranti di campagna*) working at the country seat of certain gentlemen in the area surrounding the city. However, in general, *lavoranti di campagna* figure little among those requesting relief, and even more rarely among successful suppliants. They form the category of persons whose requests were most frequently turned down, usually on the grounds of residence.

Once again, the poor who received relief prove to be those enjoying a greater measure of protection rather than the most needy or marginal poor. They were well integrated into the urban environment and its networks of protection, as was the case with the artisans of the city's workshops, or the servants with masters whose alms and legacies often financed the institutions of charity. Only a tiny proportion of those who turned to the hospital defined themselves as 'without occupation', and they are not to be confused with the high number who did not give details of their trade ('undeclared'), made up mostly of the elderly and invalids who were obviously incapable of working ('blind', 'paralytic', 'inmate of the hospital for the sick'). By contrast, among those in receipt of relief, it is possible to come across an albeit modest number of people of more elevated social status, who previously held positions of importance in the city, and had fallen on hard times: merchants and shopkeepers left 'without funds' ('traders'), notaries, lawyers, or music masters with serious illness preventing them from exercising their profession ('professions'). Respect for prestige and status enjoyed in the context of the wider society appears to mark deeply the workings of the charitable institutions.

A system of preferential treatment also seems to exist among the artisans, the occupational group best represented. If we compare the distribution by trade of the heads of families with children who turned to the hospital in the five years under consideration with the details in a list of urban trades of 1792, the *Consegna degli esercenti arti e mestieri*, we can see that requests for relief only partly reflected the different trades in the city (table 6.10).[56] Tailors, cobblers, cabinet-makers, locksmiths and many

---

[56] The 1792 *Consegna delle Arti e Mestieri* is the document nearest in time to the period under examination that provides data on all the occupations; Duboin, *Raccolta*, vol. XVI, pp. 68–9.

Table 6.10 *Trades of artisans requesting relief from the Ospedale di Carità compared with the city trades in 1792*

Trades	1792	Req.	Ref.	Trades	1792	Req.	Ref.	Trades	1792	Req.	Ref.
Silk-cloth makers^a	1,033	78	11	Hatters	153	8	—	Makers of pasta	70	2	1
Shoemakers	987	39	4	Hemp-cloth weavers	153	4	—	Tinsmiths	66	1	—
Bakers	699	14	1	Cartwrights	128	1	—	Basket makers	65	1	—
Tailors	668	39	6	Sculptors	128	1	—	Sausage-makers	62	—	—
Cabinet-makers	516	19	3	Embroiderers	125	—	—	Glaziers	62	1	—
Makers of strong spirits	419	1	—	Butchers	127	1	—	Coppersmiths	61	3	—
Stone cutters	399	1	—	Dyers	111	3	1	Chocolate-makers	60	—	—
Silk spinners	382	15	2	Curriers	106	1	—	Rag and bonemen	54	—	—
Wig-makers	363	9	1	Bookbinders	98	6	—	Watchmen	44	2	—
Silk-stocking weavers	273	17	3	Brass workers	93	1	1	Tripe preparers	40	—	—
Locksmiths	252	10	1	Turners	86	1	—	Cutlers	39	—	—
Cheesemongers	231	—	—	Woollen-cloth workers	84	8	1	Armourers	36	—	—
Barbers	203	4	1	Braid weavers	81	7	1	Straw-hatters	30	—	—
Goldsmiths	200	3	1	Upholsterers	79	4	—	Wax chandlers	29	—	—
Printers	194	2	—	Mattress makers	78	4	—	Coopers	27	—	—
Ribbon weavers	190	12	3	Glovers	77	4	1	Rope makers	26	—	—
Gilders	168	4	1	Farriers	73	—	—	Sword makers	21	1	—
Saddlers	162	2	1	Tanners	70	—	—	Miscellaneous^b	—	43	6

Notes:

^a This category includes those who called themselves 'velvet weavers', 'draw-boys for the velvet weavers', 'journeymen [or] workers in silk manufacture'.

^b Trades that do not appear in the 1792 census: building workers and master builders; clog makers; buckle makers, etc.

Req. = Requests
Ref. = Refusals
All requests and refusals refer to the sample of five years, 1743, 1753, 1763, 1773, 1783.

workers linked with the silk industry are conspicuous. Other trades are less consistently represented and many prominent groups in the local industries are entirely absent. Particularly striking is the predominance of silk workers. These include not only the 'makers of silk cloth' (or 'velvet weavers') and 'spinners', the most numerous groups, but also the 'stocking weavers' and 'ribbon weavers', specialized trades of modest proportion compared with others in the city. Did this mean that relief went to the most insecure and least-well-paid occupational group?

The silk industry was certainly particularly vulnerable to conjunctural crises which caused extensive unemployment in the sector. The 1770s and 1780s were especially crisis-ridden. However, the production of silk fabrics (a leading export of Piedmont), was also the particular object of attention of contemporaries, as well as of scholars in more recent times. Hence the documentation and analysis of its fortunes are very rich, while little is known about other trades in terms of the conditions of employment and earnings.[57]

In reality, the impoverishment of workers in the silk industry in this period was not entirely the result of temporary crises (due to shortages in the cocoon crop), but also to a long-term process of restructuring that hit the city's industries in general. In the silk sector, violent conflicts broke out between masters and merchants from the 1730s, as a result of the creation by the latter of a separate company of their own. However, similar conflicts were also taking place in other sectors: they should be seen as a clash between strong and weak producers, with the latter trying to avoid separation of sales from production and prevent control of the market falling into the hands of a restricted oligarchy of the most powerful merchant entrepreneurs.[58] As we shall see, loss of status was experienced by artisans in many productive sectors in the mid eighteenth century and not just in silk. The privileged position enjoyed by certain trades in the eyes of the hospital cannot thus be explained by reactions to sectorial and conjunctural crises.[59] At least for the silk

[57] On the silk industry, see G. Prato, *La Vita economica in Piemonte a mezzo del secolo XVIII*, Turin 1908; and, in particular, G. Arese, *L'Industria serica piemontese dal secolo XVII alla metà del XIX*, Turin 1922.

[58] The most important documents for reconstructing these processes in the silk industry are to be found in AST, Sez. I, Commercio, cat. IV, m. 7, 8, 9. An outline of these conflicts can be found in E. De Fort, 'Mastri e lavoranti nelle università di mestiere fra Settecento e Ottocento', in A. Agosti and G.M. Bravo (eds.), *Storia del movimento operaio, del socialismo, delle lotte sociali in Piemonte*, vol. I, Bari 1979.

[59] It is worth noting that the distribution of trades remains roughly constant in all the samples. Moreover, the proportion of silk workers among those requesting relief did not rise significantly in the crisis years. In fact, they were responsible for 40 per cent of the requests from artisans in 1743, 21 per cent in 1753, 34 per cent in 1763, 39.6 per cent in 1773 and 27.5 per cent in 1783.

workers, it is evident that special treatment was accorded in the second half of the century because the industry had become, to some extent, a 'state industry'.

The aim of turning Piedmont into an important centre for processing silk, taking advantage of the plentiful local production of cocoons, formed a central plank in the house of Savoy's economic policy. Since the late seventeenth century, it had led the government to concede special favours and exemptions to whoever established silk industries in the realm. But the most important developments took place in the second half of the eighteenth century, when the state itself assumed the role of entrepreneur, first with the Fabbrica della Carità per le opere e negozi di seta (later Compagnia reale), established in 1751, then, in 1761, with the Manifattura della Venaria.[60] Furthermore, silk fabric manufactories were established within the buildings of the institutions. From 1756, at royal behest, a succession of *Ritiri* (retreats) for girls of the lower classes were founded, not only in Turin, but in several centres of Piedmont. These took the form of royal manufactures, which were under the direct control of government bodies and used supplies coming from the state. In the Turin Ritiro di San Giovanni di Dio (where the number of inmates rose from 100 in 1756 to 230 in 1787), a spinning room operated, and apart from woollen cloth and silk products including fabrics, gloves, stockings and ribbons were produced.[61] In the 1780s, moreover, three manufactures were set up in the new Ritiro degli oziosi e vagabondi (Retreat for the Idle and Vagabonds, founded in 1786), in the Martinetto for fallen women (1776) and in the Figlie dei Militari (Soldiers' Daughters) (1779) to increase the production of fabrics using 'moresca' (silk floss). The spread of this type of work, which was easy to learn and required a minimum of capital outlay on machinery and materials, was officially promoted in this period as an answer to the pressing problems of poverty and unemployment.[62]

---

[60] The development of these enterprises, together with information on the fiscal privileges and economic concessions granted to various entrepreneurs in the silk industry, are documented in Arese, *L'Industria serica*; Prato, *La Vita economica*, p. 215 and Prato, *Il Costo della guerra di successione spagnola*, Turin 1907, p. 351.

[61] AST, Sez. I, Luoghi Pii di quà dai Monti, m. 20 and m. 19 d'addizione (additional series). On the characteristics of these institutions, see also Cavallo 'Assistenza femminile'.

[62] AST, Sez. I, Luoghi Pii di quà dai Monti, m. 17 d'addizione, fasc. 6, *Memoria per lo stabilimento della manifattura del Ritiro degli oziosi e vagabondi*; fasc. 10, *Parere per la fondazione di tre ritiri nelle vicinanze di Torino per le donne di mala vita, per gli oziosi e vagabondi e per l'onorevole e caritatevole ritiro dei figli dei soldati*. The 'moresca' was the stuffing extracted from the cocoons and then from the silk material, which was abundant in Piedmont but until then unused; it could be employed for producing fabrics. The processing of the floss is described by C. Ghiliossi, senator and magistrate of the Consolato, the main person responsible for its diffusion, in *Mezzi per provvedere ai mendici volontari e necessari ed agli operai disoccupati*, 1788, Turin, Biblioteca Reale, Storia Patria 879.

Yet the behaviour of the state proved full of ambiguities. On the one hand, the new initiatives seemed to be designed to deal with the unemployment problem caused in this period by changes affecting the organization of work. On the other, they represented an important confirmation of these very transformations. The institutions played, in fact, an important role in the establishment of an oligopolistic control of orders and the development of new forms of production outside the guilds. The charitable purpose of such undertakings constituted a justification for the special exemptions from tax and customs duties, not to mention the privileges claimed by entrepreneurs with respect to the regulations established by the guilds and the Consolato di Commercio.[63] The manufactories set up within the charitable institutions (whether on contract to private interests or run directly by the state) were, in fact, normally exempt from inspection visits by the officers of the guilds. This enabled them to circumvent the regulations designed to safeguard the equitable distribution of orders by setting a ceiling on the number of looms in use and apprentices per master.[64] The institutions also favoured the transformation of many poor masters into 'casual workers, waged men, or day labourers', for the employment of masters as waged workers allowed a higher concentration of looms, giving the appearance that the ratio of masters to looms was being safeguarded.[65]

In the charitable institutions, irregularities were especially numerous and frequent. A special general inspection, ordered at the request of poor masters in 1773, found eighty-five looms in excess of regulations and seventy-six apprentices instead of the requisite twenty-four at the Albergo di Virtù.[66] Sometimes entrepreneurs also enjoyed formal exemptions; in 1747, for example, two manufacturers of the Albergo di

---

[63] The *Consolato di Commercio* (Commercial Tribunal) was the body with jurisdiction over disputes in industry and craft organizations; it also had an advisory role on economic questions, in the production and commercial sectors. It was established in 1676, and from 1733 was staffed by state functionaries.

[64] The limit of four looms had been imposed through royal edict in the crisis year of 1730. This was a defensive measure obtained by small producers at a time when the divisions between the artisans and the guild were already deep. The institutional separation of producer and merchant was beginning to be discussed. Furthermore, according to the *Regolamenti dell'Università* of 1686, apprentices were limited to a maximum of two per master. However, the regulations were subject to suspensions and extensions; in periods in which orders from other countries were particularly profitable, the number of looms permitted rose from four to five and then to six (as in 1731 and 1743), while during crises there were demands for their restriction (as in 1738). For a summary of the measures, see AST, Sez. I, Commercio, cat. IV, m. 10, fasc. 4, *Parere sopra le provvidenze che si potevano dare provisionalmente affine di procurare agli operai di stoffe in seta qualche lavoro*, 1773.

[65] Ibid., m. 8, fasc. 21, *Ricorso di trecento circa giovani lavoranti di stoffe d'oro sulla pretesa contravvenzione del capo 17 dell'Editto dal mercante Carlo Vanetto*, 1741.

[66] Ibid., m. 10, fasc. 4, *Ricavo dell'ultima visita*, 18 March 1773.

Virtù were allowed to exceed the regulation number of looms 'on account of the special protection His Majesty affords the Regio Albergo which is to have a greater income and number of pupils'.[67]

There was a strong connection, therefore, between the eighteenth-century reorganization of relief and the transformation of forms of production which was taking place in urban industry in this period. Charity provided a legitimation for the concession of privileges which, by granting independence from corporate controls, favoured the creation of larger productive units. It was not by chance that the manufacturers with contracts in the institutions were the most powerful in Piedmont.

Despite such ambiguities, the link running between the silk industry and the mercantilist policies of the state resulted in the workers of the silk sector being granted a certain privileged status, which was also reflected in their favoured treatment by the charitable institutions. So the silk workers, thanks to their employment in an industry maintained by the state, had a share in the prestige attached to state employment, which grew in this period with centralization and the expansion of the bureaucracy.[68] The favours shown to them are also evidenced by the fact that they were the only group of artisans on whose behalf the state directly intervened on several occasions during the recurring economic crises of the second half of the eighteenth century.

In 1750, 3,000 lire drawn from the Cassa del Consolato di Commercio were distributed to the silk workers, with amounts dependent on the size of their families; in 1750–1, grain from royal granaries was used to feed about 1,000 people (silk workers and their families) for an eighteen-week period; temporary work in the Fabbrica della Compagnia Reale was provided in 1754, and again in 1776–7, to those out of work, thanks to a special royal gift. Similarly, in 1787 and in 1790, velvet weavers and silk spinners without work were offered employment in processing floss in the new Ritiro degli oziosi e vagabondi, in exchange for board and (if desired) lodging, and a modest wage.[69]

---

[67] Ibid., fasc. 33, *Sentimenti del Consolato sui ricorsi dei mastri di stoffe in seta nell'Albergo*, Carlo Francesco Vanetto e Felice Grosso, 14 April 1747. For the privileges enjoyed by the Ritiro di San Gioanni di Dio, see the appeal of the director, Rosa Govone, for exemption from the articles of the guilds, AST, Sez. I, Luoghi Pii di quà dai Monti, m. 19 d'addizione, 1758, and the later *Regolamenti dell'Opera* in Duboin, *Raccolta*, vol. XVI, 7 September 1758, pp. 353 ff.

[68] In the second half of the eighteenth century, petitions for relief make frequent mention of the presence in the family of a state employee as a sign of special distinction. For reference to this phenomenon, Cavallo, 'Charity', pp. 100–1, 118.

[69] AST, Sez. I, cat. IV, m. 21 da ordinare, *Riepilogo di tutte le provvidenze emanate per soccorrere gli operai disoccupati senza loro colpa*; ibid., fasc. 32, *Filatojeri disoccupati senza lor colpa, soccorsi nel 1787* and

Charitable activity, therefore, reflected structures of privilege rather than scales of need. As shown by the favours bestowed on the citizen, servant or silk worker, access to charity was shaped by the logic of preferential treatment and constituted one of the means whereby forms of protection were exercised on behalf of certain sections of the poor.

New definitions of poverty in the late eighteenth century

A comparison of figures over ten-year periods invites a number of observations. Apart from showing new developments in the forms of relief provided by the Ospedale di Carità, they throw light on the changes in the social composition and family structure of the suppliants, pointing to a shift in the boundaries defining the 'poor'.

The year 1743, which saw the beginning of the Austrian succession war and came in the wake of the harvest failures that had hit Piedmont in the 1730s, was marked by crises resulting from both. This can be seen in the unstable nature of the population in receipt of relief, the remarkably high number of women heads of household 'left' by their soldier husbands, and the increase of men with notably younger wives, suggesting the recent occurrence of remarriage. In 1743, the age differences between partners in families in which one spouse was over fifty reached a peak (in 82.3 per cent of cases the men were over ten years older, while in 50 per cent the age imbalance exceeded twenty years; see table 6.8). Even if we do not know the timing of the remarriage, we can assume that the very frequent imbalance of age between the couple, recorded in 1743, indicates that an increase in the number of remarriages had occurred in the long period of crisis of the 1730s and early 1740s. The frantic multiplication of marriages seems to be the result of older men seeking a solution to their subsistence problems in these difficult years (10 per cent of children under the age of eight had a father over sixty).

In 1743 the institution's measures on behalf of households were extremely temporary – in 60 per cent of cases the family's relationship to the charity did not last longer than two years. In itself, this is not revealing of a specific pattern of intervention, since often those receiving poor-relief themselves disappeared, failing to turn up for the June inspection. However, such temporary measures of poor-relief can be seen

Soccorso ai disoccupati filatojeri senza lor colpa, 29 October 1790. According to this last proposal, the workers' wages should have been anticipated through a loan from the King, and then repaid on the sale of the goods. However, from a workers' petition conserved together with the project, we find that they had no money, 'not even enough to buy a flask of wine, tobacco, to go to the barber or pay for the washing of shirts'.

to recur in 1753, a year of peace and relative stability. In this case, the temporary nature of support is not imputable to population movements provoked by war, but seems to be a feature of the hospital's provision in 'normal times'. In fact, relief remained linked mainly to difficult moments in the life-cycle, in which incidental factors (illness, absence of a partner) upset the delicate balance between consumers and producers inside the family. A great number of requests was made by widowed heads of household and wives in charge of families due to the temporary absence of the husband (see table 6.11), especially in the case of servants and some artisans. Hence, provision was limited to passing periods of difficulty, particularly for the distribution of bread, which in almost half of the cases did not exceed two years (table 6.13). The limited number of requests for relief (the lowest for the decades under consideration), and the prevalence of single people among the suppliants, confirm the impression that the early 1750s were a period of relative stability, in which the standard of living of the urban poor does not appear to have worsened as a consequence of conjunctural crises.

In 1773, by contrast, the situation was drastically altered. The crisis of the silk industry, which was to continue with brief respites for the rest of the century, started in these years. Food prices soared to levels which were among the highest for the century.[70] The composition of the suppliants for relief had changed considerably: families predominated (table 6.6), along with an increased percentage of artisans. At the same time, the distribution of bread increased enormously in importance, and was now provided over lengthy periods, becoming a fixed source of support for many households (see table 6.13).

These features are found anew in the figures for 1773, but they are already in evidence in 1763, even if in a less marked form. At this earlier date the burden represented by the families, on the one hand, and the artisans, on the other, already made itself felt. Above all, the reasons given for requesting relief underwent changes. The number of widows and absent husbands fell markedly as compared with the previous period. The proportion of male heads of household among those requesting relief grew, especially in the 20 to 39 age group (see table 6.11). Even the sickness of one of the partners became less frequent as a reason for requesting relief, compared to references to a 'large family', while bread was distributed on a regular basis, and not just prior to

---

[70] See the movement of prices as reconstructed by S.J. Woolf, 'Sviluppo economico e struttura sociale in Piemonte da Emanuele Filiberto a Carlo Emanuele III', *Nuova Rivista Storica*, 46, 1962.

Table 6.11 *Distribution of heads of family by sex and age*

	20–9			30–9			40–9			50–9			60–9			All ages		Total
	M.	F.		M.	F.		M.	F.		M.	F.		M.	F.		M.	F.	
		Wid.	Abs.H.		Wid.	Abs.H		Wid.	Abs.H.		Wid.	Abs.H		Wid.	Abs.H				
1743	3	2	5	14	15	11	9	6	7	8	9	2	17	1	—	51	58	109
1753	4	3	7	13	9	4	14	4	4	6	—	—	9	—	—	46	31	77
1763	12	6	6	29	2	5	20	7	3	9	3	3	9	—	—	79	35	114
1773	12	4	12	63	16	24	63	17	7	42	2	9	18	4	—	198	95	293
1783	28	15	8	68	18	1	54	8	6	30	4	—	22	5	—	202	65	267

Wid. = Widows
Abs.H. = Women temporarily head of family due to the absence of the husband

children's admittance to the hospital. Moreover, since 1773 reference was frequently made to the shortage of work as the primary reason for needing help.

The model of poor-relief adopted by the hospital already tended, therefore, to change in the 1760s, before the prolonged crisis of the following decades. The shift towards a broader definition of poverty, in which family size, unemployment and critical conditions of life became sufficient factors in providing need, does not have to be attributed to the crises. Severe crises had occurred earlier (notably in the 1730s to 1740s) without causing the same shift in the nature and characteristics of the support given.

I would suggest that in the second half of the century more radical transformations were affecting the poor population of the city. Demographic factors, combined with longer-term changes in the structure of work relations in the city's industries, seem to lie behind the progressive impoverishment of households in this period, especially among artisans. The size of families increased; in fact, the average number of children per family rose (2.5 in 1743, 2.7 in 1753, 3.1 in 1763, 3.3 in 1773, 3.0 in 1783). But their age distribution also changed in accordance with the age of the head of household. The number of children under seven with a father or widowed mother in the 30 to 59 age bracket rose continuously, while the proportion of children aged eight to twelve rose only slightly. However, it was above all the number of children over twelve living with their parents that increased from 1763 onwards. Many apprentices were now registered together with their family, suggesting a steady decline in the custom of moving to the workshop for apprenticeships. On the other hand, many other young males, who had already reached the age traditionally considered as that appropriate for leaving home, made no mention of an occupation.

Even if one excludes the apprentices (who perhaps received some kind of payment for work done and maintenance), and those declaring an occupation, the number of children over twelve living with the family was still on the increase. In fact, in 1763 one in three families included children of working age, and in 1773 one in every two, compared to only one in five families in 1753 (table 6.12).[71]

---

[71] Table 6.12 refers only to the male heads of household aged 30 to 59 (and their children). Female heads of household are not included because, in the case of single mothers, of a slight tendency of children to postpone leaving home. Moreover, male heads of household over sixty are excluded because, in this instance, cohabitation could easily have been motivated by the needs of the parents. On the other hand, heads of households aged 20 to 29 did not have children over twelve years old.

Table 6.12 *Children of working age living with their families (excluding apprentices and those in work)*

	Male family-heads 30–59	Children over 12	Ratio of male heads to children
1743	51	12	4.3
1753	41	8	5.1
1763	68	23	3.0
1773	208	97	2.1
1783	169	62	2.7

The changed composition of the households requesting relief can partly be explained by the new demographic equilibrium established in the mid eighteenth century.[72] The rising birth rate, combined with the fall in infant mortality (until the 1770s), might explain the increase in family size that aggravated the imbalance between producers and consumers, particularly in families at a more advanced stage in the cycle with adolescent children. Moreover, the decrease in the average number of children per family found in the 1783 figures can be linked to the dramatic rise in mortality.

Nevertheless, the poverty of adult workers and, above all, the postponement of the sons' departure from home at the age of apprenticeship seem to call for other explanations, related to work opportunities and the state of the labour market for artisans.

The loss of status of masters in the silk industry, and the concentration of power and production in the hands of an oligarchy of merchant entrepreneurs, starting from the late 1730s, have already been mentioned. Yet in this period many other crafts experienced a similar widening of the gap separating weak and strong producers, a reduction in opportunities for advancement, and a levelling of the traditional divisions in the hierarchy of jobs or, at least, in their status.

The parameters of the conflicts can be sketchily drawn from the disputes between groups of entrepreneurs, between masters and journeymen, and between journeymen and apprentices – conflicts that multiplied in the second half of the eighteenth century. On the one hand,

[72] See R. Davico, 'Démographie et economie. Ville et campagne en Piémont à l'epoque française', *Annales de Démographie Historique*, 4, 1968; G. Levi, 'Gli aritmetici politici et la demografia piemontese del Settecento', *Rivista Storica Italiana*, 2, 1974; G. Moriondo Busso, 'Evoluzione demografica in una parocchia torinese del Settecento', *Bollettino Storico Bibliografico Subalpino*, 68, 1970.

the conflicts hinged on eliminating the barriers to membership of the guilds and to the attainment of masterships which some groups of entrepreneurs had managed to erect, taking advantage of their domination of the guilds. In fact, certain individuals and families had established full control of craft administration, holding onto key posts for years at a time. This monopoly of power represented another cause of sharp conflicts. On the other hand, there was constant complaint about the instability and turnover in jobs, about the employment of apprentices in the place of journeymen, and the increasing difficulty in obtaining promotion to a superior rank (apprentices often being sacked before they had served their time). Nor were the poor masters exempt from adopting such strategies in their attempts to bolster their weakening position.[73]

In many instances, the new stratification came to be expressed on an institutional level as well. In fact, from the late 1730s a process of fragmentation affected the guilds, creating a multiplicity of distinct groupings which expressed the interest of particular sections or strata within the crafts. Especially striking is the tendency of the journeymen to set up separate horizontal organizations in their attempt to construct an identity for themselves and forms of self-defence to oppose this trend. The first examples of this are found in the 1730s, with the granting of authorization to raise funds to be used in aid of sick and out-of-work members. In 1736–7, the stocking weavers, cobblers, hatters and printers were further authorized to have their own patron saint, independently of the masters.[74] There was still a benevolent attitude towards the journeymen in this period that was subsequently eroded. Later, when the goldsmiths requested permission to set up their own company, this was refused, as were the makers of silk cloth in 1771. But even associations for religious and charitable purposes now met with opposition; in the second half of the century, the tailors, locksmiths, wig-makers and silk workers were prohibited, more than once, from celebrating their saint's day and making a collection on behalf of members. Such gatherings were now described as occasions for 'disorder and incitement', for 'driving one another to change masters', and for instigating the 'rise of a factious and independent spirit'.[75]

[73] The information used has mainly been drawn from De Fort, 'Mastri e lavoranti'.
[74] Duboin, *Raccolta*, vol. XVI, p. 875, p. 995, p. 1164; and De Fort, 'Mastri e lavoranti', p. 105.
[75] De Fort, 'Mastri e lavoranti', p. 119; for the case of the silk workers, see AST, Sez. I, Commercio, cat. IV, m. 10, fasc. 3, *Sentimenti dell'Avvocato Graneri sulla supplica dell'Università dei mastri*, 27 November 1771.

The measures against journeymen's gatherings testify to a now consolidated identity that set them apart from, and in conflict with, other levels of the crafts. It is not by chance that they were able, in this period, to impose rights, such as 'Saint Monday', and the payment of the *fricasse* (a sum every apprentice had to pay to the journeymen on starting his apprenticeship), which can be interpreted as symbolic attempts to establish control over the labour market and competition from apprentices.[76]

Hence it is possible to posit a connection between the difficulties experienced by groups of artisans registered in the poor-relief records for the 1760s and the changes outlined above. It seems that the crisis in the standard of living of urban workers was not caused solely by the fall in the value of wages (due to the high prices of the 1770s),[77] as is often stated, but by longer-term developments. The impoverishment of urban families appears understandable, given the erosion of the craft hierarchies and the competition between journeymen and apprentices that grew more acute in these decades. The impediments put in the path of advancement and the new unstable nature of apprenticeship contracts seem, in part, to explain the increase in the number of children of working age who remained in the charge of the family on account of their difficulty in finding employment.

Even the extensions of length of provision adopted by the hospital, which now tended to take responsibility for families over long periods rather than just in emergencies, testify to the chronic distress. In fact, the poor's relationship to charity now lasted for years at a time. Furthermore, the distribution of bread took on massive proportions. It did not substitute for the admission of inmates; if anything, the hospital was always overcrowded in the last decades of the century. Bread distributions were extended in the 1780s to include old people who could no longer be immediately admitted on request and had to wait for a place to become vacant.

As for families, the regular distribution of bread was increasingly

---

76 The royal edict which laid down penalties for holding 'Saint Monday' was issued on 24 March 1783. On the *fricasse* imposed in all the woollen mills (including those of the Ospedale di Carità, the Regio Albergo and the Opera di San Giovanni di Dio), see the *Relazione dell' Illustrissimo Conte di Palormo per levar l'abuso delle Fricasse e per il buon ordine dei folloni*, 1771, Biblioteca Reale, *Storia Patria* 907.

77 From 1772 to 1793 there was a continuous rise in grain prices in the capital, the average price for the 20 year period being 3,719 lire per emina (one emina equalling just over three pecks), whereas it had been 2,919 lire over the previous 40 years. High points had already been reached during the century, but in single years and due to war or shortages.

added to the use of admissions and wet-nursing. Already in the accounts of lives of families recorded in 1763, the provision of bread had been extended for longer periods (for 23.5 per cent it lasted for ten to thirty years; for 33.5 per cent for five to nine years). Figures in table 6.13 show that the phenomenon spread considerably and vastly increased in scale in the subsequent decades, both in terms of numbers of beneficiaries and length of provision. However, our data do not give a picture of the actual scale of bread distribution. As I have already pointed out, it refers only to those newly in receipt of poor-relief and not to the whole of the population receiving relief. It is possible to deduce from occasional pieces of information about the number of people getting assistance that the families receiving bread every week from the hospital totalled 1,287 in 1785, whereas there were 187 in 1758, 379 in 1766 and 874 in 1782.[78]

This development represented a significant change. In a sense, it affirmed a less restricted conception of poverty, as against one linked to accidental natural causes (sickness, the death or absence of the head of household), or difficulties of a temporary or seasonal nature. The hospital's provision aimed at gearing itself to the new needs and changed structure of the urban family, weighed down and impoverished by a rise in population and by the redefinition of work relationships. Relief previously directed mainly at old people and children, widows and disabled (and only episodically at the family) had become a regular factor in many 'normal' families' subsistence equilibrium.

However, changes in the forms of intervention were also more complex. In general terms, one can note the emergence of new recipients of relief – the adult and the young. A shift in concern for new groups of recipients was expressed, at the time, not only in the activities of the Ospedale di Carità, but in the wider context of urban poor-relief. The rise of new institutions from the 1750s on, organized around inmates' work, has already been mentioned. It should be noted that these were directed at age groups previously excluded from relief, namely youths of working age and adults out of work. Unlike the pre-existing Albergo di Virtù and Ritiri for women, which can be seen as forerunners, the new institutions were no longer designed to provide a craft training for males and a dowry for females. Their preoccupation was, above all, to supply work for the young able-bodied and those without employment. The

[78] The figure for 1785 is the average of a series of months (AOC, Cat. IV, Parte I, 1, *Ricoverati e poveri* 1715–1864); for 1766 and 1782, AST, Sez. I, Luoghi Pii, m. 16 d'add., fasc. 5 and 14; for 1758, ibid., fasc. 27; for 1739, ibid., Opere Pie, m. 237, fasc. 16.

Table 6.13 *Variations in bread provision to families with children*

| | Length of bread provision, in years | | | | | | No. of families receiving bread | | |
	1–2	3–4	5–9	10–14	15–19	20 and over	Total	Numbers	% of requests granted
1743	22	5	3	1	1	—	32	32	29.4
1753	10	6	6	1	—	—	23	23	30.0
1763	17	5	17	7	2	3	51	51	44.7
1773	49	29	27	28	9	17	159	159	53.4
1783	38	18	58	32	6	—	152	152	54.9

inmates had to do basic tasks, such as working wool or silk floss, which could be learnt in a few days, or were occupied in more traditional forms of production, but in conditions where the artisanal workshop's divisions by hierarchy and job had been levelled and simplified.

Moreover, an important change in the language used in dealing with inmates in the institutions was introduced in this period. Not only did the first forms of coercive institutionalization appear – with the Casa di Correzione of 1756, then with the Ritiro degli oziosi e vagabondi and the Ritiro del Martinetto of 1776 – but, even where inmates were voluntary, as in the Opera di San Giovanni di Dio, surveillance and segregation increased.[79]

At the Ospedale di Carità, too, the need was recognized for new regulations which would make it more difficult to maintain contacts with the outside, which would lay down severe disciplinary restrictions on life within the institution and which would set up a system for controlling each stage of daily activity through spot checks and a network of foremen and spies chosen from among the inmates.[80] Evidently, the change in tone reflected a preoccupation with governing a population which is described, both inside and outside the institution, as increasingly dangerous and turbulent. It should not be forgotten that the capital at this time was also affected by the processes of impoverishment and proletarianization that were hitting the rural population. The introduction of new forms of managing farms provoked a reduction in the number of smallholders and tenants, driving them to become wage labourers, and led to people leaving the land. Emigration ceased to be

[79] S. Cavallo, 'Assistenza femminile', pp. 151–4.
[80] AOC, Cat. III, *Ordinati* 1664–1945, vol. 18, 28.7.1774. The previous Regulations concerning internal life had been very different; they tended to set out the obligations of the rector, the steward, the housekeeper and so on, but remained vague about inmates' behaviour, limiting themselves to the time-tabling of meals, mass, prayers and other activities.

seasonal and limited to certain areas, as in the past, and became a mass phenomenon that was widespread, especially among the active labour force.[81] Not by chance, the 1750s and 1760s are marked by significant shifts in the wording of edicts against begging. Indeed, the person of the 'beggar from outside' or the 'able-bodied beggar' tends to be replaced by that of the 'vagabond' – a category which, by its imprecision, seems to point to the very mobility of the population in search of work (whether engaged in begging or not) as representing a threat.[82]

A growing sense of ungovernability can be seen to characterize the urban situation in the second half of the eighteenth century. Economic crises, unemployment, emigration new in type and scale, and labour conflicts created a state of insecurity and social tension without precedent. Moreover, these factors brought about more general changes, under-mining the established relations between elites and labouring classes and creating new antagonisms between social groups. The breakdown in the codified ordering of roles inside the crafts, the transformations that affected relations of work in the countryside, and more generally the restrictions placed on traditional spheres of patronage due to the centralization of seats of power and prestige in the hands of state officials, all had a destabilizing effect on the social fabric. These developments helped to tear apart the web of interdependence and exchange of favours which knit together the different levels of the social hierarchy. As we have seen in relation to the city crafts, society was breaking up into a series of 'horizontal' identities and solidarities which were counter-poised to one another.

A new system of poor-relief, in comparison with the model that had prevailed throughout the previous century, was thus beginning to take shape in the second half of the eighteenth century, laying the foundations for developments in the nineteenth century. In fact, French rule in Piedmont, during the period of Napoleonic occupation, was to propose changes in name rather than substance, and did no more than expand the system set up by the Savoyard state in the previous decades. The provisions adopted remained based on the admission to institutions of persons disabled through age and illness (the *hospices*), the distribution of

[81] G. Prato, 'L'Evoluzione Agricola nel Secolo XVIII e le Cause Economiche dei Moti del 1792–98 in Piemonte', *Memorie dell'Accademia delle Scienze di Torino*, series II, vol. LV, 1909.
[82] See, for example, the edicts of 32 January 1750 and 20 May 1766 in Duboin, *Raccolta*, vol. IV, pp. 273, 282. The increase and the renewal of measures against vagabonds is also borne out by D. Balani, *Il Vicario tra città e stato. L'ordine pubblico e l'annona nella Torino del Settecento*, Turin 1987, p. 157.

bread to poor families (administered by the Bureau de bienfaisance), and the employment of the out-of-work in public works (a policy already begun in Piedmont in the 1770s)[83] and in specific institutions (the Dépôts de mendicité).[84] The case appears especially important if one bears in mind that the actions and critiques of enlightened thinkers are usually seen as responsible for introducing radical reforms in the system of welfare.[85] An analysis of the Piedmontese case, however, shows how important changes in policies towards the poor took place in a state which was said to have been untouched by enlightened thinking and impervious to reforms. It also shows that these changes are best understood as the result of shifts in social relations rather than of an ideological revolution.

The new features characterizing initiatives towards the poor and the repressive turn they took appear to be linked to the changed pattern of vertical relations in society, to the weakening of paternalist social bonds, which hinged to no small degree on charitable institutions. Significantly, they made special provision for the young – those most affected by the crisis in roles and the transformation of the codes governing relations between social classes and age groups. Towards the end of the century, the charitable institutions no longer represented a locus for the exercise of patronage and protection in relation to the labouring classes. Instead, they had been reduced to systems of control and intimidation directed at a population seen as alien and dangerous.

[83] See the edict of 15 May 1773 in Duboin, *Raccolta*, vol. XII, p. 327.
[84] For information on the structure of poor relief during the period of French rule, see D. Maldini, 'La legislazione napoleonica e il pauperismo in Piemonte', in E. Sori (ed.), *Città e controllo sociale* and, by the same author, 'Il Dépôt de Mendicité del Dipartimento del Po: analisi di una struttura assistenziale nel Piemonte napoleonico', in G. Politi, M. Rosa and F. Della Peruta (eds.), *Timore e carità. I poveri nell'Italia moderna*, Cremona 1982.
[85] See, for example, L. Cajani, 'L'assistenza ai poveri nella Toscana Settecentesca', in Politi, Rosa, Della Peruta (eds.), *Timore e carità*, and more generally Rosa, 'Chiesa'.

Studies in modern capitalism

Index